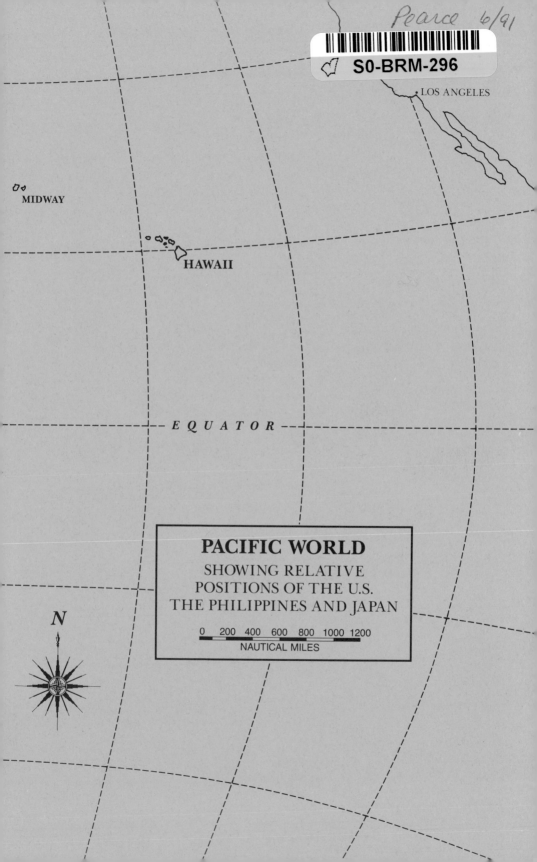

• LOS ANGELES

MIDWAY

HAWAII

E Q U A T O R

PACIFIC WORLD
SHOWING RELATIVE
POSITIONS OF THE U.S.
THE PHILIPPINES AND JAPAN

0   200   400   600   800   1000 1200
NAUTICAL MILES

N

APOCALYPSE UNDONE

My Survival of Japanese Imprisonment
During World War II

by
Preston John Hubbard

Vanderbilt University Press

Nashville, Tennessee
1990

Contents

Illustrations

Maps

Plates

Preface

Because the principal title of this book suggests more than one meaning, some explanation may be helpful. In the twentieth century, *apocalypse* has lost contact with the idea of the cataclysmic struggle between good and evil that ends in a vision of perfection. Today, *apocalypse* suggests the dark vision of the monstrous, hateful disruptions of civilization by world war and its attending horrors. Ever since Vicente Blasco Ibañez's *Four Horsemen of the Apocalypse*, we of the twentieth century have appropriated the old strictly theological usage to speak of modern war. War is now apocalyptic primarily for two reasons: the size to which war can grow and the destructive efficiency that science and technology provide for our weapons. The sides in war are no longer taken along lines dividing states or kingdoms, but along those dividing global regions. Strategies are no longer dictated by whose cannon shoots farther, but by who is willing to fire the ultimate cannon and under what circumstances.

The twentieth century has, oddly enough, also miniaturized the idea of the apocalypse. Though the potential theater of war has grown larger and larger, war's horrors are recalled on ever smaller, more personal stages. Francis Ford Coppola's *Apocalypse Now* is surely not so much about a titanic military struggle of immeasurable force as about the irresistible, twisting forces of evil that thrive in war on even the smallest scale. The American antiwar movement in the late 1930s, led by such notable figures as Charles Lindbergh, seemed to sense at a personal level the horror of the coming apocalypse. Though I had no sympathy with that view at the time, I came to know the enormity and absoluteness of human evil in my private experience of the war. The horrors unleashed by the Japanese during World War II against civilians and prisoners of war in the Philippines and Japan were apocalyptic to me, not only because the context of those horrors was a *world* war but because I felt that what was happening to me ushered in a new and darker age.

This book is not fiction or art in any sense. It is history from a personal viewpoint; that is, I watched unfold what textual history documents. What I watched was apocalyptic in both a personal and a global sense. Likewise, the apocalypse is *undone* in two senses. It is undone, both globally and personally, because we (Western civilization and I) survived (i.e., undid) the apocalypse that erupted distantly in 1939 and more dramatically for America and me in 1941. What we survived was apocalyptic on a national and international scale. Nations, international economies, and cultures struggled to withstand the shockwaves of war. On a personal level, I survived the Japanese military's apocalypse of destruction, hunger, pestilence, and death visited on the American and Allied prisoners of war. *Apocalypse Undone* refers not only to my struggle for survival in the face of those horrors, but also to the price paid for my deliverance. Though I survived and forced the enemy to undo his grip on me, my victory was not overwhelming. I paid a high price for my survival, and I am still paying.

The apocalypse is also *undone* in the sense that it is unfinished, incomplete, still threatening me and American society. It looms dangerously in my recurring nightmares of personal suffering and in the international nightmare of a weirdly glowing atomic cloud. More immediately, it threatens all of us through a new attitude toward the usefulness, indeed the necessity, of war, an attitude openly embraced by many high in our government since 1945.

My apocalypse is both personal and national, both survived and still threatening. Perhaps it is appropriate that the title, like the book, is burdened with these ambiguities. It may well be that such an ambiguous tone speaks best for veterans like me who, since World War II, have come to equate love of country with an intense hatred of war and the peacetime military domination of so much of our economic and political lives.

Apocalypse Undone

1

As We Were

When World War II erupted across Europe in September 1939, I was an enrollee in the Civilian Conservation Corps (CCC) in Oregon. The CCC was a nationwide federal welfare program for unemployed, untrained male youth. Many enrollees from the poor South and the ethnic slums of Northern cities invaded state and national forests and parks all over the country. In July of 1939 I found myself a member of a small group of CCC transfers from Tennessee on my way to join a group in the West. Our destination was Camp Sherman, Oregon's main summer camp located on the shore of beautiful Lake Odell between Crescent Lake and Willamette Pass in the Oregon Cascades. The scenery was spectacular, but the work was hard. CCC enrollees at Lake Odell mainly fought forest fires. We arrived in camp almost simultaneously with the return of a CCC unit that had been battling a great fire in northern California. When I learned that they had sustained several injuries, including serious burns, I immediately concluded that fighting fires in the national forests of the American West was serious business.

As soon as we arrived at Lake Odell, I, along with most of the other newcomers, was dispatched to a side camp located at the summer resort on the western shore of Elk Lake, a small body of water in the heart of the Oregon Cascades about thirty miles west of Bend. Resembling a great blue diamond, Elk Lake is surrounded by spectacular mountain scenery dominated by South Sister Mountain on the north and Bachelor Butte across the lake on the east. It surely is one of the most beautiful places in the world. We were under the supervision of a forest ranger, and our primary duties were maintaining the resort area and extinguishing lightning-caused forest fires.

In late August 1939 I was called back to the Lake Odell camp to assume the position of assistant educational adviser. My duties included editing a monthly camp newspaper. All in all, my situation was about as remote as possible from the incipient apocalypse. There, in the shivering cold of the small tent city on the shore of windy Lake Odell, I learned of the beginning of World War II in Europe.

Since radio reception at Lake Odell was poor and accessibility to radios was limited for most of the enrollees, I got most of my significant information about the coming of the war from Portland newspapers, as I recall the *Journal* and the *Oregonian*. I seemed to be the only person in camp who was excited about the war. The prevailing national sentiment at that time was still strongly antiwar. Almost everyone with whom I talked in the camp and in adjacent Oregon villages not only felt that the war was none of our business and we should stay out of it, but almost instinctively assumed the United States would not become involved.

We closed the Lake Odell camp as well as all side camps in September and withdrew to the company's permanent post at Camp Sherman on the Metolius River, a stream created by the snows of Three Fingered Jack and Mt. Jefferson. By the time we had settled in at Camp Sherman, Hitler had crushed Poland and the war had begun. But in Oregon, interest in the war declined to just about zero. Even in Bend, the cultural and economic capital of central Oregon and the principal recreational center for all CCC camps in the area, World War II as a subject of curiosity ranked just slightly above the Australian platypus.

During one of my recreational trips to Bend, I had the good fortune to see for the first time Lewis Milestone's magnificent antiwar movie *All Quiet on the Western Front*. I was captivated and emotionally moved by that film classic, and I wondered how the world of the film connected with my own. I raised the question with some of my comrades who also had seen the movie, but their response did little to stimulate further discussion. They saw the movie as just another interesting story about World War I with no import for current events. Throughout the late fall, Oregonians showed little concern about British-German naval activities, not even about the spectacular affair of the *Graf Spee*, a German battleship scuttled by its own crew to prevent capture by the British.

At the end of December 1939, my term in the CCC ended and I came home to Tennessee, where I found opinions about the war more homespun in their phrasing but in all other respects identical to those in Oregon. By that time the media had successfully dubbed events in Europe "the phony war." At great expense, the newspapers and radio networks had placed reporters on the scene ready to transmit blow-by-blow accounts of dramatic international exchanges—real war. The failure of other European nations to mount any serious resistance to Hitler's blitzkrieg eventually produced the press's favorite term for the events in Europe—*sitzkrieg*. Tennesseans paid little attention to the sitzkrieg, although the news media were able to drum up a little interest in the Winter War between Russia and Finland. Tennesseans strongly supported the Finns, a fact revealing less about their knowledge of the Finns than their dislike of the Russians.

Most people in Tennessee, like the American news media, were bored with the sitzkrieg and felt we were being deprived of a good fight. Hitler's blitzkrieg against Scandinavia on April 9 aroused considerable attention for a while. In spite of the widespread feeling that such developments should have no effect on American policy, affairs in Scandinavia noticeably improved the war's popularity as a news story. At the beginning of the Anglo-French invasion of Norway, Tennesseans' interest climbed fairly high, but their enthusiasm tumbled as the Germans quickly smashed that venture.

The event destined to break the power of American antiwar sentiment began on May 10, 1940, when Hitler hurled his forces against western Europe. I had just reenrolled at Austin Peay Normal in Clarksville, Tennessee, a small school I had briefly attended in 1938-39 under the auspices of the CCC program. Though I was a pauper, my poverty qualified me for educational aid under the National Youth Administration, a federal program of relief for youth of high school and college age. Just as I settled in at Austin Peay, the German forces broke through the Allied lines in Belgium and France and raced to the English Channel. At Austin Peay the war generated great excitement, and for me the momentous events leading to the collapse of the Allies on the Continent were heady stuff.

The intense excitement at Austin Peay Normal and throughout middle Tennessee reached a climax with the Dunkirk evacuation, but after that, the emotional ride was downhill. The fall of France in June 1940 produced a profound shock followed by a pall of disappointment that lasted most of the summer. One thing was certain: Hitler's blitzkrieg in western Europe in the spring of 1940 had profoundly changed the American attitude toward the war in Europe. The feeling that the war did not concern the United States was gone, and the interventionists, who in varying degrees wanted us to become involved, had gained enough support and respectability to challenge the still powerful isolationists.

During that summer, following the unbelievable fall of France, the American people focused their attention on two distant but related events: the Battle of Britain and the beginning of the long debate between the isolationists and the interventionists that continued until Pearl Harbor. We were inspired by the Battle of Britain, by the spectacle of the gutsy and underdog British withstanding the hell from their heavens that the Luftwaffe daily rained upon them. We were stirred by the words of Winston Churchill, who, as John Kennedy would later say, mobilized the English language and sent it into battle. Churchill's eulogy of the Royal Air Force and other memorable speeches greatly stirred the emotions. Not since Franklin D. Roosevelt's acceptance speech at the Democratic National Convention in 1932 had words so inspired the American people. For me and millions of others, Winston Churchill and the Royal Air Force pilots became the superstars of the movie newsreels.

In spite of the growing power of the interventionists during the summer of 1940, the isolationists were not to be sold short. They probably still represented the majority, and the rallying leadership of Charles A. Lindbergh, America's greatest living hero, along with a group of distinguished Republican politicians such as Robert A. Taft and Arthur H. Vandenberg made them extremely formidable. I admired the Lone Eagle and I had often fantasized I was the pilot of *The Spirit of St. Louis*, but I strongly opposed the isolationists. I especially hated their venomous attacks on President Roosevelt. Anyone who insulted FDR insulted me. I felt somewhat vindicated by Roosevelt's victory in the election of 1940 but was disappointed that he did not repeat the electoral knockouts of 1932 and 1936.

From the summer of 1940 to Pearl Harbor, I was in favor of the war, and so were most Southern white males of my generation whom I knew. If my friends and I were representative of Southern thinking in 1940-41, Francis Butler Simkins's assertion in *A History of the South* (1972) that the South was strongly prowar during this period is certainly valid. Simkins, however, had his list of reasons upside down. His last two reasons— opportunity for economic betterment and loyalty to FDR—should rank one and two, respectively. And Simkins failed to include another fundamental reason for the South's prowar attitude, one that should rank third, i.e., the possibility of adventure. Economic depression is extremely boring, producing mental weariness and intellectual fatigue, and the South was the most depressed of any region in the nation. If nothing else, the prospect of war diverted attention from problems at home and created a sense of excitement across the South.

The Burke-Wadsworth Selective Training and Service Act of September 1940 was important, too, in dispelling the malaise into which the nation had fallen in the early summer. That legislation, America's first peacetime draft act, was hugely popular with the public, even with those young men who would be affected. As a matter of fact, the draft seems to have been warmly supported by American women as well. After all, they, too, sensed opportunities that the coming war might offer. Some of my female friends at Austin Peay told me that they wished they could register for the draft. Even without that possibility, many of them, because of close family attachments to brothers and cousins, felt themselves to be participants in the national defense effort.

I was pleased and excited about the Burke-Wadsworth Act, and so were my male friends at Austin Peay and elsewhere in middle Tennessee. The Draft Act was obviously good for American morale since it gave the impression that the President was beginning to assert control over foreign policy. Franklin D. Roosevelt was one of those natural leaders whom the majority of the people instinctively wanted to follow, once he had clearly set out toward his goal.

By October 1940 the structure of the Selective Service System had been established, and local draft boards had begun registration. I was among those required to register in the first round, as were most of the male students at Austin Peay, but we all tried to remain nonchalant about it, as if our registration were a matter of little consequence. In reality, we felt proud of ourselves and secretly welcomed compliments and congratulations from members of the faculty and from coeds. Of course, we responded to such expressions with great modesty and self-effacement. A major reason I felt good about registering for the draft was that I believed it was a way of helping President Roosevelt, my hero, whom I supported without limitation or reservation.

During the late winter of 1941, the debate between isolationists and interventionists focused on the fight in Congress over the Lend-Lease Bill. Public interest in the debate, at least in middle Tennessee, seemed to wane, perhaps because people grew weary of the repetitious, cliché-ridden controversy. Though some interventionists argued at the time that the Lend-Lease Bill was a way to keep us out of war, in retrospect I think most Americans probably accepted the fact that the bill was, for all practical purposes, a declaration of war against Nazi Germany. At any rate, the passage of the bill was an enormous victory for the interventionists and largely rendered meaningless their continuing debate with the isolationists.

About the middle of the winter quarter of 1941, two memorable things happened to me. First, I lost my roommate to the National Guard. Robert Taylor, now a Nashville attorney, was a member of the Clarksville National Guard unit suddenly called up for active service and dispatched to Camp Forrest at Tullahoma, Tennessee. The process was quick and Taylor was gone within hours, not really having time to dispose of all of his personal effects. Many other students at Austin Peay Normal were also carried away by the call-up of the local National Guard. We did not even have time to give them a farewell reception.

Second, the Clarksville draft board came up with my number. Since I was classified 1A, I felt a tingle of excitement, knowing that I, too, would soon be on my way to an Army camp. It was common knowledge that to fail the draft board's physical one had to be a hopeless wreck and blind—unless, of course, one had political clout. But I did not want to be turned down; I was ready to go. When I appeared before the draft board, however, I was informed that since I was a student I would be deferred automatically until the end of the school year in June. I had not applied for the deferment and felt some disappointment at its being granted. Some of the other male students at Austin Peay went through the same routine; as far as I know, all of them would have preferred to enter military service.

Soon after the beginning of the summer quarter in June of 1941, I discussed the situation with a friend, Jim DePriest, whose draft status was the same as mine. We decided we could better control our lives if we beat the draft by volunteering for service. Perhaps we could negotiate with the Army recruiting office for some kind of preferential duty, or at least avoid being sent to the infantry. The next day Jim and I hitchhiked to Nashville and quickly made our way to the U.S. Army recruiting office in the old Federal Building on Broadway. There we found the Army recruiters eager to negotiate for recruits. They made a number of offers, but the most attractive to us was the chance to join the Army Air Force Signal Corps in the Philippines. The idea of going to the mysterious Philippines, a place largely unknown to most Americans, appealed to our sense of romance and adventure. After collecting our enlistment papers and passing a cursory physical exam, we hitchhiked back to Clarksville with orders to report back the next morning for transportation to Ft. McPherson in Atlanta where we would be sworn in.

Filled with enthusiasm, Jim and I spent the evening packing and taking care of personal affairs before beginning our long journey to the Philippines. Most of our comrades thought we were crazy and advised against the venture. The next morning before breakfast, Jim came to my room with a downcast look on his face. I knew what it meant. It took great courage for him to tell me that he had changed his mind. His decision offered me a face-saving opportunity to back out also, but I was determined to go, come hell or high water. Many times during the coming years I would wish that I had followed Jim's lead; I concede that he was the wise one.

As I left for Nashville via Greyhound bus the next morning, I felt lonely because Jim was not with me, but I also felt proud. I was going to have an opportunity to help protect America from the ruthless dictators of the world and preserve freedom for America and her allies. I was a product of the times, clearly reflecting in my own thinking the most popular notions of the day—notions about the United States, about our place in the world, about a citizen's responsibility, and about the American dream. I felt no great threat from forces larger than myself. The threat I had felt was from the economic despair of the Great Depression, and that dark force seemed to be waning. Nothing in my limited understanding of myself, of my country, or of history suggested to me that I was walking unshielded toward a national and personal apocalypse.

Egotistically and self-righteously, I told myself that grateful citizens yet unborn would honor me and the other youth of my generation who were preparing to make the supreme sacrifice to secure their liberty. Nearly a half century has elapsed since that day, and millions of those citizens have been born and grown up. Even though hundreds of thousands of the youth of my generation did make the supreme sacrifice to preserve the heritage of the world's oldest democracy, modern youth seem unimpressed or unaware. It is hard to say which is more dangerous, untutored and idealistic notions of the future or ignorance of history. I have been guilty of the first; this book is one of the ways I have fought against the second.

2

Journey to the Philippines

At 8:00 A.M. on June 12, 1941, I reported to the U.S. Army recruitment office in Nashville. I was informed that I would be sent to Ft. McPherson in Atlanta to be sworn into the Army and processed for the next leg of my journey to the Philippines. The paperwork for my trip to Atlanta was soon completed, but unfortunately I had a whole day to kill since my train would not be leaving until late that night. After a long day of window shopping, movie going, restaurant sitting, and tiresome waiting at Union Station, I finally boarded the train for Atlanta at midnight.

The train ride to Atlanta seemed interminable, and I slept little during the entire trip. There were few passengers and no one I could talk to. As the night wore on, I felt increasingly lonely and homesick. I was keenly disappointed that my friend Jim DePriest had backed out, and I considered scrapping my plans altogether. I had not yet been sworn into the Army, so I thought I could still return to Clarksville and await my future at the hands of the Clarksville draft board. But since the Army had paid for two meals and my transportation to Atlanta, I decided that abandoning the project would be dishonorable. Furthermore, I did not know exactly what my legal rights were—whether I could be charged with desertion even though I had not been officially sworn in. I finally resolved to stick it out and tried to revive the feeling that I was beginning an exciting adventure.

The train arrived at the Atlanta station about daylight, and shortly afterward I boarded an Army truck for Ft. McPherson. After waiting around with a group of other recruits and draftees, I was sworn into the U.S. Army. The date was Friday the 13th, June 1941. I was twenty-two years old.

I was billeted in an extensive tent city set up for Army rookies. Since I was the only one in the group slated for the Philippines, my orders attached me to a group of Army Air Corps recruits (the Air Force was not a separate service until after the war) bound for San Francisco. Until our departure from Ft. McPherson, we performed various duties around

8

the post, including working on a KP detail in an officers' training school mess and stacking live shells in an ordnance depot. On the morning of the third day, I reported for sick call. I must have had a little fever since I was sent to a nearby clinic and put to bed.

I actually enjoyed my stay at the clinic, meeting a lot of interesting people, eating well, and doing nothing. I recall that it was located in a stately old plantation-style mansion, which had a large porch with big white columns and beautiful shrubbery all around. I enjoyed lounging, sleeping, reading, and listening to the birds singing in the magnolias and pines. Perhaps the highlight of my respite was the Joe Louis-Billy Conn heavyweight championship fight on June 18. It was obvious that Billy was the great white hope of the entire ward, which was, of course, all white. Billy did not win, but he went all the way and put up a terrific fight. We were proud of him.

During the week I spent in the post clinic, I was somewhat torn emotionally: I was still homesick for Clarksville and Austin Peay, but I felt a growing excitement about the coming journey to California and the Philippines. The first few days, I entertained vague hopes that I would be found medically unfit. In such an event I knew I could take advantage of the growing prosperity in the civilian economy that was being fueled by the accelerating defense expenditures. All at once the depression seemed to be over, and good-paying jobs were becoming plentiful. However, I was unable to convince the Army medics that I had any serious illness; furthermore, by the end of the week when I was unceremoniously sent back to the tent city, my homesickness had largely disappeared. In fact, I never had a problem adjusting to Army life, mainly because of my experiences in the Civilian Conservation Corps and in dormitory life at Austin Peay Normal.

When I returned to the tent city, I discovered that my erstwhile Air Corps companions, to whom I had been attached, had already left for California. Instead, I joined another group going to the Golden State, some U.S. Army Air Corps recruits soon to leave for Hamilton Field in the San Francisco Bay area. On the following morning, June 23, my new comrades and I were thrilled by the bold headlines in an Atlanta newspaper: "Hitler invades Russia." Suddenly the evil Stalin became good old Joe, our ally. Around Ft. McPherson were defense posters containing caricatures of Hitler, Stalin, Mussolini, and Emperor Hirohito, each with a hand cupped behind an ear. The caption read, "Be careful what you say—don't give away vital secrets." Arriving in California a few days later, we found the same placards on military posts there, but Joe Stalin's portrait had been taped out.

The next day I boarded the train for California. Our group of Air

Corps rookies, about thirty men, was large enough to fill one railway car. Most members of the group were from north Georgia and east Tennessee, and I enjoyed immensely being with them, so much so that I played poker with them from time to time even though I detested gambling. When we left Ft. McPherson, the authorities chose a recruit who seemed to be a natural leader to handle everyone's railway tickets. For some reason, I was given my tickets and was expected to keep up with them. I put the tickets in my suitcase and promptly forgot about them.

We changed trains from the Southern Railway to the Union Pacific at St. Louis, and we were click-clacking across Kansas before the conductor began checking tickets. The check came up one short. After the third check, he became irritable. Suddenly it dawned on me that none of my tickets had been properly processed. When I showed my ticket to the conductor, he really boiled over and screamed at me. In return, I became angry and dared him to put me off the train. For a moment I thought he was going to do it, but he soon cooled off.

We did not have to change trains in Denver, but we had a two-hour stopover there before the ride north to Cheyenne and the junction with the main Union Pacific line, which runs through southern Wyoming to Ogden, Utah. There the railroad begins the crossing of the Great Salt Lake, then meanders through the Humboldt River valley of Nevada, and, just beyond Reno, winds toward the pass through the Sierras to California.

While we were waiting in Denver, the first of several incidents occurred that began to form in me a feeling for the important difference between officers and enlisted men. For whatever reason, it has to do not so much with good or bad behavior as with different ways of seeing the world. I was leaning against a post just outside our Pullman car along with several other members of our group when an Army captain approached us. Singling me out, he demanded to know who we were and where we were going. He chewed me out for permitting my colleagues to lounge around the station, allegedly giving the Army a bad image. When I tried to explain that I had no authority and was not the group's leader, he angrily retorted that he was putting me in charge and would hold me responsible for the group's discipline. Along with the others who overheard the conversation, I was completely dumbfounded. Though reason dictates that the differences between the two eternal classes of Army personnel were learned, I soon had the feeling that personalities somehow came packaged with the uniforms and that an unbridgeable gulf separated how officers and enlisted men saw, thought, and felt about the world around them.

Later, an episode demonstrated how it was possible to take advantage of that gulf and exploit it. After we had pulled out of the Denver station, two other Army officers came into our car and informed us that they were on duty maintaining the discipline of new Army recruits on the train. At first they were courteous and walked along the aisle of the car talking to the recruits. At the time, a poker game was in progress in a small lounge at the end of the car, and the two visiting officers nonchalantly sauntered in as if to join the kibitzing. Before long, the officers had taken seats at the gaming table, joining with the flow of cards, liquor, and chatter in a manner indicating that they were accustomed to socializing with enlisted personnel. When the two officers began to lose, their courtesy vanished. I had already discovered that two or three members of our group were highly skilled card sharks. It was now the officers' turn to make that discovery.

The officers were soon losing heavily and became increasingly unhappy. They jumped up from their seats, accused their hosts of cheating, and shouted all kinds of threats. They stormed out of the compartment into the aisle of the Pullman car, ordering everyone to assemble in that area. They informed us that they were military police and that when we arrived at the Oakland waterfront, all of us would be arrested and charged with violating Army regulations regarding gambling. They then disappeared, and we never saw them again. For a while, I, along with some others, was shaken by the strange affair, but our card sharks, who proved to be more worldly wise than the rank and file of our group, knew a piratical gambling scam when they saw it. Apparently, the two officers were phonies, con men skilled at exploiting the psychological and sociological differences between officers and enlisted personnel. Unfortunately for them, they picked the wrong group to victimize and got caught in their own trap.

All the way across the country our group of recruits was segregated in a railroad car hitched to regularly scheduled passenger trains; in short, it was not a troop train. From Atlanta to St. Louis on the Southern and from St. Louis to Denver on the Union Pacific, we were permitted to move about the train, going through the other passenger cars and lounging in the club car. We were not particularly conspicuous because we had not been issued Army uniforms. Our main objective in moving about the train was to flirt with the girls.

Beyond Denver, however, our diplomatic relations with the Union Pacific Railroad became severely strained. The conductor declared all of the train outside our car, except for the dining car, to be off limits for us. That harsh ruling came at an inopportune time for me since another recruit and I had grown fond of a couple of girls with whom we had been sitting. My girl on the Union Pacific was an angel in pink pants, an angel that was sexually captivating. In those days few women wore slacks in public. In fact, the only women I had seen wearing pants in public were west of the Mississippi; in the East, women were not so bold. Certainly, I was not going to submit to the conductor's edict without a struggle. On the occasions when he plucked me and my friend from the sides of our girlfriends, we set Olympic records getting back into action. Finally, the conductor, weary and bedraggled, gave up trying to protect the civilian passengers from the Army scum.

The Union Pacific journey came to an end at the Oakland waterfront. There we said good-bye to our girlfriends and boarded a ferry for the Ft. Mason dock area where I was to board another ferry for Angel Island. It was dusk, and the lights of San Francisco across the bay beckoned us like a magnetic lure. The ferry landed at a terminal near lower Market Street, and Army trucks soon arrived to carry the Army Air Corps recruits to Hamilton Field, leaving me in the dark all alone. Even the people at the terminal had closed their office and gone home. I began to wonder if anyone knew where I was or even cared. Finally, an Army truck showed up, the driver explaining that some normal Army snafu had caused the delay. He dropped me, his only customer, at the Alcatraz ferry terminal to await the next leg of my journey.

Getting to Ft. McDowell was another series of delays and boring waits. When we finally did arrive at Angel Island on the west side of San Francisco Bay, it was midnight. After I spent a cold night in an empty barracks without benefit of blankets or other bedclothes, someone came for me, and I was assigned to a large barracks full of recruits with overseas assignments. I soon struck up a friendship with my neighbor in an adjacent bunk—Bob Donald of New York, who had been assigned to a signal company located at Manila Port Area. Donald was one of those people at home anywhere, regardless of circumstances. Before long he made me feel at home, too.

After breakfast we were ordered to line up on the parade ground to be assigned daily tasks. In a formation consisting of several rows, we waited for members of the first permanent party to select the number of men desired. The first day, I was drafted to work on a pothole crew. Since there were few potholes to fill, we spent most of the day sitting and talking. All of the other members of the work party were Cajuns from Louisiana. They were the first people from that culture I had met, and I enjoyed their tales of south Louisiana in their strange Anglo-French patois.

The second day, I was requisitioned by a fat corporal who served as a manservant in a small house occupied by a group of high-ranking officers. The corporal, a typical Old-Army enlisted man, seemed arro-

gantly proud to perform his menial tasks, and he viewed me with the
same respect most people show a mangy dog. My first assignment was to
make up a major's bed, a job for which I was ill-suited since I had no bed-
making skills whatever. After assigning me the bed-making duty as well
as other cleaning tasks in the major's quarters, the corporal left, saying
he would check in later.

I made the bed, but it looked more disheveled than when it was
unmade. After a few feeble efforts at sweeping the floor, I discovered the
major's liquor cabinet, which contained the best Scotch whisky and some
snacks. Normally, I never drank intoxicants in the morning and rarely
hard liquor at all, but the major's Scotch looked so good I could not resist
it. I poured myself a glass, opened a can of peanuts, and turned on
the radio to catch the latest big band numbers. After a few belts of the
major's Haig and Haig, my perspective on the world changed: being
the fat corporal's flunky was not so bad after all.

Just before I finished sipping my third glass of that delicious whisky,
the corporal returned. Right away I knew he was not pleased. The
bawling out I got pretty well covered where I came from and where I was
going. The blue-laced reprimand was for my having helped myself to the
major's private stock and for drinking on duty. Then he saw the bed.
That unsightly mess only fueled his rage; it was apoplexy time in the
major's quarters. The corporal literally jumped at the bed and ripped
the covers off, ordering me to redo it at once. While I was remaking the
bed, he was shouting instructions step by step, but when I completed the
task, the bed looked no better than the first time.

The corporal could not take it anymore. He fired me, ordering me to
return to my barracks where, he said, punishment would be waiting for
me. He shouted that none of the current crop of rookies at McDowell was
any good. They were too weak and soft. He had just recently returned
from a hitch in Hawaii, he said, and it was obvious that the flabby recruits
at Ft. McDowell would not be able to stand up to the rigors of overseas
duty. As I left the major's quarters, I did not really believe that the
fatuous orderly was going to put me on report; he could not easily do
that without also turning the spotlight on himself. I never saw or heard
from him again.

At the barracks, I found my new friend, Bob Donald, lounging on his
bunk. I asked why he was not on a work detail, and he informed me that
only the stupid permitted themselves to be caught in the trap of make-
work projects. The next morning, when we fell out to be chosen for a
work detail, I stuck by Bob's side. When the first big party was drafted,
we quickly joined the group, bringing up the rear. As the leader disappeared around the first corner, we absconded. We did this two or three

consecutive mornings. It was so easy it was boring; furthermore, it was tiring just trying to think of something to do to kill time, like lounging on the south beach enjoying the view of San Francisco and the Golden Gate.

After a few days, our section of the barracks was drafted for kitchen police. I saw no way to evade that call for duty, but Bob Donald somehow got out of it. Working KP at Ft. McDowell at that time was rough. Three different groups were fed three times a day, and each group at its sitting filled the huge mess hall. I was assigned to work a table. Each person in charge of a table was required to cart the food from the kitchen at each sitting, refill empty vessels, and otherwise respond to the men's demands. Following each sitting, the table manager had to carry dirty dishes as well as all food containers back to the kitchen, then quickly scrub down the tables, benches, and the floor around and underneath the table. By then it was time to bring out the food for the next sitting. That procedure had to be repeated for all three sittings and for all three meals.

We KPs were permitted to eat after the completion of the third sitting of each meal. One morning at the KPs' breakfast I met a fellow worker named Richard Murray. Murray was a big Irishman from Wisconsin via Cut Bank, Montana. My first encounter with Murray was an unfriendly one. The *casus belli* was Murray's charge that I had committed an unpardonable violation of mess hall procedure. He accused me of taking the last helping from a platter of S.O.S. (creamed chipped beef on toast) and then failing to hold it up so the working KPs could see and refill it. Whether I was actually innocent or guilty I do not remember, but I vehemently denied it and pretended to hold my ground. Murray was much bigger than I, and thank goodness he did not suspect that I was prepared to run should he become more aggressive. Fortunately, Murray's Irish temper cooled, but we glared at each other for the next few days. There was no way for either of us to know how important to my survival Richard Murray would become.

Before that day on KP was over, I began trying desperately to find some way to get off that onerous duty. I knew that each group assigned to KP had to do a three- or four-day stint before being relieved. During a rest period after lunch, I happened to glance at a bulletin board and saw a note from one of the administrative offices asking for typists. I hurried to that office and applied for a position even though I had no formal training in typing. I just hunted and pecked, but that was standard for the Army before the coming of the deft-fingered WACs (Women's Army Corps). I was hired on the spot, assured that my name would be removed from the KP list, and told to report for work the next morning. I finished my KP duties for the evening meal feeling better about everything. I remained on the typing job until I left for the Philippines.

During the short time I was at the Ft. McDowell replacement center, I received one midweek afternoon pass before the July 4 weekend. On that first pass I went with some fellow barracks mates to girlie shows in the Latin Quarter and to the San Francisco beach, where it was uncomfortably cold. I drank a lot of beer and felt bad the next day. All in all, my first military leave was a time-wasting, headache-producing failure.

Friday of the same week was July 4, and we were given passes for the long holiday weekend. After enduring a lecture from Bob Donald on the evils of running around with a bunch of Army drunks, I decided to spend the holiday with him. His idea was to head for Sausalito, a small village on San Francisco Bay. Sausalito was a center of yachting, and Bob bragged that back east on Long Island he had become an expert yachtsman. He predicted that some rich Sausalito sailor would likely invite us to spend the weekend on the family yacht. Since I knew nothing about boats of any kind, Bob told me to keep my mouth shut and let him do the talking.

At 11:00 A.M. on July 4 we boarded a bus in San Francisco for Sausalito. The bus route was spectacular, crossing the Golden Gate Bridge, at that time only two years old, and winding around the bay shore to Sausalito. After lunch we asked for directions to the Sausalito Yacht Club. That was where Bob was determined to go. I tagged along but with increasing reluctance. At the gate to the club grounds, an imposing sign declared that only members could enter; others would be prosecuted and no doubt sent to nearby San Quentin. Bob opened the gate and strolled in as if he were a charter member, with me creeping timidly behind. When we got to the wide boardwalk at the dock, I could see an armada of beautiful yachts. At first no one seemed to pay any attention to us until some smart-alecky kid on one of the yachts screamed out, "Hey, this is no Army base!" I cringed. I wanted to run back to the gate, but Bob paid absolutely no attention to him.

We walked down to the end of the boardwalk where a distinguished-looking man of middle age was working with some ropes. He greeted us in a friendly manner, and Bob introduced us. After that I followed the code of etiquette Bob had prescribed for me: I kept my mouth shut. Bob and the man immediately became engaged in boating talk. I was surprised to see that Bob really knew enough about yachting to draw this man into an animated conversation. After a while the man told us that his daughter and son had sailed his yacht up the bay on a sort of shakedown cruise. They were due to return at 5:00 P.M. when he, his wife, and another daughter would be boarding the yacht for the holiday weekend. Then, out of the blue he invited us to join them. It happened just as Bob said it would. Bob was jubilant, but only half of me was joyful.

The other half was scared to death. On the one hand, the invitation was a wonderful gesture, and according to the man's description, his daughters were about our age. On the other hand, Bob had told the man that I also knew a lot about boats.

We left our newly won host with the understanding that we would meet back there about five o'clock. Having time to kill, I suggested that we hang around Sausalito, but Bob cynically suggested that we walk down the road about three miles to the San Francisco Yacht Club to see if we could get a better offer. His attitude irritated me. It seemed calculating and ungrateful. Besides, I could not imagine an offer better than the one in hand. We did walk down to the San Francisco Yacht Club, but it was a major disappointment; there was little activity, and the membership seemed to be composed largely of retired Army officers. But I encountered a retired colonel who told several fascinating stories about his experiences in France during World War I.

After nearly half a century, I can still remember one of the them. It sticks in my mind, I suppose, because my response to it then was so different from what it soon would be. The time was shortly after the Armistice (November 11, 1918), and the colonel was in France killing time, waiting for orders to return to the States. The place was rural Normandy, where the ravages of war had taken their toll and the people had nothing. Just before dark, he came to a farmhouse where a peasant farmer and his wife, delighted to meet an American, invited him to be their guest for the night. For a few moments the three lingered in the living room engaged in conversation, a portion of which concerned a yellow cat that had wandered into the room. The colonel complimented the French couple's beautiful animal, and he picked up the cat and held it in his lap. Soon the farmer went outside to complete his chores while his wife scurried about her kitchen beginning preparations for dinner. The colonel put down the cat and went outside to take a walk around his hosts' homestead. Before long, he was called to dinner. The fare was stew, and the colonel found it to be *délicieux*; he ate heartily. After supper when the three reassembled in the living room, the colonel looked around for the cat. His hosts informed him that the cat had been the principal ingredient in the stew *magnifique* he had so much enjoyed. The colonel had to go outside and vomit. The story shocked me, too. I had trouble imagining conditions bad enough to force people to eat their pets. Before long, I would see men eat far worse.

Bob was bored stiff with the colonel's reminiscences. He was definitely not one for history. We soon began our trudge in the hot California sun back to Sausalito, but the journey was made bearable by the low humidity and occasional breezes from the bay.

As we walked along, an automobile going our way stopped, and the driver invited us to ride. We climbed into the back seat and exchanged introductions. The driver was a socially polished young man who appeared to be in his late twenties, and the other passenger was a lady of elegant bearing, his mother. The mother soon invited us to spend the holidays at her home. The invitation created an emotional problem for me. The lady was perfectly charming, and I found her and her son genuinely magnetic people, but we already had a commitment at the Sausalito Yacht Club. I started to thank her for the invitation and offer our regrets because of the previous engagement, but I had hardly uttered a word before Bob gave me a vicious kick and took charge of the conversation. He quickly spoke up: "Oh! we are very happy to accept your invitation!" Actually, I was glad and felt relieved that Bob had been so decisive in that social emergency, although I still have a guilty feeling about standing up our would-be host at the Sausalito Yacht Club. We continued up the valley road to the impressive home of our hostess in the most beautiful town I had ever seen, Larkspur, California.

Bob and I had a wonderful time as guests of the hospitable family on that July 4 weekend. Our hostess was a widow with four grown children in the area, all of whom we met that weekend. On Friday evening the Larkspur Volunteer Fire Department, a favorite charity among the Larkspur wealthy, sponsored an Independence Day dance in an outdoor area decorated with garlands of flowers and Chinese lanterns. There were dozens of beautiful girls at the dance, and Bob danced until he was worn out. The girls, in turn, wore themselves out trying to teach me, a poor Tennessee boy from a rural community where dancing was a sin, how to dance in spite of two left feet.

For the remainder of the weekend, our hostess and her son drove us around to see the sights. At her insistence, our first stop was Hamilton Field to look up the Army Air Corps recruits with whom I had come to California. She seemed to be genuinely pleased to meet them. Those young Southern boys of common origin had had no experience with *noblesse oblige*, but they conducted themselves well and showed great respect for the lady. On Sunday morning following a late breakfast, our hostess and her son took us for a day's outing in San Francisco. After a tour of Golden Gate Park, we drove to the famous Cliff House Restaurant at Point Lobos on the Pacific Coast for lunch. While we ate, we gazed at the Pacific through large plate glass windows and observed the sea lions cavorting on the rocks nearby.

That afternoon our hostess especially wanted us to see the site of her former San Francisco home, which was located not far south of Ft. Mason. She was living there at the time of the great earthquake of 1906 and had just begun cooking breakfast when the quake struck. Her account was fascinating. Even after nearly fifty years, I clearly recall her words and tone of voice. Our hostess then decided that Bob and I should conclude our visit with some good seafood; so off we went to a large restaurant on Fisherman's Wharf.

It was only a short drive from Fisherman's Wharf to the Ft. Mason docks, where Bob and I said our good-byes to our gracious hostess and her son. It had been an absolutely wonderful holiday weekend, except that it passed all too quickly. Our hostess invited us to spend the next weekend with them, and we gladly accepted; but the Army had other plans for Bob and me. We were keenly disappointed when, over the next weekend, all Army personnel slated for overseas were confined to base to begin a sort of countdown. Bob, who was destined to die on Bataan, and I would never see that charming lady again, but she kept in close touch with us until Pearl Harbor and even established contact with our families after the onset of the apocalypse. Even as I write, the image of our elegant hostess of Larkspur connects me with a time when my world was young.

Instead of spending the weekend having a good time with our friends in Larkspur, we spent it preparing for overseas departure. About the middle of the following week, we were given immunization shots, which made me sick. The day after, still feeling sick, I had to stand at attention in the hot afternoon sun for a general's inspection. Immediately following the noon meal on the next day (Thursday, July 17), we boarded a special ferry for the Ft. Mason docks.

When we arrived at the Ft. Mason docks and disembarked, we were immediately ordered to line up before boarding our ship, but it was the usual Army routine of hurry up and wait. I felt as if I had the world's worst hangover. Finally, the line began to move, and a few minutes later I was boarding the luxury liner *President Coolidge* bound for the Philippines. The Army had not formally taken over the *Coolidge* but had merely requisitioned it for that particular voyage; hence, the great ship was not a true troopship because it still retained its staterooms and its civilian crew and staff. All five hundred military personnel going to the Philippines were assigned to staterooms, while most of the twenty-five hundred troops going to Hawaii were put in the hold.

I was assigned to a stateroom already occupied by four other people, all members of my company. Normally, no more than two or three civilians would have shared the space. Since I was the last of the five to enter our compartment, I got the least desirable top bunk. Still feeling bad but somewhat better than earlier in the day, I climbed into my bunk hardly noticing who my shipmates were. I soon dozed off but was awakened by the soldier in the bunk below mine; he had a loud voice and a raucous laugh that alternated with his harmonica playing. He was a real pest, especially for someone as sick as I was. Yet the voice seemed familiar; I leaned over the side of my bunk to take a look. Lo and behold, it was my old enemy from the Ft. McDowell mess hall, Richard Murray. At first I was disgusted, but after a while I could not resist Murray's crude jokes and infectious laughter. I found myself laughing and feeling better.

The voyage from San Francisco to Honolulu took five days. The principal event for me on that leg of the journey was that Richard Murray and I became fast friends and spent a good deal of time in cooperative projects, like playing tricks on our comrades. I also became acquainted with Alfred Eckles of Hopkinsville, Kentucky, another member of my Company.

The voyage on the *President Coolidge* was luxurious for Army troops. Though we had to line up for our meals cafeteria style, we ate in the ship's dining hall where the waiters did much of the serving. At all the evening meals and at some noon meals, the ship's orchestra played. Murray and I crudely shouted our favorite big band numbers, and the orchestra obligingly played them. After Hawaii, with twenty-five hundred fewer passengers, accommodations were even more splendid. Until then, conditions were crowded, but not painfully so. The next time I sailed by troop carrier, conditions would be different. Aboard the Japanese POW ship, space would be at such a premium that men would not have room enough to lie down, even to die.

On the day of the *President Coolidge*'s arrival in Hawaii, the ship docked at Honolulu Harbor at 7:00 A.M., giving those of us going on to Manila seventeen hours of shore leave. As we stepped from the gangplank, pretty Hawaiian girls put leis around our necks. They gave off a fragrance like honeysuckle. In fact, all of Honolulu was permeated by that same delicate odor.

Bob Donald had planned his and my itinerary for the day. To begin with, we were to go to Waikiki and spend the day surfing and lounging on the beach. That would keep me away from the rowdies who spent their day in the bar. I was not at all keen about the idea. I was not a good swimmer and knew nothing about surfing, but I went along.

The day began badly for me: I cut my foot on a piece of coral while wading in front of the Royal Hawaiian Hotel. Later, we rented surfboards and lugged them while wading toward the distant breakers. Bob soon left me behind. As I struggled to keep up, I stepped into a deep hole and almost strangled beneath my surfboard. There was no one around to help me, and I felt certain that I would drown. I finally calmed myself and gripped the surfboard for support instead of fighting it. Slowly I made my way out of the hole to wait for Bob. After a while he came in riding his surfboard like a champion. I informed him that I was giving up my surfing career and returning to town. He was unhappy with my decision and declared that he was remaining at Waikiki for the day.

Back in downtown Honolulu, I met a *Coolidge* passenger I knew, and we decided to have a beer in a nearby bar. There we met a couple of civilian hardrock miners from Oregon on their way to Wake Island where they had been hired for a military construction project. They bragged about how much money they had and invited us to join them. After a number of drinks and some additional barhopping at their expense, we went to a Chinese restaurant where we were the only occidental patrons. We were served by a beautiful Chinese waitress whose image I often recalled while a POW, not as a sexual fantasy but as my Chinese Mona Lisa. There I was fascinated as I watched an old Chinese man eating noodles with chopsticks. It was incredible to me that anyone could so deftly pick up even small food particles with such crude utensils. I could not know that by 1945 I would be equally skilled.

During the afternoon, the miners felt the need for sex and began asking passersby where the nearest house of prostitution was. They began their inquiries with a group of passing women, who appeared horrified. A Japanese taxi driver drove up and assured us that he could take us to a high-quality Japanese whorehouse. They and the other soldier jumped into the taxi, but I held back. Not only had I never been in a whorehouse; I had never had sexual relations. Though I lusted mightily, I was nervous around women and afraid of getting too close to them. The miners literally dragged me into the car. To them, real men took their sex wherever and whenever they could. So off we went to the whorehouse, the Oregon boys declaring that they preferred Japanese girls above all others.

The Japanese house was located in an attractive middle-class residential section. The taxi driver opened the front door for us, and we stepped into the front parlor. A man and a woman, both with Japanese features, came into the parlor and informed us that they were closed for the day because they were having a wedding. The miners vehemently protested, but it did no good; we were told firmly to leave. Meanwhile, I could see the wedding preparations going on in the backyard. Feeling brash from the liquor, I begged the host and hostess to permit us to stay for the wedding, but they coldly rejected my plea. The Oregon boys, who liked immensely the idea of our staying for the wedding, became engaged in a hot argument with the Japanese, insisting that at least they could let us stay for the wedding if we promised to behave properly and not disturb the proceedings. Even the taxi driver interceded in Japanese, but there was no relenting. Finally, like naughty children sent home from a party, we slunk out of what was probably the prettiest little whorehouse in Honolulu.

Back downtown, the streets were full of sailors of the U.S. Pacific fleet, just returned from maneuvers in Australian waters. We stumbled onto what was obviously one of the largest houses of prostitution in Honolulu. We could see the line of sailors extending from the front door across the front yard walkway and almost a block down the street. That scene excited the Oregon boys, but they had no intention of waiting in line. Instead, they boldly stalked to the front door (with the other soldier and me following) and started up the stairs toward the head of the line. By then the sailors had begun to complain and make loud threats, but the single-minded boys from Oregon paid no attention. I was scared even though I was drunk. I realized that bucking a line of sailors in an urgent situation like that was crazy. I tried to convince the sailors that we were not clients but news reporters.

When we reached the head of the stairs, the madam, strangely enough, opened the door and let us in despite the clamoring of the sailors on the stairs below. Soon the Oregon boys and the soldier were assigned to girls, but I held back. The madam seemed a little taken aback, but she probably had dealt with reluctant lovers before. Without hesitation, she invited me to have a seat in the parlor to wait for my friends.

I found the whorehouse parlor a sociological circus. The madam brought out the girls to meet their assigned clients. None of those I saw was native (i.e., Polynesian or other oriental); they were all Caucasians with Midwestern accents. The introductory periods were sometimes punctuated by amorous sailors pawing over the girls. One drunken sailor, when introduced to his entertainment, immediately pulled down his pants and tried to jump the girl in the parlor. The girl and the madam, demonstrating a lot of experience and skill, finally brought the sailor, a prime example of modern *Homo erectus*, under control and marched him off to his room. When our group finally reassembled, we went to dinner at a Chinese restaurant, and then I bade them goodnight. Over their protests I made my escape, worn out after a long day.

After returning to the *President Coolidge*, I lounged on the deck to enjoy the cool sea breezes. Richard Murray came back to the ship that night having done some serious drinking. He and I carried deck chairs high up on the ship's bridge and soon went to sleep. Later on around midnight, I was awakened by Murray's screams during a prophetic dream. A flight of about ten P-40s, probably from nearby Hickam Field, was roaring low directly over the *Coolidge*. Murray was screaming, "The Japs are here! The Japs are here!"

The *President Coolidge* slipped from her berth about 2:00 A.M. and began the long voyage to Manila. The remainder of the passage to the Philippines was uneventful—good weather, good food, good companionship. Beyond Hawaii, the *Coolidge* seemed to be almost an empty ship. The greatest pleasure for me was the ship's library, where I discovered the works of Richard Halliburton, including the volume published posthumously after he failed to complete his projected voyage in a Chinese junk from Hong Kong to San Francisco. Aboard the *President Coolidge* out in the Pacific Ocean seemed an appropriate place to read the works of a fellow adventurer from Tennessee.

Left: Plate 1. Preston Hubbard and Bob Donald in Larkspur, California, July 1941.

Bottom: Plate 2. SS *President Coolidge*

3

At Ease on the Eve of the Apocalypse

The beautiful days of sunshine on our voyage from Honolulu to the Philippines came to an end in the South China Sea not far outside Manila Bay. During the night, the *President Coolidge* had completed its run down the east coast of Luzon and by daylight was approaching the entrance to the bay. As we entered that magnificent body of water, one of the world's great havens for ships, I was completely ignorant of the island fortress of El Corregidor and of Bataan peninsula, which lay to our port side. The trip from the mouth of the bay to Manila, about thirty miles, took place under leaden skies, for it was early August and the Philippine monsoon was reaching its climax. As we approached Manila Port Area, poor visibility prevented us from seeing off the starboard side the home of the U.S. Navy's Asiatic Squadron, Cavite Naval Base, the scene of the first landing of American troops in the Philippines during the Spanish-American War. The misty air also prevented us from seeing the exposed remains of the Spanish fleet sunk by Commodore George Dewey in the Battle of Manila Bay in 1898. Those rusting relics, jutting from the grayish green waters of the bay, would become familiar to me while traveling along Dewey Boulevard on frequent occasions before Pearl Harbor. During World War II, the Japanese salvaged the remains of the Spanish fleet for scrap iron.

As the *President Coolidge* was awaiting tow for docking at Pier Seven, the most important facility in Manila Port Area, all military personnel, with barracks bags and other personal properties, assembled on the main deck and prepared to disembark. We were wearing our raincoats because a steady rain was falling, but as we completed our sloppy formation the clouds seemed to burst, introducing us to the real Philippine monsoon. In that sheet of falling water a raincoat was worthless; I could not have imagined such a heavy downpour.

Once the *President Coolidge* tied up at the pier, we disembarked quickly, boarded waiting Army trucks, and were on our way to our respective companies. I was among at least two truckloads of new personnel headed for Nichols Field. Soon our trucks moved from the Port Area through the city and headed south on Taft Avenue, the most prominent street in Manila. We rolled through the fantastic suburb of Pasay, a place I would soon come to love. Just south of Pasay we came to Barrio (village) Baclaran, where we turned left and crossed a bridge straddling a murky stream marking the perimeter of Nichols Field. In all, the trip from the port was five to seven miles.

Nichols Field, the principal base in the Philippines for fighter aircraft, was located on the western side of a large U.S. military reservation that covered the entire southeast quadrant of metropolitan Manila. The reservation extended from the Parañaque Road on the west toward Laguna de Bay, a lake to the east nearly half the size of Manila Bay. Most of this mammoth piece of government property was under the jurisdiction of Ft. McKinley, a major U.S. military installation in the Philippines. Its barracks and other main buildings were located three or four miles northeast of Nichols Field. Adjoining Nichols on the northeast was Nielson Field, headquarters of the Far East Air Force.[1]

When I arrived at Nichols, the Far East Air Force was in the process of replacing older fighter planes (P-35s, etc.) with America's top fighter, the P-40. The capacities of that craft were badly exaggerated by almost everyone concerned; to make matters worse, there seems to have been no awareness at Nichols Field of Japan's principal pursuit plane, the Zero. Apparently, everyone assumed that the P-40 was the best fighter in the world. It had to be so, surely, for that awkward, nose-heavy bird was a product of American "know-how" technology. Morale among the personnel seemed to be quite high, and soldiers greeted each other using the Army Air Corps' slogan, "Keep 'em flying, buddy!"

Though there was an old B-12 bomber at Nichols, the field was too small for the big bombers; however, a large construction project was under way to enable Nichols to handle B-17s.[2] Despite its position as the number one pursuit airfield in the Far East Air Force, the base was not large, consisting of a small cluster of buildings and a few hangars located just beyond the entry bridge at Barrio Baclaran. In addition, there were a handful of barracks, a few concessionary shops, an unair-conditioned movie theater, a tiny library, and the post exchange. A small hamburger joint, apparently operated by the concessionaire who managed the restaurant in the PX, was called the Tenth Hole because it was positioned near a nine-hole golf course. For the most part, everything in the main cluster was on one of two streets that formed a "T." I could see that Nichols Field was a small backwater post in the world of the U.S. Army Air Corps.

My company barracks at Nichols Field was situated on the extreme west side of the main cluster on the bank of the sluggish, mosquito-laden

Parañaque River, which formed a portion of the western boundary of the military post. From the back porch, we could see across the river the backs of the shops in Barrio Baclaran. The design of our barracks was similar to that of most military buildings in the tropics, a low-angled roof with widely overhanging eaves and long latticed windows that remained open except in a storm. Mosquito nets protected us from most flying insects, but we had to treat our bedsprings regularly to kill off the bedbugs that flourished in the damp, tropical climate. The toilet facilities were located in a detached building behind the barracks on the edge of the nearly stagnant river. The facilities (commodes, wash basins, showers, etc.) were fairly modern, but accessibility was a problem during the night and monsoon storms. Our Army outhouse may not have been convenient, but it was, at least, shaded by some beautiful mango trees. The Army officers considered this outdoor privy more than adequate for people (i.e., enlisted personnel) with limited social aspirations and opportunities.

My company was founded in April 1941 as the 330th Signal Company (Aviation). However, a few weeks after my arrival the number was changed to the 409th for reasons never explained to the company's rank and file. The word *Aviation* indicated attachment to the Army's Far East Air Force (FEAF). It was my understanding that our outfit was assigned directly to the Commanding Officer, FEAF, and that we were supposed to provide the ground communications for his office. In fact, we had none of the equipment necessary for that task. We were told that the mobile radio vans, telephone trucks, and dispatch motorcycles we needed were on the way, but they failed to arrive before Doomsday in the Philippines. When the war began, we borrowed various pieces of equipment here and there.

The members of the 409th ate with four or five other companies in a detached mess about a hundred yards from our barracks. No one at Nichols Field was required to perform kitchen police duties because of the availability of cheap Filipino labor. A small fee was deducted from the pay of all privates and corporals, permitting the hiring of Filipino kitchen workers. They served us family style, bringing the food to us at the tables.

One of the irritating problems of Army mess halls was caused by those men known as "chowhounds." Apparently, there were many of them in the Old Army. At our mess detachment at Nichols Field, chowhounds began hanging around the kitchen door an hour and a half before the noon and evening meals, peeping and sniffing. The smell of food drove them into a frenzy. When the workers finally opened the mess hall door, the chowhounds, already at the head of the line, would rush in and quickly inspect the tables for desserts. The cooks at our mess generally provided two pies for each table of ten men at noon and evening, each of the pies being cut into five equal pieces. The chowhounds would grab a whole pie unless the kitchen staff stood guard, prepared to beat them off.

The renewed Selective Service Act of September 1941 contained a provision lowering the upper-age limits. That act affected some members of the National Guard units in the Philippines. Eight or nine Apache Indians above the age limit from the New Mexico National Guard were assigned to our mess while awaiting the first available transportation to the States. I often ate with them because I was generally late in arriving, and a seat was always available at the Apaches' table. The Apaches were serious eaters and did not engage in frivolous conversation during the meal. They signaled for passage of a particular bowl of food by grunting and pointing. I kept alert for their signals in order to oblige.

Two other fees were deducted from the private's pay at Nichols Field—one for barracks cleaning and the other for laundry services. In the 409th the company housekeeper was an efficient, hardworking, handsome Filipino named Alfredo. The pay he received was enough for him to hire additional Filipinos from time to time. Though we were supposed to make up our bunks, Alfredo frequently added a deft touch to untidy bedclothes. He kept the floor polished, shined our shoes, and inspected our extra clothing to see if it needed repair or cleaning. In addition, he managed the company's entire laundry, gathering the items, checking them out with the contract laundry service off-post, and checking in and distributing the clean laundry.

Special laundry services could be obtained at one of the concessions on the post owned by a Chinese entrepreneur named Charlie Corn. At Charlie Corn's shops, military personnel could get custom-made shoes, tailored Army fatigues and fatigue hats, and tailored civilian clothing at remarkably low prices. Most soldiers used Charlie Corn's tailoring services only for the fitting of fancy fatigues (denims). We generally preferred to buy civilian items from the master Chinese tailors in Pasay.

Until mid-November 1941, only a few members of the 409th were assigned regular duties. Our daily routine, Monday through Friday, consisted of an hour's close order drill, an hour's recuperation in the PX, and then an hour in class struggling with Morse code and studying maintenance procedures for radios and other equipment. We were off duty during the afternoons, which, I understood, was standard for tropical duty in the Old Army.

The close order drill was performed halfheartedly at best. Except for one aggressive drill corporal who had grandiose dreams of military advancement and who loved to bully and humiliate lowly privates, the drill instructors did not browbeat their students. Close order drill could be fun on occasion. I remember that Lou Honstein of San Francisco made a diligent effort to perform the exercises correctly, but he was handicapped by a hearing problem. Honstein always seemed to be on the right end of his squad, and he loved leading a march when we were given the order "right march!" The drillmaster would often lower his voice for a "halt" order, stopping everyone except poor Lou, who, much to our delight, would keep on marching across the field. Outside of my bosom friends, Lou Honstein was one of my favorites. Sadly, Lou succumbed to Japanese atrocities at Cabanatuan, and the drill corporal dreamed his last at Camp O'Donnell.

Occasionally, we used a part of the morning schedule for a hike. I loved the hike but hated preparing for it. The worst part of the preparation was the packing; I had trouble getting all of the required materials into my pack, especially the ax and the spade. Once the hike began it was fun for me, but some members always fell out along the way from hypochondria or hangovers. We marched from the Nichols gate bridge up the Parañaque Road to the outskirts of Barrio Baclaran where we turned left and ambled across to the Manila Bay beach. There, in the struggle through the sand, was where most of our casualties occurred, but I enjoyed hiking the beach where I could look for stranded marine life, especially baby octopuses. After a mile or two along the shore, we turned back to a point on the Parañaque Road just south of Baclaran. By the time we got to Baclaran proper, we attracted a lot of children, both boys and girls. The kids knew many of us personally because we saw them frequently around Baclaran. As we marched through the barrio from the south, those lovable urchins would line up and march behind us or run along our flanks calling out our names and poking fun at us. I have always felt that scene had something significant to say about the nature of the American Empire in 1941, but I am not sure what it was.

At that time all soldiers in noncombatant units were required to qualify in the use of a side arm on the shooting range. The day the unqualified members of the 409th went to the range was not a high point in American military history. In fact, it was more like a tour de farce. Like the policy setters of many American public schools today, the sergeants conducting the shoot saw to it that everyone, no matter how incompetent, qualified. They succeeded through hard work and imagination, but there were some sad cases. Our weapon was the old .45 automatic, allegedly invented to stop the Moros in Mindanao who ran amuck. My gun was so loose it sounded like a child's toy. Because it was badly pitted from age and metal fatigue, it looked dirty. More than once the company commander chewed me out for not properly cleaning my weapon. One member of the group panicked and dropped his .45, which discharged along a line just beyond the feet of the men sitting on the ground pulling the targets with ropes. None of our group learned to shoot the .45 automatic well, but I was amazed at the shooting demonstration put on by some of the Old Army sergeants. At any rate, the sergeants carried out their mission impossible, qualifying everyone even though some of us could not have hit the broad side of a coconut palm.

On Saturday mornings we were required to stand a post inspection. To prepare for the event, we had to clean up our bunk areas, neatly arrange the contents of our lockers according to a precise plan, and go outside and line up to await the inspecting officer. Every Saturday morning the noncoms went through hell getting all the drunks ready for inspection. The drunks (including me on at least one occasion) had to be dragged out of bed, dressed, and led outside while their sober brothers made ready their bunk areas and lockers. Some literally had to be held up until the officer arrived. Inspection never took long, however. The officer always came through like a whirlwind, giving the line of soldiers, theoretically at attention, only a cursory glance and never entering the barracks. If we had placed a full-grown rhinoceros in line, he would not have noticed. The inspector left as quickly as he came, never pausing to look back. He had no intention of wasting a Saturday morning loitering in the enlisted slums of Nichols Field when he could be drinking gin slings at the Army and Navy Club with his kind of people—and we were thankful.

Most military personnel in the prewar Philippines were on a relaxed work schedule—one that required only half-day service from 8:00 A.M. to 12:00 noon. Consequently, we had the afternoons and evenings off. As I recall, however, the tropical duty standard was already in decline when I arrived; for example, the Army engineers engaged in construction at Nichols worked a full day, Monday through Friday. Most of the other troops were glad they were not in the engineers, and they even avoided association with the them, fearing that the full-day workweek might be contagious.

Military personnel on the tropical standard had a lot of time on their hands, and they spent it pursuing one of three main activities, depending on their personality type: the barracks siesta, on-base lounging, and off-base entertainment. Personality type one, perhaps 15 to 20 percent of 409th membership, regularly took the after-lunch siesta from about 1:00 to 3:00 P.M. During siesta hours, other members were forbidden to talk loudly or make noise in or around the dormitory. Those who took siesta, however, made plenty of noise themselves; they made the dormitory sound like a contest at a sawmillers' convention. Adding a surreal touch, many of the siesta group were also health nuts and physical culture devotees who neither smoked nor drank and whose conversations constituted, for the rest of us, lethal threats to sanity.

Some of the 409th personnel who did not participate in the siesta program, "type two," rarely went off the base, except on occasional evenings. In the afternoons they lounged in the barracks basement recreation room or around the base. The third group was the off-base foragers who spent the afternoons and evenings seeking entertainment of various kinds in the city. Many of those men became so involved in off-base activities that they spent themselves poor supporting their extra-military life-styles.

Perhaps the most popular on-base forms of entertainment took place in the company recreation room. About the time I arrived, the company's share of PX profits was allocated for new furniture and other items for the "rec" room where some company members indulged in billiards, Ping-Pong, cards, checkers, and reading. The most important activity, however, was poker, which the noncommissioned officers thoroughly controlled. Poker players often took over the section reserved for reading, and despite protests by some of us, the noncoms had their way because they had the authority. Furthermore, a vast majority of those who used the rec room agreed that poker should have priority over reading. Poker involved excitement and money; reading involved books and boredom. The more experienced noncoms consistently cleaned the company suckers and stood first in the line of creditors on payday to collect the gambling debts from their victims. Those gulled by the noncoms seemed to relish their role as dupes in that continuous economic swindle. The two company officers, who were rarely seen around the barracks, followed a policy of benign neglect, delegating the oversight of "recreational" activities to the first sergeant.

During our first three months at Nichols, Cal Borden,[3] a friend of mine in the 409th, and I both closely observed the corrupt gambling in the rec room. After discussing the subject, Borden and I decided to do something about it. As long as gambling was going to take precedence over all other recreational activities, we figured that it ought to be legitimate and we ought to enjoy some of the profit. In early November, we established a football pool, hoping not only to divert some of the easy money from the poker games but perhaps to entice the noncoms to invest a portion of their winnings in our scheme. Cal had access to money, and he financed it. At the time, I was an expert on American collegiate football, which I had studied avidly since I was about ten years old. We chose for our pool each week a list of toss-up games, betting heavy odds that our clients could not pick the winners of all the games on the list. The first couple of weeks we had only a few clients, but by the end of November we were attracting many of the suckers. We did not lose a single bet. As weak as I was in mathematics, I realized that the odds were astronomical against anyone's picking all the winners. The Japanese, however, soon put an end to the Borden-Hubbard antipoker project.

Other kinds of on-base recreation included reading in the library, which was never crowded, browsing in the concession shops where the specialty was custom tailoring, and gymnastics and sports. But the two most popular spots were the post movie and the PX beer garden and restaurant. Recruits became familiar with those two diversions during the standard three-week quarantine for new troops. Most members of the quarantined group went to the movie theater almost every night, a shed with chicken wire walls. There were, however, few breezes in the early evenings, making movie watching a sweating experience. After the quarantine was over, I rarely attended the post movie, going instead to see the newer movies in the large, first-run theaters with comfortable seats and air conditioning in Manila.

While in quarantine, some young members of the 409th followed the lead of a few older veterans who had no scruples about violating post regulations. After swimming across the muddy, polluted Parañaque, the boys followed the veterans to a Baclaran whorehouse, which operated under primitive conditions. One of my best friends was in this group, and I was horrified by his account of the affair.

In the PX beer garden, most patrons drank only one brand of beer: the world-famous San Miguel, brewed in Manila by German brewers. A later generation of American youth in Vietnam would come to appreciate the merits of that fine brew. I shall always remember the large San Miguel sign in neon letters atop the old Manila wall. The sign and much of the wall were destroyed during the Battle of Manila in 1945.

There was a vast difference between the social life of the officer and the enlisted man. The officers and a few white American civilians constituted a tightly knit unit of the American upper class who ruled the Philippines in much the same way the British ruled India. American officers had the privilege of bringing their families to the Philippines, and that greatly reinforced the role of the officer portion of the American raj. Truly, the ruling class in the Philippines was composed largely of the white officers of the U.S. Army and Navy and their families. In 1936, Manuel Quezon, president of the Philippine Commonwealth, complained to the U.S. High Commissioner that U.S. Army and Navy officers were running the Philippines and ignoring him.[4] The American raj heightened their sense of imperial dignity by living aloof from both the Philippine people and the enlisted class. The military families, along with a relatively small number of upper-class American civilians, "insulated themselves from the life of the country as much as possible and institutionalized their color prejudice by establishing their own schools, churches and clubs."[5]

The American raj not only held the Filipinos in contempt; they also viewed American enlisted men as crude peasants to be kept in their place by rigid military and social restrictions. The officer class did not use enlisted men as servants, as was the custom at military installations in the States, because of the inexhaustible supply of cheap Filipino labor, a situation that further isolated the American raj from the common soldiers. Officers, including nurses, were forbidden to fraternize with enlisted men in even the most casual ways; other members of the white ruling-class families were off limits to enlisted personnel as well. For the most part, unmarried white women, including nurses, were reserved for officers or other members of the ruling raj. By 1941 a considerable number of Russian women, many of them engaged in the oldest profession, were coming to Manila from Shanghai and other Chinese cities, fleeing from the Japanese invasion of China. They were, of course, reserved for the raj.

The social status of the American raj in the Philippines intensified a racial myth regarding women and sex. Among the ruling officer caste as well as enlisted personnel, the belief prevailed that white women were infinitely superior and more desirable sexually than Philippine and other Asian women. Helping to perpetuate the myth was the fact that most Philippine women in their childbearing years were aging rapidly from hard work, child rearing, inadequate health care, and a poor diet. It was difficult for them to compare favorably with the pampered females of the raj caste. The myth of white female sexual superiority centered on the idea that white women developd superior, fuller breasts than Philippine and other Asian women. A common sight for American military personnel was the exposed and unsupported breasts of native women, whereas white women had the advantage of modern foundation garments. Filipino women were viewed not as oriental dragon ladies, but only as poorly dressed, inferior natives with sagging bosoms. In short, the myth of the white goddess reinforced the rule of the American raj.

Since American enlisted personnel could not bring their families to the Philippines and were denied social contact with the white ruling class in the islands, they were forced to turn to the Philippine people for female companionship and familial comfort. That social bond played an important role in the American rule of the Philippines. The relationship between the enlisted men of the Old Army and the Philippine people was much more wholesome, humane, and politically and culturally constructive than the American raj's narrow and prejudiced view of the "natives." The attitude of American enlisted men of the Old Army toward the Philippine people played an important part in winning the loyalty of Filipinos to the American flag, including the remarkable demonstration of loyalty in the Bataan campaign and during the horror of Japanese occupation. The bond of friendship, sealed in blood, between the common American soldier and the Philippine people on Bataan will likely endure no matter what happens to the formal political relationship between the United States and the Philippines.

The social constraints imposed on the enlisted soldier by the American raj led to the development of the shack-up system. The establishment, growth, and protection of this institution were covertly approved and encouraged by the U.S. Army as a means of fighting venereal diseases, the great scourge of armies, and also of defusing social tensions among the common soldiers. The Army permitted those troops who met minimum qualifications regarding service and rank to live off post with a native woman, who was required to submit to periodic medical examinations by Army medical personnel. In addition, the Army required the soldiers involved to purchase meats and other foods at the Army PX. Consequently, the soldiers in the shack-up system probably had a more healthful and wholesome diet than unattached soldiers who spent much of their free time off base and were more susceptible to dietary disorders because of a life-style that included eating disease-laden food in native restaurants.

Not long after our arrival, I witnessed the ceremony central to that institution. The ceremony was held at that time so the backlog of recently promoted on-base personnel and the newly arrived eligibles could be inducted into the sacred fraternity of shack-ups. Actually, only a handful of eligibles were candidates, but their presence provided an excuse for a festive occasion to satisfy the emotional needs of Nichols Field soldiers and the people of Barrio Baclaran.

Though there was no obvious structure or organization, the event followed a fairly set ritual. On a given day in the local village (which at Nichols Field was Barrio Baclaran), the GIs would line the main street (Parañaque Road) in front of the many gin mills, while the girls who were candidates for shack-up would parade down the street in pairs in their finest attire, averting their eyes and pretending not to notice the raucous soldiers. Those comely examples of Philippine youth always wore colorful leis around their delicate brown necks and poppies in their hair. The eligible GIs would look over the contestants and eventually approach one with a proposition, that is, an offer of a given amount of money for household expenses. Everyone knew that the amount offered should be approximately double the amount necessary for household expenses so that the girl would have money to share with her family. The girl might accept a given proposition or reject it in favor of looking further for a better monetary offer or a more handsome American. In some cases, a parading girl would be participating in the affair just for fun: perhaps her shack-up mate was returning stateside and had already bequeathed her to a friend who had recently arrived in the Philippines.

One of the newly inducted shack-ups was an arrogant, ignorant, brownnosing braggart from Nichols, who possessed absolutely no redeeming qualities. To our delight his shack-up compact concealed more than it revealed. He became the laughingstock of his company when the news leaked out that he had shacked up with a ravishing female impersonator—in the Philippines called a bini-boy.

Barrio Baclaran, just outside the front gate of Nichols Field, was a favorite and convenient place for rest and recreation. The residential section, west of the town and business district, consisted mostly of one- and two-room shacks of bamboo, though there were a few substantial houses, some of which the shack-up couples rented. The Barrio's business section was strung along both sides of the Parañaque Road on each side of the junction with the Nichols Field entrance. The business establishments included a few grocery stores and various kinds of shops, but mostly gin mills. The stores and shops were small and poorly stocked, except for a relatively large Chinese grocery located just outside Nichols's gate. Richard Murray and I, returning drunk to Nichols late in the evening, would stop by the Chinese store. Murray had a theory that eating sardines would prevent hangovers. While purchasing the canned fish, we would tease the Chinese proprietor. One night Murray, to emphasize a point in his argument, slammed his hand down on a plastic bushel bowl of shelled peanuts, splitting the container and spraying peanuts everywhere. The proprietor, shouting in Chinese, chased Murray and me all the way to the bridge at the Nichols Field gate.

The most impressive shop in Baclaran was a photographic studio owned by Norman Tant, a member of the 409th. He was the only soldier I knew at Nichols Field who moonlighted. Tant, who retired a few years ago as director of audiovisual education at Morehead (Kentucky) State University, provided an element of stability in the 409th. He and his shop stood in sharp contrast to the other personalities and diversions of the Barrio's bars, where the boys from Nichols Field went to slake their thirst.

For the most part, the men of each unit at Nichols Field tended to adopt collectively a particular saloon in Baclaran where most members of that unit hung out in their off hours. The 409th adopted a wonderful bamboo palace—I cannot remember the name—owned by a handsome Filipino woman who offered good conversation and motherly advice to the lonely men of the U.S. Army. Her role as a morale booster helped mightily in implementing Nichols Field's slogan of "Keep 'em flying."

In the Philippines the principal drink of American GIs was Philippine gin. Next in popularity was Philippine rum, totally unlike the West Indian variety. On the base, San Miguel beer was the popular drink, but beer was rarely consumed off base. American enlisted men in the Manila area rarely touched whisky. In the bars of Baclaran a gin lemonado cost the princely sum of ten centavos (five cents), and it did not take many to put the drinker under the table. After nearly fifty years I can still taste that cold, sweet, tangy liquid with the potency of a typhoon.

Parañaque Road in Baclaran seemed always to be filled with Filipino children of both sexes, from toddlers to teenagers. Many of those vivacious, lovable urchins overflowed into the gin mills where they engaged in begging and banter, shoe-shining, running errands, and pimping. I knew of no incident of Filipino kids consuming intoxicating drinks, and few of them smoked cigarettes. Most of the Nichols Field men who frequented the Baclaran bars knew many of the children personally and often by their first names. The reverse was also true: the kids knew many of the American soldiers, from whom they could solicit money, soft drinks, candy, and shoe-shining jobs. A favorite pastime of American GIs was tossing the large Philippine pennies into crowds of children, watching them scramble and fight for the windfall. Most, however, felt guilty because toddlers and girls were unable to compete with the older boys. Consequently, those events nearly always ended with the GI handing pennies directly to the girls and the little ones. Pimping was widespread among the older males, who frequently went about selling their "sisters."

The enlisted men's relationship with the children was an advantage they enjoyed over the ruling raj. Obviously, the raj had few opportunities to develop an ongoing friendship with any segment of the common people and missed an important experience. I believe that the Filipino children's friendship with the enlisted men over the years played a significant role in improving Filipino-American relations. In my case, the children of Baclaran helped to fill the void in my heart caused by my painful separation from my family, especially my baby brother and sister, the twins Kenneth and Kathryn. To some extent the Filipino children provided a temporary substitute for the young members of my family. My contact with Filipino children also helped to soften my racial and cultural prejudice regarding the Filipino people. The children formed a bridge of understanding that led me to realize that poor Filipino families, in their struggle for survival, had much in common with my own people in the American South. Later, on Bataan, when we began to suffer from isolation, I felt a new and deadly homesickness for the Manila area. Some of that homesickness was for the children of Baclaran.

Often after downing a few gin lemonados in the 409th's favorite watering hole, some of us would enact skits for the benefit of our colleagues. Richard Murray and I frequently teamed up to do imitations of movie scenes, but we never attained box-office success, being either heavily booed or thrown out. On weekend evenings, when Filipino troubadours toured the Baclaran bars singing and playing musical instruments, Murray and I often joined them, uninvited. The Filipino entertainers patiently tolerated us and at times even seemed to enjoy the farce.

Many of those who went off base for recreation in the afternoons and evenings headed for Manila or Pasay. In Manila some of them went to Escolta, the most fashionable retail district in the city, where they saw the latest films from Hollywood and flirted with Philippine girls. Others went to the enlisted section of the Army and Navy Club or roamed the quaint shops on the streets of the old walled city. A few developed professional (nonsexual) friendships with Filipinos with whom they had common interests, such as photography. Besides yachting, another of Bob Donald's surprising areas of expertise was photography. He did some work in the Philippine movie industry for a successful actress. In the evenings there was a large representation of Nichols Field soldiers at the swanky Jai Alai Club on Taft Avenue. There the troops could buy a wide variety of exotic mixed drinks while placing bets on the jai alai matches. Hardly anyone actually watched the matches, most Americans considering them boring.

On most Sundays, Al Eckles, a horse-racing fanatic, and I went to the races at either the Santa Anna or the San Lazarus racetrack. Generally, Al was absorbed with the technical aspects of betting—reading racing forms and evaluating information allegedly from reliable touts—but I was more interested in observing the fans, mostly rich Chinese. It was there that I first observed the ritual of eating baluts. The Chinese eagerly purchased baluts (boiled duck eggs) from vending boys in white Coca-Cola jackets, then delicately broke the eggs, removing the shell to expose the top of the duckling's head. The consumer drank the juice from the shell before removing and eating the duckling. Baluts were a delicious repast for the Chinese racing fans, but they were a culinary and cultural shock for me.

Libertad Street in Pasay attracted many Nichols men. Located there were the shops of incredibly skilled Chinese craftsmen and some highly skilled Filipinos, especially painters. The favorite attraction for GIs at

Pasay, however, was a large dance hall at which a Filipino orchestra played big band tunes. The great variety of bars and seductive bar girls also impressed the men from Nichols. In spite of the possibility of a painful price later, many soldiers and sailors enjoyed the forbidden fruit of prostitution. Most of the red-light districts in Manila were off limits, and military police occasionally patrolled such places. So great was the military's concern for control of venereal disease that MPs maintained prophylactic stations everywhere. Anyone found hanging around an off-limits area or wandering around after too much to drink was roughly dragged to the prophylactic station and provided with a "pro," pain and embarrassment notwithstanding.

Down the road below Baclaran in Barrio Parañaque, the favorite recreational attraction for Nichols Field men was a large military-approved whorehouse, which was operated like an assembly line. I went there a couple of times with friends who were serviced while I waited in the large parlor that was usually full of waiting customers. The demand was so great that the madam stood at the door to the service area shouting, "Next!"

There were, of course, diversions of a less seamy nature. The Philippines are islands of stunning natural beauty, and I was equally attracted by their history and culture. For off-base recreation I occasionally joined the small group of culture buffs at Nichols Field, who, led by the chaplain, explored places as diverse and interesting in their own way as Malacañang Palace—the Philippine White House and then residence of President Quezon—and a large Chinese cemetery where we watched a Buddhist priest chanting as he burned incense.

In November 1941, the enlisted men's association at Nichols Field completed the renovation of a building on Parañaque Road north of Baclaran and established an enlisted men's club. In the new club one could sit with a drink on the second floor balcony and watch the sun go down behind Bataan, but by the time of Pearl Harbor that institution had largely failed to win the men of Nichols Field away from their familiar and favorite haunts. It appeared to me that the club was becoming a front for a gambling den operated by the poker kings of Nichols Field.

At Nichols, the frenzied spending by some of our company spawned an epidemic of debt. The pay of common soldiers was paltry (thirty dollars a month for privates), and most of them were spendthrifts. Many of the prodigals consistently borrowed as much money as possible at every opportunity, staying continuously up to their ears in debt. Some of them, however, were skilled debt dodgers. On payday, creditors jostled each other for places in line just beyond the pay table where they would be the first to greet the payees. Often, soldiers were plucked clean of their money as they passed down the line of creditors; for some of the men, the month's pay was completely exhausted before all creditors were satisfied. The resulting financial stress caused some theft around the base. Some of the hard-core bankrupts stole anything in the barracks they could lay their hands on. The problem diminished after the military police arrested several civilian fences in Baclaran and Pasay and recovered some loot.

Our bankrupt comrades often put great psychological pressure on their solvent brethren, including Cal Borden and me, to lend them money for off-base recreation, e.g., whorehouses and gin mills. Both of us had lent money to deadbeats and were frustrated by their reluctance to repay. We noticed that even the worst of debtors tried to satisfy their professional creditors—loan sharks—while hesitating to repay interest-free loans from friends. Consequently, we decided in November 1941, at about the same time we were developing the football pool, to launch a small-loans business, even though such an entrepreneurial activity was illegal in the U.S. Army. At the time, some loan sharks were already operating at Nichols Field, but not in our Company. As in the case of our football pool, Cal obtained the nest egg for our scheme from home. Reportedly, the average interest rate charged by the existing firms at Nichols Field was about 50 percent per month, but Cal and I stuck to the standard Army prime rate—20 percent per month.

As a matter of fact, we found that our clients who had been sponging free loans from us tended to pay their interest-bearing debts more promptly. At the end of the November 1941 payday, Cal and I did remarkably well in collecting from our clients, but that was the last payday we would have for a long time to come. The Japanese brought the Borden-Hubbard Small Loan Company to an end. A few of our clients who still had outstanding debts to our defunct firm paid all or part of their loans during the Bataan campaign.

My greatest satisfaction during the Borden-Hubbard small loans program was in dealing with a 409th sergeant who had a habit of hitting the solvent privates for loans and then suffering a lapse of memory. An implied threat accompanied such requests for money. He had borrowed from me a couple of times, and I had had difficulty collecting the interest-free debt. When he first asked for a loan after we established our firm, I replied that I would be happy to comply and that it would cost him only 20 percent per month. Initially, he became very angry, saying, "Go to Hell. I wouldn't pay you a centavo in interest." But the sergeant had an un-wholesome recreational program to finance; he soon returned, politely applied for the loan, and repaid it in full the next payday.

Along with our small loan business, Cal and I provided a brokerage service for the Company bankrupts and others. Because of the large number of debt-ridden soldiers, the Army issued books of canteen checks at midmonth. The bankrupts could draw on them against future pay, but the scrip could be spent only for necessary items (toilet articles, cigarettes, etc.) and only in the PX. The profligates tried to convert the canteen checks into legal tender out of desperate need to finance off-base recreation; they drew the maximum amount allotted and sold the checks to brokers for fifty cents on the dollar, or even less. The brokers took them to certain parties in the administration of Nichols Field who were powerful enough to have them cashed at the PX for full value. Since Cal handled that end of it, I never knew or cared who the cashing parties were, but they charged only 5 percent for cashing the canteen checks illegally. In that way, Cal Borden and I were able to extend a helping hand in making possible off-base recreation for the deprived members of the company.

Oddly enough, despite the abundance of alcohol, both on and off the base, there were relatively few alcoholics among the soldiers at Nichols Field. Of the three or four serious cases in the 409th, two were slated for court-martial, one of them scheduled for trial on December 8. Those cases were dismissed as a result of Pearl Harbor, and the two drunks involved became extremely valuable soldiers on Bataan where liquor was virtually unobtainable.

I usually drank modestly because excessive drinking made me sick and silly—sometimes dangerously so. On one occasion, when I indulged too heavily, I was coming down Dewey Boulevard, which fronted on Manila Bay, with some other GIs when we came to a mass meeting of Filipino nationalists on the beach at the end of that grand promenade. They were cheering their intense speakers enthusiastically. After one of them had completed his talk, I abruptly and rudely intervened, asking the chairman if I could speak. Instead of cutting off my head with a bolo knife, he invited me to mount the platform. I delivered a rousing address praising the Filipino people and advocating immediate Philippine independence, despite the fact that I knew nothing about the issue and had never heard of the Hawes-Cutting or Tydings-McDuffie Acts. Nevertheless, the Philippine nationalists applauded and cheered me roundly. That story would have been quite different if the military police had caught me drunk and meddling with that delicate political issue.

November 1941 was a busy month for me. In addition to my other activities, military and private, I joined Al Eckles in developing a plan to get out of the Philippines to some place and activity more romantic than the drab, gray world of Nichols Field. One evening we were drinking at our favorite bar in Baclaran when a couple of strangers wearing civilian clothes entered and sat down beside us. Al and I fell to talking with them and found that they were en route to Burma, their ship having stopped over in Manila for a couple of days. They informed us that they had been career men in the Army but had been released to work for General Chennault's Flying Tigers in China. They told us that a goodly number of U.S. Army Air Corps personnel with certain skills (including communications) were being released for service in China.

That information excited Al and me. The very next day we began to work up a plan to take advantage of that situation. We eventually had two favorable discussions with the Chinese consul, but we probably mistook his courtesy for a genuine sign of encouragement. Al also got optimistic reports from two friends from whom he was seeking help, including a colonel on MacArthur's staff. By the first week in December, he and I were still excited about our prospects, and we began to have fantasies about Christmas in China. Amid such hopes, however, we realized that our chances of going to the Middle Kingdom were diminished by a lack of real skills—even in communications. On December 8, the Japanese abruptly ended our China project, dashing what remained of our dreams of high adventure.

While Al Eckles and I were pursuing the high road to China, we had another project in the works. We applied and were accepted for enrollment in the University of the Philippines, located on a splendid campus on Taft Avenue. Should our China project fail, we would have something challenging to do as an alternative. We had a long conversation with the admissions officer, who seemed eager to enroll American military personnel. After all these years, I recall clearly his stating that the University of the Philippines was comparable to Cornell in size and quality. Al and I doubted this; we had been under the influence of the raj too long to accept the idea that a native school on the back side of the world could compare with a great American university. Anyway, fate and the Japanese had other plans for us.

Because of increasing tension by mid-November 1941, the Army ended the leisurely tropical work policy and replaced it with regular full-duty assignments for everyone. I was assigned an eight-hour stint (2:00 P.M. to 10:00 P.M.) in the Message Center at the headquarters of the FEAF at Nielson Field, which joined Nichols Field on the northeast. Though my job was primarily delivering messages to adjacent offices, I began receiving instruction in encoding and decoding messages. Soon after I was assigned regular duties at Nielson, General MacArthur began a series of alerts, which indicated increasing Japanese activity. That made my job more exciting.

At that time the Army implemented various measures to beef up the security of Nichols Field. During the alerts, personnel were confined to post and, except for those on duty, frequently had to fall out wearing our World War I helmets and new style gas masks and bearing .45 automatics. We would stand there looking at the sky as if trying to ward off evil spirits. Though we were never told why we were engaging in this activity, apparently we were supposed to defend the post from attack by any enemy from land, sea, or air.[6] Security drills, gas masks, and .45s were useless against what lay ahead. In one twenty-four-hour period in early December, the largely untrained, class conscious military adjunct of the American Empire in the Philippines would be transformed into a battlefront army fighting for survival.

On the eve of the apocalypse, the American Army in the Philippines was not ready for war. To be sure, it suffered from the weaknesses afflicting all peacetime armies—inefficiency, boredom, and little sense of purpose, to name a few. But there was the added unhappy aspect of an American institution rife with the sense of class-conscious privilege and political self-righteousness. The American statesman, Frank Murphy, whose relationship with the American raj became one of mutual contempt, was involved in a humorous incident that epitomized the attitude of the American officer caste serving in the Philippines. On his voyage to Manila aboard the *President Coolidge* in 1935 to assume the office of Governor-General of the Philippines, Murphy came on deck in casual attire and was mistaken for an enlisted man by an Army officer who greeted him with, "Boy, bring me a deck chair." [7]

When the war alarm sounded in December 1941, the problem was not that the war came before the U.S. Army in the Philippines was ready; it would never have been ready. The Army's severest handicap in the Philippines was not a scarcity of manpower and materiel, but the officer class's anguish over the loss of a way of life based on overconfidence and a sense of superiority.

Despite my resentment of the U.S. Army officers' relationship with enlisted personnel in the Philippines, practically all of the common career soldiers at Nichols Field were apparently satisfied with their place in life. Many of them were plainly happy with their lot. They took everything for granted; they did not appear to feel oppressed by the officers. In their view the Old Army in the Philippines was a mutually beneficial compact between officers and enlisted men to lead a life that was physically and mentally undemanding. The Old Army men viewed military service in the Philippines as highly desirable, next to that in China. Thus, even though I and other new recruits despised the negative attitude of the officer caste toward enlisted men, the men of the Old Army were content to stand at ease in that island Eden in the shadow of the American raj.

Plate 3. 409th Signal Company, platoon photograph
Top row: Louis Honstein, 6 (from left)
Middle row: J. L. Whitehead, 6; Preston Hubbard, 7; Louis Bailey, 8
Bottom row: Alfred Eckles, 3

Plate 4. 409th (330th) Signal Company Barracks

4

The End of the Rainbow

On the eve of Pearl Harbor, the officers and men of the Old Army in the Pacific theater were blinded to the dangers posed by the Japanese threat. The belief in American superiority—physical, political, and moral—made difficult an understanding of, or meaningful negotiations with, the Japanese. Japan was a nation of weak little people who produced shoddy and inferior goods; America was the paragon of excellence.

A short time before my departure from Ft. McDowell for the Philippines, all of the Army personnel slated for the next troop shipment overseas were herded together for routine pep talks by various members of the McDowell permanent party. The officers who spoke gave us the standard ambiguous exhortation: America is invincible, but soldiers should be prepared to give their lives readily. The most memorable lecture was by a tough-talking stereotype of a sergeant who stole the show. With the help of other enlisted personnel, he demonstrated the proper procedures for folding and unfolding, raising and lowering the American flag. "The flag must never touch the ground," he shouted. After completing the flag ritual, the sergeant barked a rhetorical question: "Why must the American flag at all costs be prevented from touching the ground?" The answer was, he informed us, that the flag's touching mother earth was symbolic of national defeat. But the American nation, armed with might and right, had never suffered defeat at the hands of an enemy and never would.

To me the sergeant's pep talk was chilling rather than exhilarating. Perhaps because of my Southern heritage I felt the speech to be personally threatening. What if some weak grandson of the Confederacy like me should accidentally drop the flag? Would the result of such a sacrilege be simply embarrassment? Or would I find myself in genuine physical peril? My comrades seemed to share some of my concern about the implications of the speech, but I could tell that the sergeant's admonitions were going in one ear and out the other. I think I must have been alone in storing his words forever.

I also found offensive the sergeant's insolence and pomposity. Equally offensive was the air of the officers who participated in the pep talks, all of whom addressed us as if we were mentally handicapped children. Though I did not doubt that America was the most powerful nation in the world and that no one could defeat us because of our great store of skills and wealth, I felt an emotional repugnance at bragging about it; the whole argument seemed in bad taste. Deep down, I was a little intimidated by the sergeant's coarse declaration of American supremacy.

From San Francisco to Manila, I found that most American servicemen did not really believe we would have war with Japan. They could not see an American first strike against the Japanese, and they were certain that Japan would not be so foolish as to attack Uncle Sam. A minority considered it possible that the United States might become involved in a war should Japan invade British territory. But it appeared to me that most of them hoped for war; such an event would provide opportunities for adventure as well as promotion, and it would be great fun to participate in whipping the "Japs." As late as the November alerts of 1941, most members of the U.S. armed forces with whom I had contact, both officers and enlisted men, believed that in the event of war with Japan the affair would be over quickly. The consensus among my comrades in the 409th Signal Company and others at Nichols Field was that the United States would need only about six weeks to defeat Japan. I had read in the popular press about Japan's war preparations, including the stockpiling of an enormous amount of war materiel. So when I suggested that it might take as long as nine months to win a war, I was viewed as exceptionally pessimistic.

General MacArthur played a significant role in creating an atmosphere of overconfidence in the Philippines. When he was appointed Commander of U.S. Army Forces in the Far East (USAFFE)[1] on July 26, 1941, the War Department's plan for defense of the Philippines was the recent (April 1941) version of the old Orange Plan called War Plan Orange-3. In the event of war with Japan, Orange-3 called for the withdrawal of U.S. Army forces in the Philippines to Bataan and Corregidor to await reinforcements while denying the Japanese use of Manila Bay. Unhappy with the "defeatist and defensive" Orange Plan, General MacArthur proposed a change in October 1941 that would permit him to be much more aggressive against a Japanese invasion. In November of 1941, Washington accepted MacArthur's new proposal, a revision of the old Rainbow Plan. That plan greatly increased the General's authority to attack in case of enemy landings in the Philippines. MacArthur planned "to meet the Japanese at the beaches . . . and drive them back into the sea."[2] Undoubtedly, General MacArthur's unjustified optimism, promoting the change from a defensive to an offensive mission, tended to obscure reality and give further support to the illusion of American strength in the Philippines.

In November, two events focused attention on the possibility of war: the Japanese emissary Saburo Kurusu's mission to Washington to aid in peace negotiations and a series of military alerts initiated by General MacArthur. No doubt those events caused many Americans in the Philippines to consider for the first time the possibility of war with Japan. Kurusu's flight aboard the *China Clipper* came through Manila, where there was a brief stopover. The famous Japanese diplomat granted an interview with the Manila news media, which gave considerable local publicity to the event.

The MacArthur "alerts," during which we were confined to post and drilled on how to defend American soil with our .45s and gas masks, were a result of warnings from Washington. On November 24, Washington warned Navy units in the Pacific, including the Asiatic Fleet in the Philippines, that a Japanese attack anywhere in the Pacific, "including . . . the Philippines and Guam," was possible. On November 27, a strong message went out from the War Department to General Short in Hawaii and to General MacArthur in the Philippines warning that peace negotiations with the Japanese seemed to be breaking down and that "hostile action" by the Japanese could take place at any moment. Also on November 27, the Navy Department sent out another warning to naval units in the Pacific even stronger than the War Department's message of the same day. The Navy Department insisted its message be shared with the Army in Hawaii and the Philippines.[3]

Despite the alerts, I, along with many of my comrades, still did not think there would be war. We strongly believed that the Japanese would obtain some face-saving, diplomatic concession from Washington that would enable them to back down. It is my opinion that General MacArthur also did not believe the Japanese would attack. I think his professed optimism about an aggressive war against Japan and his successful promotion of the Rainbow Plan were designed to enhance his macho image with little cost to himself; all he had to do was brag, and that he did. On November 28, he reported by radio to General Marshall in Washington that "within the limitations imposed by the present state of development of this theatre of operations, everything is in readiness for the conduct of a successful defense."[4] And on December 6 (two days before Pearl Harbor), he ordered General Wainwright's North Luzon Force to get ready to move quickly to assigned positions on the beaches.[5]

During my tour of duty in the Message Center at Nielson Field from

2:00 to 10:00 P.M. on Sunday, December 7 (the Philippines being east of the international dateline and, therefore, a day ahead of the States), there was considerable talk among our officers about an apparent increase in radio traffic by the Japanese, but I paid little attention. Some grounded Air Force pilots on duty in the message center were greatly excited and predicted imminent Japanese action against the Dutch East Indies and possibly British territory. On Monday morning, December 8, as I was on my way to breakfast, someone told me that the Japanese had bombed Pearl Harbor. I hurriedly made my way into the supply office in the basement where a radio was blaring. There the best-known radio voice in Manila, Don Bell, confirmed the report. The United States was at war with the Empire of Japan.[6]

We in the Philippines did not know how badly Pearl Harbor had been hit. No one among us even suspected that we were completely isolated with no possibility of reinforcements. Instead, almost everyone assumed that the mighty Pacific Fleet would soon be steaming into Manila Bay. On the basis of radio reports and rumors, we believed that damage to American facilities had been negligible and that Japanese naval air forces had sustained massive losses. In fact, none of the military personnel in the Philippines with whom I was associated would know anything more about the Pearl Harbor debacle by the time Bataan fell. During our years as POWs, we gradually pieced together information indicating that the Pearl Harbor attack was a Japanese success, but not until after the war did we learn the full extent of the American disaster.

Following World War II, some people argued that FDR deliberately enticed the Japanese to attack so that he could bring the United States into the war.[7] However, at the time of Pearl Harbor, no one in the Philippines, so far as I was aware, believed anything except that America was an innocent victim of an unprovoked Japanese attack.

After I returned from breakfast, our first sergeant lined the company up in front of the street entrance to the barracks' supply room. We counted off and stood at attention for a moment, looking as defiant as possible. On Wednesday, December 10, when the Japanese made their first major air raid on Nichols Field, a bomb hit approximately where we had lined up. Meanwhile, news was received about GIs being killed in their bombed barracks at Hickam Field and Schofield Barracks in Hawaii. So, later in the day on December 8, all GIs at Nichols were ordered out of their barracks and into the field. Two days later the 409th barracks was destroyed. Fortunately, the dry season was upon us.

I feel compelled to disagree with Louis Morton's description of the emotional response by American enlisted personnel to the news of war. According to Morton in his classic *The Fall of the Philippines*,

By breakfast, the news of the attack on Pearl Harbor had reached all ranks. The men had for so long accepted the fact that war with Japan might come that the event itself was an anticlimax. There was no cheering and no demonstration, but "a grim, thoughtful silence."[8]

In the early hours after breakfast, shocked silence did prevail, but before noon excitement began to surge. Both responses reflected the shattering of illusion. None of us had really expected war. Its coming was the surprise of our lives.

During the morning hours we heard various rumors about Japanese air attacks in the Philippines, but we had no certain knowledge that such attacks had occurred. Of course, we were unaware that the Japanese had planned to hit the Manila area early that morning at the same time they were attacking Pearl Harbor. The plans were delayed by heavy fog at their Formosan base.[9] At noon, while I was helping to dig a small air-raid shelter on the edge of the airfield, several nearby P-40s took off. Within a few minutes we heard that Clark Field was being bombed. Soon the P-40s returned pocked with bullet holes. Some of them were as big as my fist, and I was impressed. That was my first contact with the real war.

We understood that the P-40s had participated in the action at Clark Field. Yet, Louis Morton asserts that the pursuit squadrons in the Manila area "made no effort to attack the Japanese aircraft [at Clark Field]" because Japanese bombs had hit the communications center at Clark, confusing and delaying their operation.[10] Perhaps it was not successful, but our P-40 pilots made the effort. I saw them take off. I put my fist in the holes.

On December 8, I reported for duty at the Nielson Field Message Center as usual at 2:00 P.M. About the same time, a number of personnel from Clark arrived—some of them wearing bloody bandages covering superficial wounds. For me that was the first blood of World War II. They gave us the bad news: the Japanese had obliterated our B-17 bomber force. According to their story, the Japanese came in from the west, hitting Iba Field on Luzon's west coast minutes before arriving at Clark. Since those first bombs destroyed Iba's Message Center through which air warnings from northern Luzon were transmitted, Clark Field was left naked.[11] Consequently, the Japanese air fleet had hit Clark by complete surprise.

Amid the confusion at Nielson, FEAF officers and other personnel were blaming the alleged procrastination of General MacArthur for the disaster at Clark Field. According to the story being bandied about FEAF Headquarters, General MacArthur had refused permission to General Brereton, Commander of the FEAF, to take the offensive against the Japanese (i.e., to bomb Formosa), MacArthur's alleged hesitation reflect-

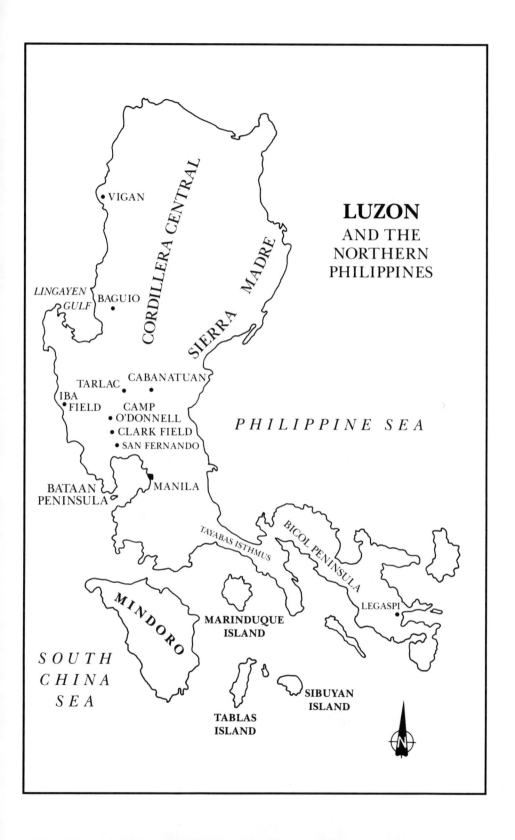

VIGAN

CORDILLERA CENTRAL

SIERRA MADRE

LUZON
AND THE
NORTHERN
PHILIPPINES

LINGAYEN
GULF
BAGUIO

TARLAC
CABANATUAN

IBA
FIELD
CAMP
O'DONNELL
CLARK FIELD
SAN FERNANDO

PHILIPPINE SEA

MANILA

BATAAN
PENINSULA

TAYABAS ISTHMUS

BICOL PENINSULA

LEGASPI

MINDORO

MARINDUQUE
ISLAND

SOUTH
CHINA
SEA

SIBUYAN
ISLAND

TABLAS
ISLAND

N

ing a period of shock and indecision. Consequently, General Brereton had ordered his B-17 fleet aloft to prevent it from being caught on the ground. At about 11:30 A.M. the fleet was forced to land for refueling. The FEAF Commander then ordered the planes armed with bombs, expecting that MacArthur's permission to attack would soon come. There apparently was no awareness at Nielson that, as Bateson claims, MacArthur had granted permission for the bombing of Formosa some thirty minutes before the B-17s landed for refueling and rearming.[12]

That Clark Field received absolutely no warning and was caught completely by surprise (contrary to later assertions) seemed to be the unanimous opinion among personnel at FEAF Headquarters during the early hours of December 8. However, later in the afternoon, Al Eckles, who was my closest friend and who had been on duty in the Message Center prior to my shift, told me that he had watched the air warning system at Nielson plot the Japanese air fleet on its way to Clark Field and that he had carried the warning message to the teletype operator. I also heard that Clark Field had been warned by telephone. Those events left me with the confused impression that there had been bungling at either Clark Field or Nielson, or both. Morton tends to confirm my suspicions.[13] My pride in the mighty Far East Air Force had been struck a serious blow.

The failure of air warning at Clark Field, the Far East Air Force's biggest base, was symbolic of the primitiveness and inefficiency of the U.S. Army in the Philippines. Primitive as it was, the system had its mysteries. For instance, it has never been clear to me why the alleged destruction of the Message Center at Iba prohibited the air warning function at Clark Field but not at Nielson. The only available advance information that a Japanese bomber armada was heading toward Clark was a formation of tiny toy planes displayed on the crude plotting board at the Air Warning Center at Nielson. The Plotting Room was close by the Message Center, my workplace. The Message Center handled all incoming and outgoing communications except air warning reports. Since there was no interoffice telephone system, the messages were delivered by runners like me to the various offices.

As I recall, the Air Warning Center had an independent system that took reports from air watchers in Luzon, who were largely Philippine government officials (postmasters, mayors, etc.), and plotted them on the air warning board, a large table about sixty to seventy feet in length cut into the shape of the Philippine archipelago. As the reports came in by telephone, telegram, and teletype, a communications officer read them aloud to the plotters, who, using cue sticks, pushed the toy planes into place. Some of the Message Center staff, including Eckles, watched the exciting event that began to unfold in the Plotting Room on the morning of December 8. A great rush of reports came in about 11:00 A.M.; shortly before 11:30 it became apparent that a large formation of Japanese planes was bearing down on Clark Field. Frantic attempts by the Message Center to warn Clark were futile.[14]

When I arrived at Nielson for my tour of duty that afternoon, the news about Clark Field drew more attention than the reports that Japanese bombers also had devastated Iba Field on the China Sea coast west of Clark as well as the town of Baguio in the mountains of northern Luzon. My only thought about Iba focused on the alleged connection between its bombing and the failure of the air warning at Clark. But Baguio was the target of the first major Japanese air strike in the Philippines, the attack coming about two hours before the Clark Field tragedy. We wondered why the Japanese would want to bomb Baguio since no military installations were there except for a few barracks for rest and recreation. But we did not cry for poor Baguio: it was the summer home of the American raj and the American Empire's attempt to imitate British India's summer capital at Simla. Anyway, the Japanese apparently paid a price for their bombing and brutal occupation of Baguio. When I came back through the Philippines in 1945, I heard reports that the Igorots (fierce local aborigines) had been taking Japanese heads and that the processed noggins could be purchased as souvenirs in Manila.

The debacle at Clark Field was a mini-Pearl Harbor with some of the same characteristics and consequences that had occurred a few hours earlier in Hawaii. But as Louis Morton points out, "The catastrophe of Pearl Harbor overshadowed at the same time and still obscures the extent of the ignominious defeat inflicted on American air forces in the Philippines on the same day."[15] The real Pearl Harbor, however, did not overshadow the significance of the Clark Field tragedy as far as the personnel of FEAF Headquarters, Nielson Field, were concerned. By 5:00 P.M., the truth had sunk in: the FEAF had been largely destroyed and would not be an effective force in the war unless reinforcements were forthcoming. MacArthur was, in our view, the villain.[16]

Sometime after midnight, a small group of Japanese bombers hit Nichols Field, which was adjacent to Nielson. Since the Air Warning Center was next door to the Message Center, I watched the Japanese planes plotted in. When the board showed them practically overhead, the bombs began to explode. Actually, the bombs hit about a mile from FEAF Headquarters. We were ordered to go out and get into the air-raid trench that had been hurriedly dug to provide some protection for the headquarters personnel. I was excited but not afraid. In fact, I lingered behind in the Message Center talking with some of the officers (probably

Captain Mason and Major Lamb) in a bold attempt to demonstrate my bravery. But when I stepped outside, tracer bullets seemed to be flying everywhere. I had never seen tracers before, and their flight like shards of lightning dazed my eyes. Then I was frightened. I ran and jumped into the air-raid ditch, landing on the back of an Air Corps lieutenant with whom I had been working in the Message Center. He complained mildly about my bad air-raid manners.

When my shift ended at 10:00 P.M. on that first day of the war (Monday December 8), there was no sign of my work relief. In fact, no relief ever came, although Eckles remained on duty from the previous shift. I was on duty, with occasional catnaps, until Thursday morning. The situation was made even worse by the FEAF's failure to arrange meals for the personnel at Nielson Headquarters. In the terrible confusion and chaos that came with war to the Philippines, we were forgotten. The debacle at Clark Field left the FEAF without prestige or priority. Since some individuals or small groups at Nielson had food delivered to them through private arrangements, Albert Stahl, who was on my work shift, and I fed ourselves and some of the other personnel in the Message Center by begging from those with food or by raiding their supplies. Though the raids were less than honest, they were our first training in scrounging, which would be so vital to us later in Bataan.

Albert Stahl and I stayed on duty together continuously until Wednesday night when he was sent to Ft. McKinley for food and rest; my turn came on Thursday. In our brief rest period at Ft. McKinley, Stahl and I discovered that some members of our Company had been assigned to a large air-raid tunnel in front of the officers' club at Ft. McKinley. Their duty was to stand ready to dash out and rout the expected Japanese paratroops. Later that week when our headquarters moved to Ft. McKinley, some help was provided for internal duties in the message Center, but Stahl and I continued to carry most, if not all, of the messages to the mobile radio unit. We divided the twenty-four workday into two twelve-hour shifts until we evacuated Manila on December 24.

While on leave at Ft. McKinley, I ran across Richard Murray, who took me to a post restaurant where we had a delicious breakfast of ham and eggs. I was amazed that such a normal thing as breakfast was still going on anywhere in the Philippines. Murray laughed and made jokes the whole time. I remembered how he made me laugh even when I was sick on board the *President Coolidge*. Now in the midst of war, he was doing it again. I stayed with Murray all day, and we had a big lunch and an evening meal. I really hated to return to Nielson; it was like going to another world.

With some members of our company holed up in the tunnel at Ft. McKinley, working long hours in the absence of proper support irritated me. The very idea that the Japanese would risk using paratroops was incredible to me, since the Philippines provided so many opportunities for beach landings. Also, an isolated paratroop operation several miles from the coast not associated with a massive coastal invasion nearby made no sense to me. Nevertheless, Col. E. B. Miller, Commander of the 194th Tank Battalion, later asserted that the fear of a Japanese paratroop invasion was widespread in the Philippines from the first day of the war.[17] My postwar conversations with various veterans of Bataan have tended to confirm Miller's view. In retrospect, I think such ideas took root because of the German conquest of Crete with paratroops, which had occurred only a few months before.

Despite draining fatigue and lack of food and sleep, I enjoyed those first days of the war at Nielson Field. Even though I knew that the FEAF had been largely destroyed on the first day, I liked to think I was playing an important role in the defense of America.

One product of the turmoil of war is the hero. We generally think of heroism as the noblest expression of human behavior. In fact, heroism and hero worship often reflect the chaos from which they spring. I recall, in this regard, some of the events surrounding the Colin Kelly affair. I personally carried teletype messages to General Brereton from Adm. Thomas C. Hart, Commander of the Asiatic Fleet, concerning reports about a Japanese carrier said to be lurking in Luzon waters. When General Brereton did not respond, Admiral Hart telephoned the Message Center demanding to speak to the General. I so informed General Brereton's office, and the General immediately came to the Message Center to take the call. Admiral Hart wanted to know what the FEAF planned to do about the alleged carrier. The result of the Brereton-Hart talk was the dispatching of Capt. Colin Kelly in a B-17 to attack the carrier. Unable to find the carrier (which did not exist), Kelly sighted what he thought was a Japanese battleship and decided to bomb it. As a result, the FEAF reported that Kelly had sunk the battleship *Haruna*. The fact is there were no battleships in the Philippine area and no large ships anywhere near the location of Kelly's bombing. Nevertheless, Captain Kelly, who died when Japanese fighters shot down his B-17, became a hero in America and in the Philippines at a time when heroes were needed.[18]

Following his telephone conversation with Admiral Hart, General Brereton turned to me and demanded to know why he had not received the teletype messages from the Admiral. When I informed him that I had delivered the messages to the Sergeant-Secretary, he seemed perturbed. I had the feeling that there were personnel problems in the General's office.

The most exciting events of the early days of the war were the Japanese air attacks on Nichols Field and, almost simultaneously, on

Manila Port Area and Cavite Naval Base on Wednesday, December 10. Though the Japanese bombed and strafed near FEAF Headquarters at Nielson Field, they missed the Headquarters building, which was still standing on December 12 when we evacuated to Ft. McKinley. But they bombed and strafed the hedgerows where many of us had taken cover.

Al Eckles and I took refuge in the hedgerow when the attack began, thinking it was a safe place from which to observe the action. As it turned out, the hedgerow was a target, and we nearly fell victim to Japanese bombers and fighters. Unfortunately, an American machine gun nest had been set up in the hedgerow, which drew the attention of a Zero fighter pilot who attacked the hedge as if it were a carrier. The bombers laid down a string of heavy bombs that hit close enough to throw dirt on us. We, along with a herd of carabao, were saved by the soft, muddy ground that largely absorbed the shock and shrapnel. During the bombing I was lying down in the hedge with my face pressed to the earth. I happened to look up, and there was a snake with its head and body coiled about two feet tall right above me. But I was not afraid of the snake; I was being attacked by Japanese bombers and had no excess capacity for fear of snakes or anything else. I merely brushed the snake backward with my arm and went about my business of sweating out the Japanese Air Force. When the strafing finally ended, Al and I lay on our backs smoking our first cigarette since the attack started. Suddenly I felt something crawling across my legs: my pal the snake. I kicked it off into the bushes and continued to enjoy my cigarette and my survival.

When we returned to the Nielson Headquarters, Sergeant Carter gave me some morale-shattering news: J. L. Whitehead of Chattanooga, Tennessee, a good friend of mine, had been killed at Nichols Field. A Zero fighter hit him with a twenty-millimeter projectile. Whitehead was the first member of the 409th Signal Company to die—the first of fifty-seven of the eighty-one-member 409th who eventually would lose their lives during World War II.

As a result of the destruction wrought by the Japanese in the attacks of December 10, especially at Nichols Field and Cavite, I was completely purged of any lingering prewar images of Japanese incompetence. There were, however, still some doubting Thomases. Their failure to accept the reality of the great air raid of December 10 probably fathered the ridiculous rumor that the Japanese Air Force was being led by German pilots. In fact, a rumor that German pilots had been shot down in that air raid led to an official American military report to Washington that "white pilots" had flown some Japanese bombers.[19] I never believed it. The idea seemed so farfetched as to be laughable.

Other groundless rumors circulated widely. On the very first day of the war, reports went around that Filipino and Japanese saboteurs were shooting flares to guide Japanese airplanes. I remember that a lieutenant with a reputation for incompetence was appointed to head an antiflare detail that scouted the environs of Nielson Field. So far as I know, the detail uncovered no saboteurs, flare-shooting or otherwise, at Nielson or anywhere else in the Philippines. Nevertheless, stories giving specific details of the alleged capture of saboteurs caught in the act of shooting flares and operating shortwave transmitters continued to circulate. Early on the first evening of the war, I was sitting on the lawn in front of FEAF Headquarters when something like a Roman candle suddenly flashed on the dark horizon. It was probably a drunken GI shooting a tracer. However, a number of my colleagues sitting beside me saw the same thing, and all agreed that it might have been a legitimate flare and should be reported. I ran through the dark to report the incident to Army Intelligence. When I arrived, the G2 Office was dark except for the dial of a shortwave radio. I dashed through the office door and breathlessly began to give my intelligence report. In the dim light I did not see an officer seated just inside the door with his broken leg propped in a chair and barring my entrance. "Sir, I . . . ." Before I got beyond that, I tripped over the barrier leg and my first effort at a report was lost in the major's pained groans. I picked myself up and began my report again: "Sir, I saw a flare!" The major, writhing in pain, answered, "Flare, hell!" He then leveled at me all of the verbal ammunition he could muster. I hurriedly withdrew, and that ended my short-lived career with Army Intelligence.

During the first days of the war, I was aware of most of the rumors later mentioned by Louis Morton. As I recall, however, the reports about poisoned water and poison gas did not reach the Nielson Field-Ft. McKinley area. We did have our own version of Morton's account of Japanese or Eurasian women being involved in a spy ring for Japan.[20] A story circulated that a beautiful Eurasian woman in Barrio Baclaran had been caught while engaged in spying. It was made more believable because such a girl had been working in a bar in the Barrio on the eve of the war, and many GIs at Nichols obviously had sexual fantasies about her.

As late as 1984, Bobette Gugliotta, in her *Pigboat 39*, gave credence to the rumors of sabotage. She asserts that a group of young Filipinos who had been students in Japan worked as plants in the Philippines to carry out sabotage or directed sabotage plots from Japan. She states that they were responsible for a good deal of damage. According to Gugliotta, a Navy man saw fifth columnists using reflectors in daylight and flashlights at night to direct Japanese bombers to strategic locations. The Navy man also allegedly saw American soldiers shooting down fifth columnists caught sending signals.[21] But since many similar stories proved to be baseless and since strong demonstrations of Philippine loyalty were so common and effective in improving and prolonging the lives of American soldiers, including mine, I cannot accept Gugliotta's arguments. I am still a nonbeliever.

My respect for the Filipinos extended to their military personnel. My contact with them from the earliest days of the war only increased that feeling. Some of those points of contact, however, were alarming. One of my duties was delivering messages to a mobile radio unit whose location was changed daily in order to confuse spies. Most of the messages were delivered at night, and I often had a problem finding the unit in the dark. Many Filipino guards were stationed around Nielson and Ft. McKinley. On moonless nights a Filipino would often jump out of the bush and stick a .45 automatic into my stomach, angrily demanding identification. Their stealth and ferocity were terrifying, and I was glad they were on my side. When we moved to Ft. McKinley, I could often get a post taxi to carry me to the hidden mobile unit.

Our living conditions were much improved when we moved to Ft. McKinley. At Nielson we had no food supply, and we could sleep only by catching a catnap in the Message Center. At Ft. McKinley, however, we had access to adequate mess facilities and were given a bunk (complete with mosquito net) in a barracks.

The approximately two-week sojourn at Ft. McKinley was for me the most pleasant period of the war. During those precious days of crisp trade winds weather, false reports stirred hopes that replacement aircraft and aircraft parts were arriving from the States, and that large quantities of those materials were piling up along the Port Area and Dewey Boulevard. Morton points out that members of the Twenty-seventh Bombardment Group rushed pell-mell to the waterfront area to secure those vital materials, which allegedly included A-20s and A-24s ready to fly. When they arrived, they found only a will-o'-the-wisp.[22] At first the stories raised my morale, but within a few days it became evident that they were baseless.

At Ft. McKinley, the reality of the war tended to fade somewhat, especially compared to the first hectic days. By the end of the first week of war, the two principal military targets in the Manila area, Nichols Field and Cavite Naval Base, had been destroyed. The Japanese obviously did not consider Ft. McKinley a serious threat. It was largely ignored, and consequently, Japanese air activity declined. I had the feeling of being in a rear area serving a vague front, which we all perceived to be on the southern shore of Lingayen Gulf, although it could just as easily have been at Batangas Province closer to Manila. Our sense of the front at Lingayen was probably due to rumors pointing to that area. Almost daily we heard that a major Japanese landing at Lingayen had been smashed. The false stories probably spread from a message on December 11 from Brig. Gen. Mateo Capinpin, Commander, Twenty-first Division, Philippine Army, that a Japanese landing had been repulsed. The report followed a vigorous attack by the 21st Division on the night of December 10 against a phantom landing force. Around December 20, a Manila newspaper tightened our focus on the Lingayen area when it printed the story that an attempted Japanese landing at Lingayen had been repelled with heavy losses by the Japanese.

All that good living at Ft. McKinley had to end. On December 22, the Japanese landed in great force at Lingayen. However, when the actual landing finally occurred, we at Ft. McKinley did not realize that anything unusual was happening. Early word was that another landing had been thwarted, but apparently there had been so little resistance that the Japanese had made a major advance southward without any real battle taking place. At any rate, by December 24 the Japanese stood poised for a dash through the great valley of Luzon toward Manila and Bataan.[23]

At Ft. McKinley, we were largely unaware of the crucial events taking place during the period of December 22-24. We did not know that General MacArthur was in the process of making major decisions. U.S. military reports and rumors led us to conclude that on the Lingayen front we were holding our own against, if not defeating, the Japanese. We expected the Battle of Lingayen to last for a while, giving time for reinforcements from the States. The truth was that in those first two days of invasion the Japanese had devastated Filipino-American defenses.

The disastrous results of the first days of the war in the Philippines apparently shook MacArthur's confidence in the ability of Filipino-American forces to carry out the offensive action authorized under the revised Rainbow Plan. As early as December 12 MacArthur shocked President Manuel Quezon by informing him that he should be ready to evacuate to Corregidor on four hours' notice. On the same day, he began scrapping the aggressive Rainbow Plan in favor of reverting to the old War Plan Orange—a retreat to Bataan and Corregidor.[24]

Gen. Masaharu Homma's massive invasion at Lingayen during the early hours of December 22 caused General MacArthur grave concern. MacArthur quickly requested permission from Washington to revert to a defensive posture, and permission was granted. On December 23, following the devastating success of Homma's landing, MacArthur took stock of his precarious situation and initiated the momentous decision to revert to War Plan Orange. It was the end of the Rainbow. Though some units, including those of the South Luzon Force, did not get the order until the next day, December 24, the retreat to Bataan had begun.[25]

Meeting with his USAFFE staff members on the morning of December 24, MacArthur informed them that he would be moving his headquarters, as well as the Philippine government, to Corregidor that evening. Also, he stated that he would "disengage" all military forces from Manila during the evening hours. After the evacuation, he asserted, Manila would be declared an open city, a gesture pleading the city's neutrality. Apparently, the decision to declare Manila an open city was made in a secret conference earlier that day between General MacArthur and President Quezon. The open-city declaration was to remain a secret until complete evacuation plans (including some demolition) could be executed. From his Corregidor headquarters, MacArthur ordered release of the open-city declaration on December 26.[26]

The decision to declare Manila an open city appears to have been one of the worst-kept secrets of the war. It was leaked all over Ft. McKinley by the afternoon of December 24. Around 2:00 P.M. I was called to the main office of the FEAF Message Center. There, two Air Corps officers (first and second lieutenants with whom I had been working at the Message Center) and I were informed that General MacArthur was declaring Manila an open city and that all military personnel were to be evacuated to an unknown destination. We were also told that General Brereton, along with most higher ranking officers of the FEAF including our top Message Center officers, was being sent to Port Darwin, Australia.[27] I begged our chief Message Center officer, Maj. Sam Lamb, to take me with them, but he responded that limited space on the outgoing planes made it impossible for me to join the airborne exodus. Naturally, since it cost him nothing, he declared that he would like to have me with him. That episode, however, led me and my Message Center colleagues to hope that our destination would also be kangaroo country.

We were ordered to return within the hour, each with a barracks bag containing only essentials. On reassembling at about 3:00 P.M., we were ordered to gather important code-processing materials into a single barracks bag and to guard the bag with great care. If we encountered the enemy, we were to destroy the contents of the bag immediately. We were to wait at the office until an Army command car came to pick us up and carry us to the Port Area.

By the morning of December 24, I had partially recovered from the shock of the Clark Field disaster. I had begun to hope that perhaps large reinforcements would soon arrive from the States. But the information that came to me in the Message Center at midafternoon was loud and clear: the game was over; we had been defeated in the Philippines. My embryonic optimism of Christmas Eve morning was stillborn in the afternoon. As I learned later, my views after 3:00 P.M. of December 24 were similar to those of Admiral Hart, who at that very moment was getting ready to leave the Philippines to join his Asiatic Fleet, which had already departed. In fact, following the destruction of Clark Field on December 8, the Admiral realistically gave the Philippines up as a lost cause.[28] Though we Army men censured the Asiatic Fleet for its apparent lack of aggressiveness against the Japanese invasion of the Philippines, I now admire the Admiral's wisdom.

On the way to Manila Port Area, I could see on my left the burning remains of Nichols Field and a few miles to the southwest a giant pall of smoke hovering over Cavite. I had been back to the 409th Barracks at Nichols only once since I left on December 8. My one return visit was made during my rest period at Ft. McKinley. It was sad. The 409th Barracks was one of the few buildings at Nichols left standing after the devastating attack of December 10, but it stood in shambles, a victim of bombing near misses and .50 caliber bullets. I wish I had never gone back.

We arrived at the Port Area about 5:00 P.M. Several small steamers were being loaded with food and military supplies. According to rumors, all of the ships were going to Bataan except one, which was being sent to Australia. The first lieutenant, the leader of our group of three, scouted around to try to find out which vessel was Australia-bound. The good lieutenant thought it would be nice if we could "mistakenly" board a ship headed for Australia.

I later learned that practically everyone being evacuated that day at Manila Port Area had hopes of going to Australia. Few, if any, of the lower echelon knew anything about the Rainbow and Orange Plans. Thus, when the evacuation of Manila took place, the vast majority of the troops involved had no specific information about their destination. That failure in communication led to the wishful speculation that they were headed for Australia instead of the peninsula of Bataan, which would be the scene of one of America's costliest and bloodiest battles.

By 6:00 P.M., the lieutenant had gathered enough evidence to convince himself that he had identified the Australia-bound ship. No military personnel were yet being permitted to board, but the lieutenant intimidated the MP by declaring that we had special orders from on high to board early for the purpose of securing our barracks bag of super-secret code material. On board ship we sought a place that would provide the maximum safety against Japanese air attack. The place we chose was deep in the "V" of the bow where the steel plating presumably would afford protection against .50 caliber bullets.

Soon after we found our accommodations, the lieutenant broke out a couple of large bottles of bourbon. By the time the troops began to board at midnight, we had stopped worrying about the ship's destination or about the war. In an advanced state of inebriation, we had come to the end of the Rainbow. Instead of a pot of gold, we got a free trip across Manila Bay to Bataan.

5

The First Battle of Bataan

The ship in which my two companions and I found ourselves on that Christmas Eve night was an interisland steamer ready to evacuate the capital city in accordance with General MacArthur's reversion to War Plan Orange. The noise of the boarding troops awakened us from our bourbon-induced slumber, and in the early hours of Christmas Day 1941 our ship weighed anchor. As we sailed westward across Manila Bay, the troops aboard wanted to believe that we were Australia-bound.[1] The fact that the majority of the troops were in high spirits because they were full of spirits helped to sustain that belief. The rumor spread that even the ship's captain, a Dutchman, was under the influence.

Well into our trip across the Bay, signal lights from Corregidor began to blink at us frantically. Word was passed around that our ship's signal lights were not working and that the captain was asking for someone who could signal with a flashlight. Coincidentally, a sergeant in my outfit had formerly operated the same signal light now wildly trying to attract our attention. The sergeant, having at the time a high alcoholic blood count, inadvertently signed off with the signature of the Corregidor signal light. That led to another round of signaling to clear up the confusion. Meanwhile, the sergeant had received and interpreted the message from the island fortress—"Stop! Let down your anchor where you are! You are in a mine field." That message had a sobering effect. Most of us were aware that only a few days earlier, a Philippine Army troopship had wandered into this mine field and been blown to bits with a heavy loss of life.

Immediately, the captain stopped the ship and dropped anchor. After sunrise, a small boat came out from Corregidor and led us out of the mine field. Our ship slowly plowed through the north channel between Corregidor on the port side and Bataan Peninsula on the starboard. About 10:00 A.M. the ship edged into Mariveles Bay and dropped anchor offshore near a smoldering wreck. The village of Mariveles, about a half mile away, appeared to have burned. Smoke was still rising from various locations in the village area. Officers informed us that Japanese bombers had struck Mariveles and the harbor the previous day and hit the ship still pouring smoke near our own. Fortunately for our nerves, they did not tell us until sometime later that the smoldering ship was loaded with military explosives. They did tell us, however, that we would be put ashore as quickly as possible because the approaching noon hour was considered the likely time for the Japanese to resume their bombing.

The unloading began shortly after a transport barge pulled alongside. As we waited our turn, we peered nervously at the blue Philippine sky, hoping that we would neither see nor hear Japanese bombers. The waiting seemed interminable, but finally our turn came to scramble down to the barge. We were happy to reach shore and avoid being caught on a ship during a bombing raid. Soon after landing at Mariveles, my party stopped at a small restaurant, one of the few establishments in the area that had escaped the previous day's bombing. There the Philippine proprietor gave each of us a bottle of San Miguel beer for a Christmas present and recounted for us the terrors of the previous day.[2]

And so, on Christmas Day 1941, we were dumped on the docks of Mariveles, which seemed to me to be very near the end of the world. Since most of the troops had imagined they were being sent to Australia, few who arrived in Mariveles knew what they were supposed to do. No one was under any specific orders to go anywhere. There was little organization or direction because the hurried evacuation from Manila had torn military units asunder. Since Mariveles lay at the southern extremity of one main road on Bataan, we instinctively drifted up the road toward Cabcaben looking for our respective outfits or commands. Occasionally, some of the troops would catch rides, but there was little traffic and most of us continued to walk.

At nightfall, the lieutenant decided that our party of three should make camp. It was clear that he had not given up on Australia. He felt that we should keep ourselves isolated from other troops as much as possible in order to facilitate our escape from the Philippines. Presumably, a policy of isolationism, both physical and psychological, would advance our plans of departure for Australia.

We made camp beside a small stream in a wooded area well hidden from the road. After a cold supper of canned rations, the lieutenant ordered me to guard our possessions while he and the second lieutenant went back to Mariveles Harbor to search for a *banca* (a Philippine fishing boat) in which we could sail to Australia. As darkness came on, I felt a growing fear of being alone in that particular environment. It was a dense jungle, a tropical habitat of eerie sounds and invisible, nocturnal animal life. John Coleman, another survivor of Bataan who had slept near the same spot the previous night, records similar feelings in his book: "This exact area was where I had read about Frank Buck capturing the world's largest python snake in 1928."[3]

After a long period of frightful waiting and monitoring the strange jungle sounds, I finally dozed into a fitful sleep. About midnight, I was awakened by the return of the two officers. The lieutenant's optimism seemed considerably reduced. He described their frustrating and unsuccessful search around Mariveles Harbor for a boat. Since they failed to find a seaworthy craft, he decided to abandon the Australian quest. He directed that each of us seek and rejoin our basic units in the morning, leaving him responsible for the classified materials we were carrying. Soon after daybreak we began moving up the road toward Cabcaben. Many troops were on the road, most searching for their respective companies. Chaos prevailed, but as the day wore on, troops gradually reformed their companies and reestablished some sense of mission. Finally, we found the nucleus of the 409th, and there on the road to Cabcaben I bade good-bye to the Air Corps lieutenants.

The members of my Company in this group greeted me warmly, and over the next couple of days others straggled in. Some of them had come by truck through San Fernando and had brought some household equipment (gas stoves, bedding, etc.) and food. The truck returned to Manila for more food before the Japanese could capture San Fernando and gain control of all the main roads. During the time the 409th was located in the jungle alongside the Cabcaben Road, the Japanese bombed Corregidor daily, the planes coming directly over our camp. On one occasion I took cover beside the concrete foundation of one of the many low green buildings in the area. Just as the bombers were overhead, someone informed me that the building contained thousand-pound bombs. My fragile sense of security vanished quickly, but as the Bataan campaign wore on I adjusted to life among the ammunition dumps, or bodegas.

After a few days in the main road camp, most of the men in our Company had been reunited. We then received orders to move to the Far East Air Force Headquarters camp at Little Baguio, located about a mile north of the main road on the slope of the Mariveles Mountains. The camp was about half way between Mariveles and Cabcaben, and there we settled in for the duration of the Bataan campaign.

Theoretically, the 409th was now ready to resume communications services for the commanding officer of the FEAF. However, the original commander, Gen. Lewis H. Brereton, and most of his staff had been dispatched to Australia on December 24 by General MacArthur. The remaining FEAF staff in the Philippines was headed by Gen. Harold H. George, who would shortly accompany General MacArthur to Aus-

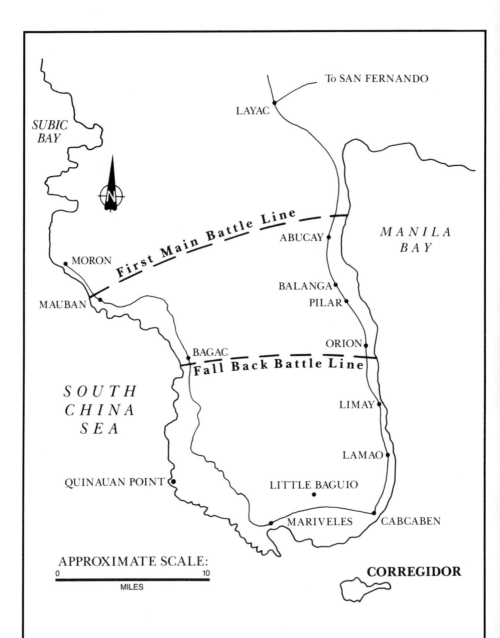

BATAAN PENINSULA AND CORREGIDOR
DURING THE FIRST BATTLE OF BATAAN

Map shows route 110 from Moron to Layac.

The East Road (Mariveles to Layac) was paved.

The West Road (Mariveles to Moron) was poorly surfaced.

tralia.[4] Following the withdrawal to Bataan, some preparations were initially made to carry on extensive air operations, but the failure to receive any reinforcements of men or materiel led to the disintegration of the once proud FEAF. Throughout the First Battle of Bataan, the FEAF consisted of six P-40s and a few Philippine Army training planes.[5]

On January 7, 1942, Generals Wainwright and Jones, through brilliant maneuvers, completed the withdrawal to Bataan. The successful withdrawal gave an enormous morale boost to the American-Philippine forces on the peninsula. On the same day, however, General Homma's Fourteenth Japanese Army closed the door to Bataan by smashing the Layac Junction Line. Two days later, January 9, the Japanese launched the First Battle of Bataan, America's first extensive military operation of World War II.[6]

The main American battle position at the beginning of the First Battle of Bataan was the Abucay-Mauban Line. Technically, "Abucay" designated the defense line on our right in front of General Parker's II Corps. That line ran from the central mountains across the eastern plain of Bataan to Manila Bay. The "Mauban" line referred to the complicated defense points of General Wainwright's I Corps in the rugged terrain of western Bataan. However, at Little Baguio (where I was located) and other places in the rear, the men used the term "Abucay Line" to refer to the whole defense system in the north. Indeed, the major Japanese thrust was on the east against the Abucay Line.[7]

The Japanese attack against the Abucay Line was the beginning of six weeks of hard, bloody fighting that constituted the First Battle of Bataan. Despite the shortages of food, medicine, and military supplies, the sheer excitement of the gigantic struggle emotionally and psychologically carried us through the ordeal. Even in the rear areas, almost everyone was extremely busy with the battle action in one way or another. Being in the rear area on Bataan was no picnic. Since the Japanese possessed absolute air superiority, the Imperial Wild Eagles could constantly harass the rear areas with bombing and strafing.

General MacArthur was not personally popular with the troops on Bataan, and many FEAF personnel with whom I was associated still carried a grudge against him because of the Clark Field disaster. Still, we had enormous respect for the majesty of the man and, indeed, a profound faith in his ultimate ability despite the early catastrophes that had forced the great retreat. MacArthur's charisma may have prevented a general panic during the first two weeks of the Battle. During that period the Philippine-American defenses of Bataan were in grave peril as General Homma hurled his Army against the Abucay Line. Yet confidence and morale remained high.

The Japanese were expected to make their major thrust against our right flank along the Manila Bay coast. Instead, the major attack came against the left flank of General Parker's II Corps in the rugged and weakly defended country east of Mt. Natib. From January 9 to 22, the Japanese pressed deeper and deeper into the II Corps' left flank, despite heroic counterattacks by II Corps troops to regain lost territory. Each thrust and counterthrust resulted in net gains for the Japanese. Finally, by January 22 it appeared the Japanese Army was positioned to overwhelm the entire II Corps line and smash it against Manila Bay. In response, on the evening of January 22 General MacArthur decided to withdraw in order to straighten his line. The bloody withdrawal battle took four days, but by January 26 a new and relatively strong line had been formed—the Orion-Bagac Line, popularly called the Orion Line. Wainwright's I Corps west of the central mountains also withdrew, connecting more firmly with General Parker's II Corps in the east.[8]

In retrospect, the tremendous struggle over the Abucay Line during the first two weeks of the Battle seems to have been a much greater threat to MacArthur's hold on Bataan than we thought at the time. Not only did troop faith in MacArthur help allay in our minds the seriousness of our condition, but MacArthur's communiqués to the troops, worded in majestic military language, apparently overstated our situation and understated the Japanese position. The result was that practically no one in the rear areas felt severely threatened. General MacArthur was sending a different message to Washington to justify his decision to withdraw to the Orion Line.[9]

That withdrawal in late January by no means ended the First Battle of Bataan. The Japanese did not let up on their attack, and MacArthur's forces continued to fight with the same fervor as in early January. The struggle over the Abucay Line was probably a greater shock for General Homma than for MacArthur. General Homma had expected to sweep through Bataan with ease.[10] Instead, the Philippine-American forces, although forced to abandon the Abucay Line, had inflicted severe wounds on the Japanese Fourteenth Army and had completed the withdrawal to the Orion Line with little apparent loss of fighting spirit.

During the confusion that attended the withdrawal from the Abucay Line to the Orion Line, the Japanese initiated two sets of operations that would continue the bitter fighting of the First Battle of Bataan. One set of maneuvers depended on amphibious assaults to occupy some key places or points along the west coast of Bataan deep in Wainwright's rear position. The contest over those positions came to be called the Battle of the Points. The other set of Japanese operations was the so-called Battle of the Pockets. Taking advantage of the confusion in Wainwright's lines, the Japanese infiltrated his right (i.e., mountain) flank with troops that formed several pockets inside the new defense line.[11] The Battle of the Pockets wound its tortuous and bloody way until the middle of February, largely without our attention. Our concern was deflected because General MacArthur's communiqués, as in the case of the battle over the Abucay Line, seemed not to portend any major threat in the Battle of the Pockets. Since none of our troops directly participated, we did not personally know many men caught up in the awful battle. For those and other reasons, the personnel in my area were not all that apprehensive about the Battle of the Pockets.

On the other hand, the Battle of the Points was of immediate and constant concern to us. In the first place, a large number of Air Corps soldiers were involved. Having no planes to service, many Air Force troops had been retrained as infantry troops. The Air Force's connection brought the Points affair close to home (i.e., Little Baguio). Furthermore, some members of the 409th, including me, were involved tangentially. Shortly after the outbreak of battle, I was assigned to the motor pool, and my job became a busy one.

Soon after the beginning of the First Battle of Bataan, men attached to the Air Force Headquarters at Little Baguio but not responsible for essential services were assigned infantry training in the immediate vicinity. At least 10 percent or more of Army personnel at Little Baguio had no real duties except an occasional stint as guards. Those men drew on scarce resources, especially food; they also adversely affected the morale of the other troops at Little Baguio who were performing essential duties. Many of the redundant Air Force troops were engaged in infantry training, and some were already in combat. Since my Company and the other groups similarly attached to Air Force Headquarters were considered noncombatant, the principal mission of the training was to teach those unassigned men, whose only firearms training had been in the use of the .45 automatic handgun, how to handle .30 caliber rifles and machine guns. The infantry training was highly contrived if not a farce, and the trainees became the butt of jokes.

The call for 409th combat support came during the "Points" crisis. Air Force troops had already gone up to the fighting front on the west coast. Our newly appointed company commander, who was ordered to lead our Company in combat, quickly pressed into service a group of men that had never received combat training. The group was comprised entirely of people who held essential jobs. I had just been transferred over my protest from the position of motor pool clerk to assistant company clerk. We were now considered combat-ready troops. For most of us, the first introduction to .30-30 rifles was when we took them out of the packing and cleaned off the Cosmoline just a few hours before leaving for the front.

The destination of the 409th makeshift combat unit was Quinauan Point, the location of one of the major Japanese amphibious landings. There a motley array of noncombatant troops (including a large number of Air Force personnel) was trying to contain the Japanese invasion, which posed a grave threat to General Wainwright's forces. At the time, we were confused about the place-name of the battle location. Quinauan Point was being referred to as Agloloma Point because of a nearby village and creek named Agloloma. There was something darkly comic in this. Was it Army training or human instinct that wanted the right place-names along the road to Hell?

Around 9:00 P.M. one evening in late January, we members of the 409th Point boarded a truck and awaited orders to move out to Quinauan Point. While we were waiting, our company commander gave us a lecture on the techniques of early American Indian fighting, which he declared would suit the combat at Quinauan Point. After a while we moved out with a small convoy of trucks, going through Mariveles and up the West Road of Bataan toward Wainwright country. Somewhere beyond Mariveles, the convoy turned to the left off the main road and soon came to a small Army camp hidden among the trees and bushes. A small unit of Wainwright's I Philippine Corps occupied the camp, apparently assigned to coast-watching duties. We stayed during the remainder of the night and most of the next day, enduring two Japanese dive-bomber attacks. There was absolutely no American anti-aircraft protection along the West Road, but we made the best of it under the forest's heavy cover. Having brought along enough food for a day or two, the 409th group cooked its own meals. The plan called for each outfit to send food to Quinauan Point to supply its own men via daily trucks from Little Baguio. As soon as the 409th supply group arrived at its destination, our truck returned to Little Baguio for supplies and personnel replacements.

Late in the afternoon of the next day, our convoy pulled out into the narrow, winding West Road, which had been cut out of the hillsides. We had traveled only a short distance when two Japanese dive-bombers spotted us. The convoy quickly stopped, and everyone scrambled off the trucks and climbed down the left shoulder of the road, a bluff of about ten feet. As the circling planes began their whining dive, we took cover at the foot of the bluff among some small trees and brush.

The Japanese, obviously having observed our actions, went after us rather than the trucks. No sooner had we gotten in place at the foot of the bluff than the lead pilot pulled out of his dive at a low altitude and came right down the bluff line. He strafed our position with .50 caliber bullets and a string of bombs. As the plane came over our hiding place, we were standing single file pressed against the bluff. Suddenly, a bomb exploded almost in my face and flattened me against the bluff like a pancake. The explosion violently threw my head back against the rock, injuring my throat as a result of the pressure from my helmet's chin strap. The atmosphere became a thick fog of dust filled with debris and shrapnel. It seemed that almost every person near me on either side had been hit with shrapnel; blood coated everything—men, bluff, vegetation. I did not even know at the time whether I had been hit. It all seemed like a wild nightmare, surreal and incomplete in sensation and meaning.

Just seconds later I heard the second plane diving and people screaming that we were being hit again. Decisions made in nightmares are not governed by reason: I bolted and ran, trying to get to the jungle away from the road. As I came out of the bushes at the foot of the bluff, I had to cross about twenty feet of cleared area. The dive-bomber caught me in the middle of that area, the .50 caliber bullets kicking up dust all around me. That was the last thing I remember of the dive-bombing episode.

Some time later, about sunset, I regained consciousness and found myself trying to dig my rifle out of the mud of a marshy bog. There was hardly a sound anywhere; the truck convoy had gone, leaving me stranded in the jungle. I tried to piece things together in my mind. Obviously, I had made it across the clearing into the bushes on the other side, but as I entered the bushes I apparently fell over a twenty-foot cliff into the bog below. I have never remembered any of this; my mind stopped functioning in the middle of the clearing where the dive-bomber's bullets danced around my feet.

Feeling desperately alone and not knowing what to do, I climbed out of the bog and up the slope, making for the camp where we had spent the night. As I emerged from the bog, I heard a strange noise ahead. A member of my Company was wandering in circles, dazed and confused, mumbling to himself. It was Charles McMahon of California, who looked as if he were only fifteen or sixteen years of age. Most members of the 409th believed McMahon lied about his age to get into the Army. He was a gentle soul, and I was fond of him. He barely survived the bombing raid only to die shortly at Camp O'Donnell as a result of Japanese atrocities.

After I talked with McMahon awhile, he regained his composure and we set out to find the Army campsite we had left that afternoon. After walking about two miles, we came upon it just at dusk. Because food was so scarce on Bataan, we feared that the members of the Army unit at the camp might resent our return. Just the contrary was true: they greeted us warmly, enthusiastically helped us, and shared what they had. We related our story to the commanding officer, who was extremely kind. We hoped he would be able to provide us transportation so we could rejoin our comrades at Quinauan Point. He told us to stay with them that night and said that he would arrange a ride for us in the morning. After a delicious hot supper, we fell asleep.

The next morning the commanding officer decided to send us back to Little Baguio aboard one of his trucks. From there he knew a daily supply truck would leave for Quinauan Point. When we arrived, McMahon and I found that a truck would be going to Quinauan Point again the next morning. We cleaned up, got a change of clothes, and were ready to rejoin our group. The next morning, however, word was received from Quinauan Point that the 409th group was coming back to Little Baguio. McMahon's and my return to the battlefield was canceled.

Later that day when the 409th group arrived, we learned the full story. Several of our men had been seriously wounded in the dive-bombing attack on our convoy. The man who had been standing on my left against the bluff had to have his leg amputated. By the time the 409th unit arrived at Quinauan Point, Filipino Scouts of the Forty-fifth Infantry had relieved all of the makeshift troops except for a unit of the Air Corps from the Fifth Interceptor Command. The fierce Filipino Scouts, some of them Moros from Mindanao, had the situation well in hand. All of us were thankful for the magnificent Filipino Scouts, probably the best combat unit in the Philippines during World War II.

Some time after the Battle of the Points, a lieutenant at Little Baguio had an unfortunate conflict with an ancient master sergeant, Wolfe Boney.[12] Sergeant Boney was one of the top-ranking noncommissioned officers in the Signal Detachment, which was attached to Air Force headquarters at Little Baguio. Boney had been spending the night with some civilian and Navy friends in the Navy tunnel at Mariveles. The lieutenant accused Boney of stealing .45 automatics (in short supply), blankets, and other items and trading or giving them to his Navy tunnel friends. The lieutenant ordered a court-martial for Boney. I remember that a sergeant from the 409th, who coveted Sergeant Boney's position, boasted that the old master sergeant would be deposed as well as defrocked. But the lieutenant underrated his adversary. Sergeant Boney, who was well known in the Army's Pacific theater, was not defenseless. He claimed to be a personal friend of General MacArthur, and indeed there was a lot of talk around Little Baguio to that effect. More important for the moment, Boney had excellent relations with other officers at Little Baguio. When the lieutenant hurled his court-martial orders at Sergeant

Boney, the accused appealed to higher-ranking authorities. Immediately, things happened. The lieutenant was relieved of his duties at Little Baguio and dispatched forthwith to join a telephone party stringing wires on the front line. That comic farce in the Bataan jungle had no influence on the outcome of the Battle of Bataan, but it did result in Sergeant Boney's becoming probably the most powerful person in the Signal Detachment at Little Baguio.

At that time I was putting out an illegal sheet entitled *The Little Baguio Gossiper*, each issue of which consisted of a typed page with a couple of carbon copies. Just for fun and to relieve my tension, I treated as hard news the ridiculous rumors about the arrival or expected arrival of American convoys. The ironic force of those fun-poking publications seemed to defuse rumors and delight readers. One day I wrote an article intended as a flowery parody of some earthy comments Sergeant Boney had made in praise of American-Philippine political relations. My piece was something of cruel joke because everyone knew that Boney was illiterate. When the article was read to him, Sergeant Boney had me brought before him. Actually, I would rather have faced General Homma than Sergeant Boney. The Sergeant, who was sitting in the kitchen tent where he ate separately and at a different time from everyone else, gave me a glowering look that made me quake in my boots. When I fearfully admitted authorship of the article in question, Boney said, "Son, them's not exactly my words, but them's my sentiments." He invited me to share some of his special food, things I did not even suspect still existed on Bataan. He then told me we would be having frequent press conferences; we met several times, during which the Sergeant presented ideas for articles that he wanted written. At those meetings he invariably shared his special rations with me.

When he heard that General MacArthur had left for Australia, Sergeant Boney called me in for a press conference. He told me about his personal friendship with MacArthur, but he thought the General had betrayed us. He felt he could not directly criticize MacArthur because of their friendship, but he wanted me to write an article that by implication would be critical of the General. His solution was to order an article praising Gen. Lewis Brereton, the former head of the FEAF whom MacArthur had sent to Australia at the time of the evacuation of Manila. In Boney's view, MacArthur would be offended by an article praising Brereton but not mentioning him. The result was a copy of *The Little Baguio Gossiper* in which the lead article stated that "Sergeant Wolfe Boney eulogizes General Brereton." Boney had the article radioed to American headquarters in Port Darwin, Australia.

My relations with Sergeant Boney were nearing an end. A couple of

days later the Sergeant, weary of air attacks in the vicinity of the Little
Baguio headquarters, had himself transferred to a signal unit located
underground.

By the end of the First Battle of Bataan (late February 1942), food was
getting critically scarce. Because half rations became the order of the day
for all personnel on January 6, the troops had been hungry since the
beginning of the battle; rations had gradually declined in quantity and
greatly in quality. But by the end of January, many of the troops had
found ways, at least temporarily, to augment their supplies. For example,
many companies had been able to procure extra food and establish
company caches during the early stages of the retreat to Bataan. Units
that had such private reserves of food (most of which had been acquired
during the confusion of the withdrawal to Bataan) were ordered to
surrender the illegal holdings to the quartermaster. So far as I know,
none obeyed. Also, during January some individuals and groups took
food illegally from supply dumps and trucks. For a short period midway
through the First Battle of Bataan, when I was motor pool clerk at Little
Baguio and Richard Murray was a mechanic, our job was to make nightly
runs from a nearby supply dump, carrying supplies to the front lines.
Murray, whose skill as a con man was legendary in the 409th, was able to
purloin a couple of cans of food each night simply by confusing the
Filipino supply officer in the count-off.

Though our theft was petty, it appears likely that the looting of
supplies in rear areas was so extensive that it caused suffering among the
frontline troops. Bataan troops believed that the closer to the front line,
the less there was to eat, but that the closer to General MacArthur's
headquarters on Corregidor, the better the cuisine. By early February,
the company caches were empty and looting became more difficult. By
the end of February, the daily ration for our Signal Detachment mess at
Little Baguio (approximately 120 men) was ten or less cans of salmon and
enough raw rice to fill one-third of a medium-size dishpan.

It was difficult to supplement food supplies from domestic or natural
sources. Agricultural produce was scarce mainly because most of Bataan's terrain was too rugged for cultivation. Only a small area in the
northeast contained farms. A limited quantity of domestic produce (rice,
chickens, pork, and sweet potatoes) could be obtained in the early days
of the First Battle of Bataan. By the middle of the Battle, that source had
completely vanished.

The idea of subsisting on the wildlife and other resources of the
fecund forest I believe to be largely a myth given a major boost by
Morton's account. I heard a few stories about American troops eating
monkeys and snakes, but none proved more than rumor. Monkey stories

always contained a standard paradigm: the revulsion felt in preparing the feast because of the resemblance of a freshly skinned monkey to a human newborn. To my knowledge, however, monkey eating did not occur in the Little Baguio area or any other place I happened to be during the Bataan affair. Actually, wildlife appeared to be unnaturally scarce on Bataan. The noise and other polluting effects of battle apparently reduced and scattered wildlife with devastating efficiency. Though I spent much time in Bataan forests and jungles, I saw amazingly few wild creatures.

During the First Battle of Bataan, there were many monkeys at Little Baguio and other rear areas. They had been driven back by the terrible noise of the artillery battles. For a full month from mid-January to mid-February 1942, the great mahogany trees at Little Baguio were filled with monkeys seeking refuge from battle, some trees supporting as many as one hundred of the chattering creatures. At the time there was still enough food to suppress most latent desires for prime primate. But when the din of battle ceased, the monkeys had largely disappeared. During the lull following the Battle, the pangs of hunger began seriously to stalk Bataan. By mid-March, probably many monkeys would have been eaten had they been available. Where were the monkeys when we needed them?

As for snakes, I saw only one during the entire Bataan campaign, and it was a puny little reptile with a frog in its mouth—also the only frog I saw on Bataan. Since I did not see a single iguana, I never had the opportunity to find out if that prehistoric creature really did taste like breast of chicken. Even the ubiquitous gecko lizard did a vanishing act. During the First Battle of Bataan, the only truly fresh meat my detachment mess prepared was our share of the Twenty-sixth Cavalry horses. Those noble animals, no longer needed by the military after their heroic role in the withdrawal to Bataan, continued their service after slaughter. Also, on one occasion Japanese bombers hit a meat storage refrigerator on Corregidor. The meat had to be eaten or it would spoil. Some of it was shipped over to us at Little Baguio, and we received some semifresh beef as a result.[13]

As food and other supplies became desperately scarce by mid-February, many units established scrounge committees whose function was to acquire food and cigarettes by any method short of murder. On one occasion, a member of our detachment, of whom Charles Dickens's Fagin would have been proud, turned up with a complete case of cigarettes. He said that a nurse at one of the field hospitals had given them to him. We did not even open the case in our detachment, the precious tobacco being traded for rice, flour, and other food items that were shared by all the members of our Company at Little Baguio.

The shortage of cigarettes was itself the cause of a significant morale problem on Bataan. To many of the troops, cigarettes were more essential than food. As in the case of food, the supply of cigarettes decreased as one proceeded from Corregidor toward the front line on Bataan. Cigarettes could be purchased on the black market, but few common soldiers had the money. According to Louis Morton, Bataan soldiers received an average of one cigarette per day during the entire Bataan campaign.

The First Battle resulted in a severe depletion of another nonrenewable resource—clothing. By the end of February, Bataan troops grew increasingly ragtag and threadbare in appearance. The uniform of the day was any apparel one was lucky enough to have. Our World-War-I-issue Shoes were wearing out and were irreplaceable. Socks were almost nonexistent. Many men were hesitant to take off their shoes during bathing or sleeping for fear of theft. Blankets and other bedclothes were also scarce.

At Little Baguio, in the foothills of the Mariveles Mountains, troop health appeared to remain relatively good during the First Battle of Bataan despite the scarcity of food. By early February, however, there were signs of worsening conditions on the fighting fronts: increasing instances of malaria, dysentery, and general malnutrition. And by the end of that month, it was clear that the desperate struggle had taken a greater health toll than we had realized during the heat of combat. Apparently, a sort of nervous energy had kept us going, and the excitement of battle had diverted our minds from health problems. Fortunately, troops in the Little Baguio area were spared high rates of dysentery and malaria, but by the end of the First Battle of Bataan, Madame Malnutrition had raised her ugly head.

Morale during the First Battle would likely have been much lower but for the frequently heard theme that "help is on the way." During the battle it was official policy in Washington that the U.S. military forces would run the Japanese blockade and bring reinforcements and relief to the beleaguered troops on Bataan. Accordingly, General MacArthur strongly reinforced the idea that the convoys would soon arrive when, on January 15, he released his famous communiqué to the men on Bataan promising that

help is on the way from the United States. Thousands of troops and hundreds of planes are being dispatched. The exact time of arrival of reinforcements is unknown as they will have to fight their way through Japanese attempts against them. It is imperative that our troops hold until these reinforcements arrive.

... Our supplies are ample; a determined defense will defeat the enemy's attack.[14]

Few of little faith were left on Bataan as a result of General MacArthur's "help is on the way" message. Unfortunately for my psychological welfare, I was one of the few surviving doubters. A factor undermining my faith was the abysmal ignorance of geography among officers and men on Bataan. My faith in MacArthur seemed tied directly to the quality of the general troops' understanding of our strategic situation. I knew that the Japanese held apparently strong positions in the Mariana, Caroline, and Marshall Islands, all of which lay between the Philippines and Pearl Harbor. When I discovered that most of the Bataan personnel had not the foggiest notion about those Japanese strongholds or, worse, the approximate geographical location of the Philippines, I rapidly lost faith in General MacArthur's statement as a nearly absolute guarantee of deliverance. Though my view gained a few adherents over the next two months, it remained the minority opinion. The orthodox view that "help is on the way" remained intact.

Faith in General MacArthur's promise totally collapsed in mid-March when Bataan troops learned that MacArthur had left for Australia on March 12. The feeling of abandonment was reinforced at Little Baguio when we heard that our FEAF chief, General George, had gone with MacArthur. Morale on Bataan sank quickly to a low point from which it never recovered. The term "The Battling Bastards of Bataan" now really rang true. For Bataan troops, there really was "No mama, no papa, no Uncle Sam," and it surely seemed that "Nobody gives a damn."

During the first half of February, the embattled American-Filipino troops ground General Homma's Fourteenth Army like homemade sausage. The Japanese offensive in all three major sectors—the Points, the Pockets, and the II Corps' Plains front—failed. MacArthur's forces had badly pummeled the Fourteenth Japanese Army, and since the first week in January, General Homma had sustained heavy casualties. MacArthur's great victories of February forced Homma to withdraw from the battle lines in disgrace to await reinforcements.[15] At the end of February, General MacArthur's Bataan troops, having stopped and defeated one of Japan's finest armies, felt confident that they could hold Bataan until reinforcements arrived. Those men, who had lived fantasies about the arrival of convoys, were realistic enough to know that their survival as a military force depended on immediate help. They were aware that they had exhausted practically all of their resources—food, military supplies, and health—in the arduous battle of January-February 1942.

The First Battle of Bataan brought the first victory to American forces in World War II. It boosted the nation's morale in the midst of desperate times. Forcing the Japanese to increase vastly their investment in the Philippine campaign possibly saved Australia from Japanese conquest. For a while, "The Battling Bastards of Bataan" were heroes. But their splendid victory was soon forgotten in the immense labyrinth of World War II. For most of the Bataan heroes, the path of glory would lead only to a Philippine grave.

6

Defeat and Death
on the March

By the end of February, the major portion of the First Battle of Bataan was over. General Homma had withdrawn his Fourteenth Japanese Army from the Orion-Bagac Line and had dug in some distance to the north awaiting reinforcements from Japan. General MacArthur's American-Filipino forces were digging in along the Orion-Bagac Line, also awaiting reinforcements—reinforcements from the States that would never come. The air war, such as it was, continued. The FEAF had not been able to fly simultaneously more than half a dozen planes during the entire First Battle of Bataan, and was practically a nonexistent organization by the end of February. The Japanese Air Force met little resistance in its continued bombing and strafing of Bataan during the break between the two battles in March.

The March lull was deadly for the American-Filipino troops even though they desperately needed a respite from combat. General MacArthur's forces, who had received no reinforcements of either men or supplies since the beginning of the war, had expended the major portion of their resources (health, energy, and supplies) during the bloody encounter with General Homma's Army in January and February. The physical and material decline had gone too far to be halted. The fact is that the American-Filipino forces were practically in a state of collapse by the middle of March. MacArthur commanded an army in an advanced stage of terminal illness.

An inexhaustible source of jokes during the First Battle of Bataan was the official contention by MacArthur's Headquarters that Bataan troops were on half rations. The initial issues of food following the half-ration declaration of January 6 were considerably below that amount in both quantity and quality and consistently declined during the Battle. By March the American-Filipino troops literally were starving. The weakened condition of the malnourished troops made them vulnerable to those twin scourges of soldiery in the Philippines, dysentery and malaria.

Though ordnance supplies had been badly depleted by the First Battle of Bataan, the lack of guns and ammunition was a smaller factor in the fall of Bataan than exhaustion, malnutrition, and illness.[1]

In late March, my Company began to prepare for the rainy season, which normally began in May. An American civilian employee of the Army brought in a crew of Filipino carpenters to build a kitchen and mess hall for us. Since my Company, as well as the entire FEAF Headquarters at Little Baguio, was located in a forest of huge mahogany trees, we hoped that the new building would be well hidden from enemy planes. The kitchen crew somehow acquired a large wood stove and, even more remarkable, obtained and cooked a piece of semifresh carabao meat. The slightly tainted carabao flesh was tasty but tough. That enjoyable and rare repast was not only our first meal in the new mess facility; it proved to be the 409th's last supper. Never again would our Company eat an evening meal together as a unit, for on the next day (April 8) we evacuated Little Baguio, and on the next (April 9) Bataan fell.

During late March under the threat of approaching rains, soldiers in small groups or individually made feeble attempts to provide some overhead shelter. The effort was entirely a laissez-faire operation without help or direction from the company or detachment officers. During the First Battle of Bataan, practically all of the troops (combat and noncombat) slept in the open, and fortunately the anticipated rains did not come early that year. In retrospect, it seems certain that my Company's poor preparations would have offered little protection from the Philippine monsoon. We could not possibly have survived a rainy season on Bataan.

The FEAF Headquarters Group (including the 409th Signal Company) at Little Baguio did not suffer much from Japanese air attacks. We attributed our apparent security to the canopy of the great mahogany forest, which shaded the foothills of the Mariveles Mountains. As it turned out, we were not hidden. We later learned that the Japanese airmen could clearly observe all of our activities because the damaged forest undergrowth provided little cover. The Japanese spared us during that period only because they preferred to concentrate their efforts along the battle lines and against the island fortress of Corregidor. During the March wait between land battles, we were shocked to learn that we were an easy target: the Japanese bombed and strafed us at will and even had the temerity to descend to the treetops and drop propaganda leaflets on our wooded stronghold. For a while, the Japanese attacked our positions in Little Baguio only with small planes—fighters and dive-bombers. Nearby, however, they frequently used the big bombers to hit targets, including nonmilitary ones. One day late in March, Lieutenant Moore, an FEAF pilot from Chattanooga, Tennessee, and I stood on a high overlook of the Mariveles Mountains and watched in horror as a formation of Japanese bombers, with apparent malice aforethought, hit Hospital No. 1.[2]

On April 8, 1942, as Bataan was falling, the Army nurses stationed there were evacuated to Corregidor despite the desperate need for them on Bataan. At the time, Hospitals No. 1 and No. 2 were filled to the brim with the wounded and soldiers suffering dreadfully from dysentery or malaria, but the welfare of the nurses was given priority over that of the patients. During the Battle of Corregidor, many nurses, including some who had already left Bataan, were evacuated to the States via Australia, using extremely scarce space on military craft (submarine and aircraft) that might have been used for seriously wounded men. When those nurses arrived in the States, they were welcomed as war heroines. When the Japanese took Corregidor, they interned all captured nurses with American civilians in Manila and treated them reasonably well. At least, all survived and were liberated. Certainly their treatment was better than that afforded the male POWs, including the patients at Hospitals No. 1 and No. 2 on Bataan.[3]

On one occasion during the respite in March, a Japanese dive-bomber caused panic at Little Baguio by dropping a bomb on a small ammunition storage building that contained primarily tar and tar paper. The slight breeze coming from Manila Bay lifted the acrid smoke uphill through our camp. There was general alarm when someone yelled "Poison Gas!" Everyone tried to find a usable gas mask, but they were scarce because American and Filipino troops had lost their fear of gas by the time of the retreat to Bataan. Many had either discarded their masks or converted them to shoulder bags for carrying various and sundry items. I witnessed a number of quarrels and at least one fistfight over usable gas masks. After that incident, the poison gas problem quickly disappeared and, so far as I know, did not reappear during the Bataan campaign.[4]

General MacArthur's departure from the Philippines on the ides of March and the continuously deteriorating health and supply situations on Bataan during the lull had caused morale to plummet by the end of March. Yet, up to the beginning of the Second Battle of Bataan, we refused to accept the reality that we immediately faced either surrender or annihilation. Everyone assumed that we would continue to hold out under miserable conditions. Louis Morton has succinctly described the scene when Gen. Edward King, Commander of the Luzon Force, called his staff together at approximately midnight on Tuesday, April 8, to inform them that he had made the decision to surrender: "Though the decision could not have surprised the staff, it 'hit with an awful bang and had a terrible wallop.' Everyone had hoped for a happier ending to the grim tragedy of Bataan. . . . "[5]

Late in the March lull, Lieutenant Moore and I concocted a vague and fantastic plan to escape should Bataan fall to the Japanese. We would hide out in the Mariveles Mountains and work our way northward through the Zambales, the small mountain range to the west of Luzon's central plain. To facilitate the plan, we agreed that each would prepare an escape kit of food and medicine. In fact, I had no access to medical supplies and barely enough food to stay alive. Besides, I was too caught up in surviving the last hectic days of the war to attempt the almost impossible task of provisioning a supply cache. But when the fall came, Moore was not in Little Baguio. Apparently, the Lieutenant believed in the plan. According to vague bits of information picked up later, Moore did escape and was captured and executed by the Japanese at Manila's Bilibid Prison.

By mid-March, the battle- and bomb-weary troops on Bataan knew with terrible certainty that without reinforcements they could not hold out against a new Japanese offensive. What we did not know was that in mid-February General MacArthur and President Quezon had concocted a scheme to end the fighting in the Philippines and extricate American troops by an immediate grant of Philippine independence. Also, we did not know that President Roosevelt had angrily rejected the scheme and declared his willingness to sacrifice the lives of American troops on Bataan for the sake of Allied morale. Roosevelt tartly informed MacArthur that American troops would defend the Philippines "to the death" and that "resisting Japanese aggression to the last transcends in importance any other obligation now facing us in the Philippines." The purpose of the human sacrifice was to provide "complete evidence" of "American determination" to our allies for whom "we cannot display weakness." President Roosevelt's strong no-surrender order of February greatly embarrassed MacArthur, to say the least. Therefore, the General replied to Roosevelt and General Marshall that he had never entertained a thought of surrender, that he would fight "to destruction," and that he and his family "would share the fate of the garrison." One month later, however, MacArthur departed for Australia, leaving General Wainwright in command in the Philippines. Wainwright's strict no-surrender orders were directly from both MacArthur and Roosevelt.[6] We knew nothing of the matters of ego and expediency that determined our sacrifice on the steaming, fetid altar of Bataan.

Actually, it was well we did not know that our President had consigned us to slaughter. Knowledge of that ignoble affair was the last thing we needed at that particular time. Ironically, American troops on Bataan viewed MacArthur as the villain capable of sacrificing us for his military glory and Roosevelt as the good Samaritan resisting our abandonment. But it was General MacArthur, through the MacArthur-Quezon scheme, who demonstrated compassion for his troops in an attempt to provide a political solution where the military effort had failed.

During the March respite, American-Filipino forces attempted to strengthen fortifications along the Orion-Bagac Line and carried out some combat training, especially the training of noncombat units. But given the dreadful conditions, they could do little to prepare for the Japanese offensive we realized was coming. General Homma's Army had been growing progressively stronger; reinforcements of men and supplies had been pouring in since mid-February.[7] Word of the Japanese buildup came to us via the grapevine, and by late March everyone fully expected a powerful Japanese offensive to begin at any time.

General Homma launched the Second Battle of Bataan on Good Friday, April 3, 1942. News of the first few days of battle that filtered down to Little Baguio was not good, but apparently the lines were holding. Our Company was looking forward to Easter Sunday with great anticipation because sweetened oatmeal was planned for breakfast. But when that morning arrived, even the simple pleasure of breakfast was overshadowed by continued bad news from the front. Easter Sunday, 1942, was a bad day at Little Baguio.

The news that we received of the battle was necessarily incomplete and fragmentary. The situation was actually much worse than we knew. Homma's Fourteenth Japanese Army had smashed through the Orion-Bagac Line, seized some vital points, and knocked out important combat units. By rounding General Parker's left flank in the vicinity of Mt. Samat, the Japanese were in position to drive the American-Filipino II Corps into Manila Bay.[8]

At Little Baguio, we were not aware that the day's conflict would determine the bloody struggle for Bataan. Early that Easter morning, American-Filipino forces, including the bulk of remaining reserves, mustered for their final counterattack. Unfortunately, our forces clashed head-on with a new offensive the Japanese had just launched. By the end of that fateful Sunday, the American-Filipino forces were defeated— beyond repair, beyond redemption.

General MacArthur's once magnificent Army would take two more days to die. Louis Morton's account is as poignant as it is accurate:

The story of the last two days of the defense of Bataan is one of progressive disintegration and final collapse. Lines were formed and abandoned before they could be fully occupied. Communications broke down and higher headquarters often did not know the situation on the front lines. Orders were issued and revoked because they were impossible of execution. Stragglers poured to the rear in increasingly large numbers until they clogged all roads and disrupted all movement forward. Units disappeared into the jungle never to be heard from again. In two days an army evaporated into thin air.[9]

On Monday, April 6, rumors from the north created considerable confusion at Little Baguio. Unlike the First Battle of Bataan, during which official communiqués from MacArthur's Headquarters often were posted on camp bulletin boards, we received no official news during the brief and tragic Second Battle of Bataan. Grapevine reports on Monday contradicted each other, some indicating that we were holding and others that our resistance was collapsing. On that day at Little Baguio, however, we did not receive any official word that our front had fallen. About noon on Tuesday, April 7, we had grim reports of retreating troops appearing at Cabcaben about five miles to the east. Late that afternoon remnants of the defeated army began to appear on the main road below Little Baguio—the Mariveles-Cabcaben Road—and by early evening the road became too jammed with troops and vehicles to permit an orderly flow of traffic. At the 409th mess, not many were on hand at the regular evening mealtime. As weary stragglers began coming in, they were served a few at a time.

As the evening wore on, reports describing conditions on the Mariveles-Cabcaben Road were even more ominous. The fact that some members of our Company had not shown up for the evening meal caused us concern. Since we were an Air Force signal company with no air force to serve, FEAF Headquarters frequently dispatched the Company to various places to perform signal duties, and we hoped that our missing members had been delayed by the congestion on the main road.

Around 9:00 P.M. members of the 409th responded to an order to assemble immediately near FEAF Headquarters. There we were told to abandon the Little Baguio area before midnight. At that time the U.S. Army Engineers would begin the demolition of the surrounding ammunition bodegas. Furthermore, all Air Force personnel (including attached service units such as the 409th Signal Company) were to assemble at a place on the West Road, northwest of Mariveles. Since the Mariveles-Cabcaben Road was impassable, we were to reach the designated location by walking six to eight miles directly westward through the jungle. We were given a half hour to prepare a pack and report back to the assembly spot. Regrouping at FEAF Headquarters, we found ourselves again participating in the old army game of hurry up and wait. The FEAF Headquarters area was in utter turmoil—everyone talking at the same time but no one knowing what to do. Two of the three officers who were supposed to accompany us had disappeared. Their absence virtually immobilized our Company while other units were moving out.

By 10:30 P.M. the Army Engineers were already preparing to blow up the bodegas, and they demanded that we clear out. The Company's junior officer, John Mullaney, moved us up the Little Baguio hill just outside the bodega area. He ordered us to wait there while he returned to Headquarters to search for the two missing officers. We never saw him again.

All of us were tired, mentally and physically, and there under the huge mahogany trees most of us fell asleep. Soon after midnight, a terrible explosion woke me to a nightmare. I seemed to be suspended in midair by an invisible hand. Back just beyond the FEAF Headquarters area a great orange light topped by a brilliant blue flooded the horizon. The Army Engineers had begun their demolition. Since the first Japanese air attacks of the war had destroyed our air force in the Philippines, some of the bodegas stored a huge surplus of five-hundred- and thousand-pound bombs. Apparently, the engineers had blown simultaneously all of the bodegas in the FEAF Headquarters area. The dreadful explosion robbed me of sleep, but it also robbed the Japanese of the chance to use those bombs.

To my knowledge, all the members of my Company survived the shattering blast, but the horrible nightmare continued. Exploding large-caliber ammunition and shell fragments were flying through the trees above us, and fire swept across the top of the forest. Fueled by sheer panic, we ran as no one has ever run before. I feel sure that we shattered Olympic records that night. When we had escaped from the danger zone, our Company regrouped and began walking westward through the dark Philippine forest. Suddenly, a huge and spectacular display of fireworks far to the south, the Navy base at Mariveles, shared its self-destructing light with us. Other explosions continued to rend the air with noise and light to the east and south.

After about an hour's struggle through the dark jungle, illuminated from time to time by the sad and unnatural light of friendly destruction, we stopped to rest. We had no sooner stretched out on the ground than an earthquake hit Bataan. Nature herself seemed to awaken convulsively to our nightmare. We were so tired and exhausted that the quake merely rocked us to sleep. We decided not to move again until morning.

On Thursday April 9, we arose about sunrise and confronted the problem of breakfast. When we left FEAF Headquarters the previous evening, everyone carried some food in his pack. But since a few members had lost their belongings in the confusion following the deafening blast, those of us with packs had to share. Amazingly, our few hours of rest amid explosions and earth tremors left us all refreshed and hungry. We thoroughly enjoyed our cold breakfast. That morning Bataan seemed strangely quiet; we heard no gunfire or explosions and little noise from Japanese aircraft.

After breakfast, with no officer to lead us, an argument erupted over which direction to take. The dispute divided us into two almost even factions led by two sergeants. One faction favored moving in a north-westerly direction, while the other faction favored the southwest. I chose the southwest, or the Bailey faction. I respected Sergeant Bailey. Though he had been only a likable alcoholic during peacetime, after the war began he became an outstanding soldier, heading the Little Baguio motor pool where I had served as clerk during the early phases of the First Battle of Bataan. At that point the remaining members of the 409th Signal Company split up, and I moved off to the southwest with the Bailey group.

As the morning wore on, movement through the thick jungle slowed, and we became increasingly confused and frustrated about our location. Some of us believed we should veer toward the northwest, others that we should continue on our present course. About noon we reached a stream flowing south (the Paniquian River). There, after a short time for lunch, we became engaged in a heated argument. Sergeant Bailey wanted to continue in a westerly direction through the foothills of the Mariveles Mountains. I argued that we should follow the stream, which I knew would bring us out at Mariveles Bay. There we might find water transportation to Corregidor before the Japanese arrived in Mariveles. Again we split up—about half and half. As Bailey's faction crossed the Paniquian and faded into the jungle, my group began a labored and stumbling trek down the banks of that stream.

About midafternoon we reached the head of the Mariveles Valley, where we walked nervously in open country for about a mile. We felt exposed and insecure in the open, especially when we heard Japanese planes in the distance, because all Little Baguio personnel had become forest-dwelling creatures in Bataan. Since our defection from the Bailey faction at noon, we had not seen anyone, American, Filipino, or Japanese. About 3:00 P.M. we reentered the jungle for a short stretch at the end of which was an abandoned, crumbling building. Following the trail around that structure, we suddenly found ourselves amidst a contingent of the Philippine Army, and in the distance we could see Japanese soldiers milling around. I realized that we were at the end of the road.

My group just stood there, stunned and exhausted. Like the others, I was heavily armed—a Springfield rifle, my old .45 automatic pistol, three bandoleers of ammunition around my neck, and pockets laden with .45

ammunition. Meanwhile, a Philippine Army officer approached us and advised that we disarm and present ourselves to our Japanese hosts. We complied and thereby became prisoners of the Japanese Empire.

Just then I looked up the main road and saw ragged elements of the famed Thirty-first Infantry stumbling toward us flying a piece of white cloth. That tragic scene produced an emotional reaction I cannot describe. My mind wandered back to Ft. McDowell, California, in July 1941 when a tough first sergeant explained to a group of rookies why the American flag must never be permitted to touch the ground. The answer? Because it had never been dipped in defeat.

Philippine Army personnel moved us further down into the valley where captured Americans were being concentrated.[10] As yet we had had no direct contact with the Japanese. There we made camp and began swapping food and stories with other Americans. In the late afternoon our camp was rocked by a giant explosion at least as strong as that produced by the blowing of the bodegas at Little Baguio. A Japanese dive-bomber had hit a ship loaded with bombs in Mariveles Bay about a mile from our camp. So powerful was the explosion that I was thrown from a water pipeline where I had been sitting and flattened against the ground.[11]

By the time the sun set on our Mariveles Valley camp, we had set up housekeeping. Most of us still had some food and cigarettes we had brought from Little Baguio. Everyone in the American camp was relaxing for the first time since Christmas Eve, when we left Manila. We reassured each other that we had nothing to worry about because we were sure the Japanese would abide by the Geneva Convention.

Just before dusk, we had our first encounter with Japanese abuse. An American sergeant came through our area with word that the Japanese had ordered us to report immediately to a designated location nearby. We were told not to take time to gather our supplies; we should leave everything as it was since we would be returning shortly. Our captors, we were told, merely wanted to look us over. Other American officers and noncoms were going throughout the camp with that message. Within a few minutes, we reached the Mariveles-Cabcaben Road where Japanese guards took over and began herding us toward Cabcaben. None of us suspected that we had begun the first stage of one of military history's most infamous atrocities, the Bataan Death March.

As it became apparent that our move was not at all temporary, we grew alarmed and unhappy that we had been forced to leave most of our supplies at the Mariveles camp. Despite Falk's assertion that it took only about five hours to reach Cabcaben, we actually walked all night.[12] The going was extremely difficult, particularly up through the steep Mariveles zigzag, because the Japanese Army was moving men and supplies south toward Mariveles in preparation for the attack on Corregidor. We were often forced to wait alongside the road to permit Japanese military traffic to pass. During that first night, the Japanese soldiers did not overtly harass us as they would beginning the next day; indeed, they largely ignored us and neglected our needs for food and water. Slowly, the nightmare's grip began to tighten.

Near the top of the zigzag, which took us out of the Mariveles Valley up into the foothills, we witnessed an unusual incident. A Japanese soldier, who had spotted an abandoned U.S. Army motorcycle, attempted to ride the vehicle, scattering POWs right and left. But the soldier, obviously a novice at riding motorcycles, lost control as he approached a sharp downhill curve. I can still hear his fading scream as he plunged off a bluff into a canyon some 250 feet below.

Soon after sunrise, when we had reached a point about a mile east of Hospital No. 2 near Cabcaben, we were herded into an open area. Rumors abounded that we were going to be fed, but no food came. In fact, we needed water more than food. Some, like me, had had no water the previous night. Many of us had left our canteens in the Mariveles camp, and others who just happened to be wearing their canteens when we left the camp had not, of course, had the foresight to refill them before the surprise beginning of the March. During the early afternoon, the Japanese permitted a limited number to take a load of canteens and fill them in a small, badly polluted stream nearby. Not all of the canteens came back. Some of the water bearers returned to other areas so that they could keep the canteens. That happened to a friend of mine who sent his canteen and was going to share with me. As the day wore on, the shadeless camp grew hotter and hotter. In spite of the heat and all the exertion of the march that day and the previous night, I got no water and began to suffer from acute dehydration.

Within the first full day of captivity, I felt and witnessed a variety of Japanese abuses. First, there was the surprise start of the March that denied us most of our meager but essential personal supplies. Later, Japanese guards seized all the money, food, and extra clothing they could find among the prisoners.[13] Then there was the brutal first stage of forced marching without water or food. The third and most painful was the continued and inexplicable Japanese denial of access to the nearby water supply while some American and Filipino troops, as well as civilians, died of dehydration under the broiling Philippine sun. For many, the conditions were aggravated by their having left their headgear in the Mariveles camp. The most awful atrocity I witnessed that first day of the Death March was Japanese guards shooting into groups of Filipino civilians as a means of control. Ironically, during that day our numbers increased—despite deaths from exhaustion, dehydration, and murder—as more and more Americans and Filipinos (soldiers and civilians) were herded into camp.

Late in the afternoon, the Japanese began to move us onto the main road toward Cabcaben. The majority of us were frantic with thirst. About a half-mile down the road, we were shunted to the roadside and stopped a few feet to the rear of Japanese artillery that had been set up to attack Corregidor. Ominous rumors circulated that the Japanese planned to use us to protect their guns from Corregidor's artillery. Had we known that those very guns had exchanged fire with Corregidor the previous afternoon, a number of American POWs being killed in the process, panic would have consumed us. Shortly after we left the area, the Japanese ringed Hospital No. 2 with artillery that exchanged fire with Corregidor, but there were remarkably few POW casualties. Throughout the ensuing days, other POWs were killed by Corregidor's artillery.[14] After some excited conversations between the guards and military police, we proceeded toward Cabcaben.

We passed through Cabcaben at sundown, completing our first horrible twenty-four hours under the Japanese, desperate for water. At Cabcaben the main road turned north. Again we walked all night. Many were already falling out. Those who fell were at first beaten, the Japanese guards either kicking them or bashing them with rifle butts. If the fallen could not get up and walk on, the Japanese guards either bayoneted or shot them. Many Americans, themselves barely able to walk, helped their stricken comrades as much as they could. One of the most poignant untold stories of the Bataan Death March concerns those who, often to no avail, gave their lives to help their companions.

That night, we left the foothills behind and entered the plains country of eastern Bataan. On the morning of April 11 while marching through a field beside the road jammed with heavy military traffic, we came upon a stagnant stream where the guards permitted us to drink. From that creek, clogged with the rotting bodies of fallen soldiers and dead animals, I drank all I could hold.

Having relieved my acute thirst, I began to feel hunger pains. But there was no food, no rest, no more water. There was only and everywhere the ruin of war: abandoned and destroyed equipment, a scarred and scorched countryside, and the bloated bodies of dead soldiers and civilians.

During the afternoon, as returning thirst sapped my strength and clouded my sanity, I began to lose all sense of time and place. The remainder of the March to San Fernando (sixty-five miles from Mariveles) only intensified the hellishness of the nightmare—unending thirst, the struggle to keep going to avoid certain death, and delirium.

When I reached San Fernando, I did not know how long I had been on the March following the afternoon of the eleventh. Actually, I did not know the date of my arrival at San Fernando and was too near death to care. I was fully conscious of events that I witnessed during the period, but for the most part I had lost all sense of sequence—especially beyond Lamao, about seven miles north of Cabcaben. Though my mind was still fairly clear when we reached Lamao, I became thoroughly confused long before reaching Limay, just three miles farther north. My memories of the other towns along our northward march through eastern Bataan were completely disordered, both chronologically and geographically. I later learned that delirious disorientation was common among my comrades on the Death March.

Some specific events that occurred on the road between Lamao and San Fernando still stand out in my memory. Somewhere beyond Lamao a rumor cropped up that at Limay food, water, and transportation awaited us. But when, after an eternity, we reached Limay, we received nothing. We experienced the same torturing rumors of relief at each of the other important towns of eastern Bataan—especially Orion and Balanga. There was a grain of truth in the Balanga rumor. The Japanese originally had planned to assemble all Bataan POWs at Balanga, feed them, and provide transportation to Camp O'Donnell. Unfortunately for us, the plan materialized only for a few high-ranking officers who were given varying amounts of food and transportation.[15]

The only food I had on the entire March from Mariveles to San Fernando was some half-cooked rice in a dirty tin can (about seven ounces) that I purchased from a Filipino soldier, and a turnip that I found in a field during a holding period while military traffic passed by. The only water I got after filling up on the morning of the eleventh at the polluted stream near Lamao was a drink I took by force one night, probably near Limay. Two American soldiers emerged from the shadows alongside the road with a pail of water. Evidently, they were familiar with that territory. Though it was dark, I instantly smelled the water. I rushed up behind them and grabbed the bucket and began drinking from it. Though the soldier holding the container tried to snatch it away, he was clearheaded enough to realize that if he pulled too vigorously, all the water would be spilled. His concern for the water allowed me to get a fairly good drink.

On another occasion—probably at Pilar—I thought I would get water again. We were in another holding pattern when POWs began lining up at a public pump. The Japanese guards, however, immediately

Z A M B A L E S   M O U N T A I N S

CABANATUAN

• TARLAC

CAMP O'DONNELL

CAPAS

CLARK FIELD ○

**THE BATAAN
DEATH MARCH**

SAN FERNANDO

SUBIC BAY

B A T A A N
P E N I N S U L A

BALANGA

PILAR

ORION

LIMAY

M A N I L A
B A Y

MANILA

LAMAO

MARIVELES

CABCABEN

CAVITE

PASAY

NICHOLS FIELD

S O U T H

⌂ **CORREGIDOR**

PARAÑAQUE

C H I N A

LAGUNA
DE BAY

S E A

N

.... DEATH MARCH PROPER
(Mariveles to San Fernando)

++++++ SEALED BOX CARS
(San Fernando to Capas)

——— FINAL MARCH
(Capas to Camp O'Donnell)

APPROXIMATE SCALE:

0   5   10   15

MILES

dispersed the line and soon forced us to resume the March—at least all who were physically able. At every stop after Lamao, some could not rise to continue and were murdered.

On one occasion I slaked my thirst without drinking water. This occurred in the last segment of the journey when the guards forced us to march all night and until midafternoon the next day. During that period, we were not permitted to stop except when a heavy thunderstorm broke about midnight. We lay down in the road and literally absorbed moisture. When the rainstorm passed and we resumed marching, our previously dehydrated bodies enjoyed a brief respite from parching thirst. It was the first rain of the season, and it not only partially quenched our thirst but gave us a rest.

Falk states that this first group of POWs to leave Mariveles halted "to rest or sleep from time to time."[16] In fact, we never stopped for rest or sleep during the entire March. We stopped frequently to permit large groups of the Japanese Army to pass, to await other groups of POWs coming from the hinterland of Bataan, and to provide guards time to clarify communication with their superiors, but we never stopped for the benefit of the POWs. When we did stop, prevailing conditions prevented rest and sleep. Many stops were made in daylight hours in rice and cane fields where we were crowded together and exposed to the merciless Philippine sun. The stopping places often reeked with the odor of rotting bodies, and as the March progressed, those places became increasingly polluted with human feces containing deadly dysentery germs.

I later learned that there was no consistency in marching conditions for POWs. How one group was treated depended on the policy of the nearest guard. Some groups were given varying amounts of food and permitted rest and water, according to Falk. No prisoners with me on the March received any food. Shooting or bayoneting stragglers and the fallen seems to have been the rule rather than the exception. I did not see anyone buried alive, as Falk described, but I later heard stories about such things.[17]

Mixed in with the military prisoners on the March were many Filipino civilians fleeing from Bataan. They were generally in desperate condition—sick and without food or water—and they, too, were treated brutally by the Japanese. Gradually, I came to realize that since the Japanese military had no compassion for the civilian Filipinos (the aged, women, and children), their treatment of POWs was not likely to improve when we reached the internment camps.

By midafternoon of the last day, those of us still alive and walking reached San Fernando, Pampanga Province, the end of the March proper. On the outskirts of town, I was overcome by an emotional experience despite my burning thirst and delirium. Filipino women lined the road, attempting to provide food and water to POWs, American as well as Filipino. Other groups of Filipinos were accepting money for their gifts of food and water, and still others were selling goods outright. The Japanese guards stopped that welfare activity and in the process severely beat some of the people. But many, especially the women, undauntedly continued their largely futile efforts to help us. Though I never saw the Japanese kill (as Falk asserts)[18] any of the Filipinos who were either giving or selling food and water to the POWs, I did witness the terrible beatings, particularly of the women, and I was deeply moved.

Locals did not appear along the road as observers or vendors until we crossed the northern boundary of Bataan into Pampanga Province. The Bataan towns were dead, destroyed by two savage battles and apparently depopulated of all residents. At the end of the March in San Fernando, a POW holding pen awaited us. Though the conditions were nightmarish, we did receive a little food, and, even more important, plenty of water. At first, the blessing of abundant water was all I cared about. But except for the presence of plenty of water and some rice, the San Fernando holding pen was like all the other stopping places on the March north of Lamao—prisoners crowded together amid the filth of human waste and the repulsive smell of human death. From Lamao on, I noticed that more and more of the POWs, like helpless babies, had fouled themselves with their feces because of dysentery.

Of all the horrors and sorrows of the Bataan Death March, the most unforgettable for me was the sight of our fallen comrades—emaciated, filthy remnants of humanity whose plight elicited no sympathy or mercy from the Japanese and whose wasted remains in death stirred revulsion among their own kind. Falk correctly records that the POWs witnessed so many incidents of Japanese murder of stricken POWs during the Bataan Death March that they developed "blunted feelings . . . toward their fallen comrades."[19] The circumstances of their deaths were so hideously degrading as to be contemptible and ignoble. So dehumanizing were the living conditions on the March that a fellow soldier dying of dysentery and a Japanese bayonet had somehow forfeited his place among the human race and fallen beyond the reach of sympathy. We arrived at San Fernando far down the slope into the subhuman world of POWs, motivated almost exclusively by the primal urge for survival.

7

O'Donnell: Camp Death

I endured the San Fernando holding pen for only that day, that night, and a portion of the next day, April 13 and 14 as best I remember. It was little more than a day, but I cannot rid my memory of the stinking horror. The one latrine, an open ditch, was dreadful to behold; its squirming maggots and its unbearable stench have haunted my nights for over forty years. Human feces spotted the entire grounds of the holding pen. Many prisoners suffered from acute dysentery, and most of them had no control over bowel movements. Not only did they scatter their bloody flux hither and yon or wherever they lay, but most of them also badly soiled their clothing. In the crowded holding pen, we could hardly find a place to sit that was free of fecal matter.

The offensive odor of human excrement mixed easily with the sickening smell of death. When I arrived at the despicable facility, I found many of the prisoners lying on the ground either critically ill, dying, or already dead. In the hot Philippine weather, the dead flesh decayed quickly, and in the holding pen there were no burial details.

The live prisoners in the pen were emotionally dead, perfect examples of zombies. No authority or leadership (except that of the brutal Japanese guards) helped maintain order. Any vestige of Army or Navy pride had long since disappeared on the Bataan Death March. No officers, commissioned or noncommissioned, assumed command. Though some prisoners continued to give a helping hand to the weak and sick, by and large it was every man for himself. By the time we reached San Fernando, it was difficult to have any feeling of group fellowship.

We had no medical aid of any kind at San Fernando, only the limited assistance one weary or sick individual might offer another. We saw no American military medical personnel—no doctors, no corpsmen. And, of course, the Japanese provided no medical aid. I recall a poignant scene late in the afternoon of my arrival at the holding pen that illustrates the point. In an area nearby but not directly adjacent to my sitting space, a soldier, sick and friendless, was crying out in great pain. The

POWs around him identified his illness as acute appendicitis. He screamed frequently through the rest of the afternoon and evening. As the night wore on, his screams devolved into moans and eventually ceased. When morning came, I was too concerned with my own survival to give further thought to the matter. After all, I had been living with dead bodies around me since my arrival at the holding pen.

The San Fernando pen had one asset—plenty of water. After quenching my terrible thirst, I began to feel sharp jabs of hunger. I had eaten almost nothing since leaving Mariveles junction several days before. Much to my surprise, the Japanese fed us rice that evening, and I received a liberal portion. After a fitful night, I awoke at daybreak ravenously hungry, but we got no more food before our departure later that morning. The rest, water, and food received at San Fernando did wonders for me. In spite of filth, the stench of death, and hunger, I felt much better as the new day got under way.

By midmorning, Japanese guards, using their now familiar chant of "hoy-hoy," began rounding up the POWs who were able to stand. What happened to those unable to get to their feet I never knew. Heading west, we marched out of our hellish holding pen, leaving behind the dead and dying. Our march ended a few minutes later at the railroad station. There we were made deliriously happy by the news that we would have railway transportation to our permanent POW camp, the identity of which still remained a secret.

Shortly after we arrived at the railway station, the Japanese began loading us into empty boxcars. When I first entered the one assigned to me and sat down against the wall opposite the door, I was relieved, even exhilarated, about not having to march. As more and more men were herded into the car, however, alarm began to spread. Soon prisoners were packed into the car so tightly that some had to stand because they had no room to sit. Worst of all, air was becoming scarce, and we were having difficulty breathing.

At that point, the Japanese guards slammed the boxcar door shut, apparently sealing it. The POWs next to the door tried but could not open it. Panic-stricken, some prisoners screamed and flailed about, and we all feared suffocation and death. The sun in its cloudless sky made an oven of the boxcar. Apparently the only thing that saved the passengers in my car from mass suffocation was a narrow crack between the bottom and the sides, through which we could see some daylight.

The stifling heat in the boxcar was mixed with the stench of sweat and feces, but no one really noticed those things. Our minds were completely absorbed by the terror of possible death by suffocation. I hardly noticed another onset of mouth-drying thirst because of the heat and sudden dehydration. I still had no canteen and was not able to carry water with me on the railway trip to Capas.

Time is so difficult to measure when every moment is full of fear and stress. It was probably less than an hour after the door was sealed that the train finally pulled out of the station. We stopped several times during the twenty-five-mile trip to Capas, a village just south of Tarlac and near Clark Field. Though the journey to Capas seemed to last for an eternity, the actual time was about four hours. When the door was thrown open at Capas, all who were able to rise rushed pell-mell for the fresh air without looking back. I have no idea how many of my fellow travelers remained behind in the car, dead or incapacitated. My escape from that dreadful boxcar felt like a resurrection—as if I had literally risen from the dead.

As we emerged from the boxcars, Japanese guards set us on the last lap of our journey—a march of some eight miles to Camp O'Donnell, the first Japanese concentration camp for American and Filipino POWs. As we walked along the dusty road through Capas, Filipino civilians gathered and tried to give (and sometimes sell) food and water to the POWs, who were terribly dehydrated and desperately hungry and thirsty. The local citizens stood in their front yards handing food and water over their picket fences wherever Japanese guards permitted or were not looking. The food was largely rice balls, rice bread sandwiches containing carabao meat or pork, and cakes of brown sugar. Most of those delicacies were wrapped in banana leaves. In those days in the Philippines, banana leaves were the universal wrapper, performing somewhat the same function as paper towels or plastic wrap in America today.

At one of those residences, a Filipino tried to hand me a sandwich, a sort of biscuit with carabao meat inside. Just as I reached to take it, an arm came over my shoulder, and a hand snatched the sandwich out of my grasp. With the instinct and quickness of a hungry animal, I grabbed the arm of the intruder, and locked in battle, we fell down into the dust and filth of the street. In my attempt to retrieve what I believed was rightly mine, the sandwich was torn to shreds and scattered among horse droppings in the street. Suddenly, I discovered that I was wrestling with a high-ranking Army officer. His companion, another officer of equal rank, was trying to stop the fight. As soon as I realized what had happened, I backed off while the second officer began to lecture both of us about the sins of American comrades fighting each other, especially in those circumstances. The officer's firm but fraternal reprimand got to me emotionally—I began to sob, confessing that I had reached a very low state in stooping to fight with my fellow American soldier for a piece of bread. Meanwhile, my former opponent paid no attention to his fellow officer's lecture. He was down on his knees picking food particles from the horse manure.

Stanley Falk accurately describes the POWs in Capas as they began their march to Camp O'Donnell:

> The physical condition of most of the prisoners was at its worst. Some were so weak that they could barely lift their feet to walk. All the liquid in their bodies seemed to have been drained from them on the train ride from San Fernando. Some men were sure that no more than a quarter of their number would live to complete the last few miles of the march. Gaunt, haggard, dirty, unshaven, clothes torn and stained with filth, the captives looked at each other unfamiliarly. Even best friends had difficulty recognizing one another.[1]

Though my hunger and thirst seemed to increase with every step, the march to Camp O'Donnell was in some respects rejuvenating. We were coming to the end of the journey, to our place of internment. Despite the persistence of Japanese brutality, most of us still hoped that once we were interned in a permanent camp the Japanese would abide by the Geneva Convention. The fact that the Japanese guards were more relaxed and permitted a leisurely walk boosted my spirits. I walked with the officer who broke up the fight, and his companionship further brightened my mood. We had a delightful conversation all the way to Camp O'Donnell. From time to time along the way, we both helped the mad officer. By that time, he had eaten his food particles and begun to mutter senselessly as he stumbled down the road in a state of serious mental derangement.

Camp O'Donnell, a partially completed facility for General Mac-Arthur's new Philippine Army, was located on the grass plains near the center of the great valley of Luzon. The camp was a starkly uninviting place with practically no trees. Many of the barracks were roughly constructed, with sides and floors of bamboo and roofs of grass. The Philippine dry season was reaching its height, accompanied by cloudless skies and a blazing sun. The whole country seemed to be a lifeless beige.

When we arrived at Camp O'Donnell, the guards herded us up a hill to a barren area in front of Japanese headquarters. There they ordered us to sit. After we had baked on the shadeless dirt beneath a scorching sun for what seemed hours, a Japanese officer, introduced or otherwise identified as the Camp Commandant, emerged from the headquarters building, mounted a platform, and began to harangue us. After more than forty years, I do not remember whether he spoke in English or used an interpreter. The gist of his comments needed no interpretation. According to Falk, the officer was the Camp Commandant, Captain Tsuneyoshi, who greeted each new batch of prisoners arriving at Camp

O'Donnell with "essentially the same fiery speech of welcome—and warning."[2]

He told us, in effect, that we no longer even qualified as human beings. He made it clear that since we had surrendered, the Japanese Army had no obligation to provide for our welfare. Hence, any treatment we might receive from the Japanese would be better than we deserved. He declared that Japan had won the war and that the United States as well as her Western allies had been permanently defeated. He gave us little hope for survival and warned that anyone guilty of breaking a rule, no matter how minor, would immediately be shot. The camp rules, he said, required that all prisoners, regardless of rank, salute all Japanese personnel. In fact, all differences in rank among the POWs would be abolished, he informed us, and we would all be treated equally—i.e., subhumanly.[3] An ex-POW interviewed by Donald Knox in the early 1980s captured the essence and tone of the threatening speech:

A Japanese officer gave us a little talk about what we could expect. He told us that Americans were dogs, that they'd always been dogs, and that they were going to be treated like dogs. He said that Caucasians had been enemies of the Oriental for 100 years and would always be enemies. He said these things real harsh. . . . That's when I began to realize we had big problems.[4]

Despite the Commandant's statement about abolishing rank among prisoners, a few days later all POW generals and colonels were segregated and removed from camp. They were permitted one orderly each. I learned later that the officers were interned briefly in Taiwan and then in Manchuria. Generally speaking, the Japanese treated them little, if any, better than other POWs, and many of them died in the camps.[5]

Sitting there at the entrance to Camp O'Donnell in the broiling April sun listening to the officer's harangue, I suddenly felt all alone in the world for the first time during the war. No longer could I muster strength from the companionship of my comrades or from my patriotism. I felt deserted by God and country. Within a few hours, however, I recovered my faith, hope, and national pride and never again plunged into the black despair experienced at O'Donnell's gate.

Few of the nine thousand American POWs would ever forget the "welcome speech" on their arrival at Camp O'Donnell. It was one of those special events that become indelibly printed on the mind. Throughout the next three and a half years, POWs in prison camps from the Philippines to Japan frequently mentioned that speech and its effect. In his interviews with surviving POWs, Donald Knox found that the aging veterans of Bataan still remembered the "welcome speech." It is not easy to say why the Commandant's speech so impressed us. It was probably the event that dashed our hopes for decent treatment by the Japanese, the event that forced us Americans to disabuse ourselves of the notion that our conquerors would turn out to be decent people.

The Japanese provided no internal administration for the camp. Once the POWs passed through the gate behind the headquarters building, a lethargic anarchy prevailed, except for some halfhearted attempts by Army noncoms to arrange for the orderly delivery of food from the kitchens. The guards segregated the Filipinos in one area of the camp. Within the section reserved for American personnel, commissioned officers segregated themselves from the enlisted men and did not seem concerned with the administration of our section, even though the Japanese, so far as I was able to tell, did not require the separation. In fact, it appeared to me that they would not have cared if officers had lived in the barracks with enlisted men. As long as their prisoners made no trouble, the Japanese seemed content to keep their distance and let the filthy, diseased Americans organize their own hell. The only Japanese military personnel I ever saw in the American sector were a few enlisted men who came to the edge of the camp to recruit POWs for work details.

Because of the segregation, I came into contact with officers only when I was standing in the water line. The only source of water for personal use in the American section was one defective, rusty hydrant where a slowly moving line of men stood most of the day. Rank or class distinctions were never observed at the water line. Officers did not attempt to pull rank to gain quicker access to the hydrant and, to the best of my knowledge, waited their turn the same as enlisted men.

In general, the performance of Army officers at Camp O'Donnell was poorer than it might have been. For selfish reasons, I desperately wanted to see aggressive leadership from our officers. I felt that had they made a greater effort, morale among the enlisted men would have been much higher. For example, the superior performance of the U.S. Navy officers at Bilibid Prison resulted in a much higher quality of life for all the interned military personnel there. During my long imprisonment under the Japanese in several locations, I met officers whom I admired and even a few who became role models for me—but not at O'Donnell.

The value of my judgment of the officers at Camp O'Donnell must be considered in the light of some mitigating circumstances. In the first place, I was interned at O'Donnell for only the first month of its operation, a time of great uncertainty and turmoil. I suspect that internal administration there improved as time passed. In the first days everyone was in a state of shock: we had just endured the infamous Death March. We simply could not believe that a modern, civilized, industrial nation like Japan could unleash the atrocities of the Death March and Camp O'Donnell. Looking back, I am forced to admit that the officers probably could not have done anything to alleviate, in any significant way, the terrible situation there. Officers at O'Donnell, like enlisted men, were spiritless, hollow-eyed men dying of dysentery and broken hearts.

When I arrived at Camp O'Donnell, I, like my comrades, was physically drained as a result of dehydration and starvation. Up to that point I had escaped the ravages of dysentery, that killer in whose shadow I had existed since Mariveles. But as soon as I lay down in one of the bamboo buildings, the terrible malady hit me. After a couple of days I reached the point where I abandoned all hope of recovery. Once more, amid the death and dying of others, I sensed the presence of my own death. But again, as with the boxcar door, my death was suddenly pushed aside. My good friend Richard Murray arrived at Camp O'Donnell. I had not seen him since our withdrawal from Little Baguio, when Murray and I had become separated. He heard that I was in the camp, sought me out, and brought me back to life. He somehow acquired some sulfathiazole pills on the black market and made me take them. That magic drug soon killed the dysentery germs, and I was on my way to recovery. I shall never forget that during my weakest period Murray held me in his arms and force-fed me. While I was recovering, he was transferred. Later, Richard Murray, my friend and nurse, died in the prison camp at Cabanatuan— friendless, without care. He died of dysentery.

Initially, there was plenty of room on the bamboo floors or built-in wooden bunks in the barracks for everyone to bed down. By the time I recovered from my bout with dysentery, however, space was becoming scarce as more and more American and Filipino POWs poured in. Though the Medical Corps designated an area as a hospital, it was largely just a receiver of terminal cases. Increasingly, space in the barracks was used for the sick, and POWs who were not seriously ill had to find room under the barracks. Because most of the sick men above were suffering from dysentery and the accompanying problem of uncontrollable bowels, and because the bamboo poles that formed the floors had air spaces between them, the shelter beneath the barracks became a septic slum.

Any discussion of the conditions at O'Donnell must focus on the area the medical officers designated as the hospital. A basic rule was adopted early: no sick person who was fully conscious would be sent to the hospital. So primitive were the conditions and so poor the supplies and quality of care that few, if any, ever returned. Only when a sick person slipped into a coma would his friends carry him there. At the hospital, patients were processed through a crude assembly line. Friends would place the comatose patient on the ground under one end of a large L-shaped building, the first floor of which was about five feet above the ground. As dead POWs were removed for burial from the other end of the L, those still alive were gradually moved down the line. Somewhere along the L route, death was virtually certain to come to each patient. One ex-POW, in his interview with Donald Knox, called it like it was: "It was not a hospital. It was a place to put the guys that were going to die."[6]

At our barracks (mostly 409th Signal or other Signal Detachment personnel), a sort of halfway station was established for the gravely ill. Just outside the barracks was a small bamboo, thatched roof structure that resembled a gazebo. There we placed severely ill men until they lost consciousness. Several members of my Company spent their last days of awareness there. I especially remember Frank Lillard of King City, California, who had become my good friend on Bataan. We carried Frank to the halfway gazebo when he first became acutely ill. There I talked with him while he remained conscious. Frank loved the American West and talked wistfully of his Salinas Valley ranch. We exchanged western stories frequently until he lapsed into a coma and was carried to the O'Donnell Hospital to die.

As I recall, some of the U.S. Army Medical Corps personnel lived in the hospital building above the assembly line of dying men. It is possible that the assembly line included an overflow of patients from the main floor of the building. Some patients seemed to be hospitalized on the floor above, but no one I knew had been in that area. Just how the hospital was constructed and precisely how it operated are lost from or clouded in my memory. The medics working in that horrible environment had the most difficult duty at O'Donnell. They lived and worked constantly in the shadow of the death watch. I could not have faced their ordeal and maintained my sanity. The members of the Medical Corps did all they could to save the dying patients, but it was an impossible situation.

The images I carry of O'Donnell have been clouded by more than simply the passage of almost half a century. While I was there, I often turned away from the reality of the ongoing tragedy of death. Using my imagination, I went to great lengths to shut the horror out, to pretend that the awful thing was not happening. What penetrated and remains permanently in my mind is the long line of dead and dying men, their bodies horribly consumed by dysentery, and the piles of contorted corpses at the cemetery awaiting the digging of their common grave. Death at O'Donnell created images from which nightmares are made, and conscious thought of these matters is no less painful for me now.

Whenever I think about the death and burial of my fellow POWs, my brain becomes sick.

My primary work assignment there was on the burial detail, digging graves. At the time, the six-month dry season was nearing its end, so the soil in the graves area was almost as hard as concrete. The cemetery was located immediately north of the American sector in what had been sugar cane fields. To save labor, we chiseled out graves barely deep enough to contain the bodies. The graves were generally about eighteen inches deep (or less) and seven feet long by fifteen feet wide. We placed fifteen bodies in each grave. The graves were not deep enough to provide protection from roving animals, had there been any. Yet, according to testimony given to Donald Knox in 1980, graves at O'Donnell were dug three to five feet deep, where the grave diggers were stopped by the water table. One ex-POW told Knox that they stacked bodies in the grave two-deep.[7] Obviously, those men were members of the grave-digging detail after the rains came. When I was on the burial detail, dynamite would have been required for graves of such depth.

By the time the bodies of dead POWs were removed from the assembly line, the horrible effects of uncontrolled dysentery had made them unrecognizable, terribly emaciated things barely human in appearance. Borne on stretchers to the cemetery, the dead bodies were dumped in a pile unceremoniously before being placed in a mass grave. No religious or memorial services of any description were performed at the burial site. Perhaps there were chaplains who officiated at funerals of enlisted personnel at Camp O'Donnell, but I saw no evidence of it during the few weeks I was there.

The only graveside ritual performed at Camp O'Donnell was the check for dog tags. As I recall, dog tags were deliberately not removed. Our reasoning was that after the war the Army would be able to use them for identification to certify or register a grave. However, another survivor of the Camp O'Donnell burial detail "remembers" that we did collect the dog tags and that the names of those buried were written down.[8] If memory serves, we made no lists of dog tags. The members of the burial detail merely checked the tag to determine if the body was someone they knew or a member of one of their companies. In this way I identified many members of my Company at the graveside. So distorted were the bodies that it would have been difficult, if not impossible, to make the identification without the dog tags. Fifty-seven of the eighty-one members of my Company (the 409th Signal) died between the fall of Bataan and V-J Day—most of them in the assembly line at Camp O'Donnell Hospital during the few weeks I was there. In fact, a large majority of the deaths of all Bataan POWs occurred at Camp

O'Donnell, and somewhere along the assembly line under the hospital building.

Some deaths, however, occurred in and under the barracks. Deaths among the sick inside the barracks were to be expected, but occasionally some refused to declare themselves ill or were actually unaware of their condition and died beneath the barracks floor. I knew at least three men in that category. One of them slept beside me under our barracks and worked with me on the burial and latrine details. One night, we talked a long time about the harshness of conditions, the killing effect of working all day and half the night, and our chances of survival. When he failed to respond to my greeting the next morning, I saw that he was dead. A general conclusion among the survivors at O'Donnell was that many of the barracks deaths resulted from a sort of "broken heart" syndrome. Some men simply lost the will to fight for life and gave themselves up to death. They just did not have the heart to continue facing such a wretched way of life.

In addition to the enormous number of American deaths at Camp O'Donnell, the Filipinos appeared to be dying en masse. According to one observer, the Filipinos were "dying like flies. . . . Their bodies went by in an endless column."[9] Another observer stated, "Each day we would count how many of them died. If there were 400, we knew about forty Americans had died."[10] I believe the ratio of ten to one was approximately correct. The daily death toll indelibly etched in my mind for the period I spent at Camp O'Donnell is three hundred Filipinos and thirty Americans.

Though my primary work assignment was duty on the burial detail, I had a second essential job—digging latrines. Generally, I worked all day digging graves and until midnight digging latrines. I had to do double duty because so few POWs were able to work. Ex-POW Jack Brady told Donald Knox that

unfortunately, there was no such thing as being laid up for a while at O'Donnell. There were people in much worse shape than I. Water had to be hauled, people had to be buried, wood needed to be brought in—all kinds of things needed doing. So in O'Donnell, if you could move, you did something.[11]

The O'Donnell policy of filling up old latrines and digging new ones (i.e., slit trenches) was necessary to try to keep down the fly population to reduce the spread of dysentery.

O'Donnell had enormous numbers of flies, which, after feeding on dysentery-ridden feces, spread the disease further. One of Knox's interviews neatly describes the problem at chow time: "The flies were so thick. You'd get your mess kit of boiled rice and you had to fan it as fast as you could to keep the flies off. All the way to your mouth you had to fan to keep from swallowing flies."[12] In effect, we lived in the midst of a swarm of millions of flies. There was no way to fight or control them, and, as another ex-POW interviewed by Knox describes it, they were so numerous we measured them by weight instead of number:

The only thoughts I had at O'Donnell were of the flies. They were so damn thick. At night they would sit on the roofs and because there were so many of them, whole patches of thatch would fall down. . . . [B]ushes . . . were so thick with flies, they bent right down to the ground. Nowhere . . . could you get away from those damned flies.[13]

The latrines provided a breeding ground for the flies. Since many (probably the majority) of the POWs were suffering from some form of dysentery, it was essential to maintain a large number of slit-trench, open-air latrines. We concentrated the latrines in areas that we hoped would be close enough to the sick POWs and at the same time far enough away to reduce the numbers of flies around the barracks. Actually, we failed in both goals. The location of the latrines did not noticeably affect the fly population around the barracks, but for the sick the latrines were still too far away. Many of those racked with dysentery could not control their bowels long enough to reach the trenches. Some of the sick lived (and often died) in the latrine area, unable to return to the barracks. The sight of those men lying prostrate beside the latrines, badly soiled with fecal matter and covered with flies, is a recurring scene in nightmares that more than forty years have not erased from my mind.

The problem of maintaining enough latrines was severe. The dysentery-infected population was large, and the number of able-bodied men available to dig was small. Most of the members of the latrine-digging detail, like me, were also members of the grave-digging detail. In addition, we faced the same problem digging trenches that we encountered in digging graves: the ground was too hard and dry for our detail to keep pace. The plan was this: after each person used the slit trench, he was to take a shovel and cover up his waste matter with dirt. Though many POWs were too sick to do this, others tried to keep the dirt moving. The result was that the latrine was soon full of dirt and had to be replaced. The latrine-digging detail attempted to open new slit trenches as fast as the old ones were filled.

Though both of my jobs involved repulsive labor, they demanded that I get enough food to satisfy my body's demand for energy. O'Donnell was the only place during three and a half years of imprisonment where I had more than enough to eat, such as it was. The cuisine consisted largely of a steamed grain that we referred to as rice but was largely a mixture of millet and barley. Those of us on the working details had plenty to eat because so many POWs were dying or were otherwise too sick to consume their rations.

In retrospect, I do not understand how I had time to work two jobs, stand in line for food, and, worst of all, stand in line for water. The water faucet is another image that perpetuates itself in the memory of Bataan veterans. There was only one faucet for general use in the American sector, and it ran at little more than a drip. Sharing the one inefficient faucet with several thousand other POWs presented a time-consuming, mind-draining, and physically exhausting problem. In 1980, various ex-POWs shared with Donald Knox vivid memories of the O'Donnell water line. Perhaps that grim aspect of life at O'Donnell was best expressed by John Falconer: "Mostly, you stood with your canteen in line, waiting to get water. You stood for hours. I remember seeing men who had died while waiting in line." [14]

The agonizing exercise of getting water was compounded for me since I had been unable to replace my canteen, which I had been forced to leave at Mariveles. I eventually found a bamboo joint that held about a half-gallon of water. The bamboo was a piece of waste material left over from the construction of the barracks. I tied a rice straw rope around the joint so that I could carry it more easily. It served me well and long as a canteen.

At O'Donnell we cooked with water from a stagnant creek nearby that was too polluted for drinking. We heard rumors that some of the hundreds of Filipinos dying each day were thrown into the creek. There was also the speculation that a major cause of Filipino deaths was their drinking the polluted water. Some POWs recall that Filipinos drank the creek water despite warnings by Filipino and American officers.[15] In the American sector, the danger from the contaminated creek water was understood and assured the steady line at the faucet, while water-carrying details provided creek water to the kitchens for cooking.

By the time I left O'Donnell in early May, the clothing shortage had become critical. The Japanese, of course, did not provide any clothing allowance. Each POW was responsible for maintaining his own wardrobe. Some of the clothing left by those who died became available, but there was no organized effort to assure fair distribution of the personal properties of the dead. Many of the articles went into the black market. Then, too, most of the dead POWs possessed precious little clothing not being worn when they went to their graves. According to an account in Knox's book, the dead were buried "nude because their clothes, after being boiled, had been passed on to other prisoners." [16] Perhaps the policy of recycling the dead's clothing was adopted after I left O'Donnell, but we buried the deceased in their clothes. We felt that since our dead comrades had already been stripped of their dignity by Japanese atrocities, we should not add another indignity by stripping them of their only remaining earthly possession—their stained and stinking tattered clothes.

The uniform of the day at O'Donnell (and from then forward) was anything we could find to wear. Soon after I arrived at the camp, someone stole my shirt. Fortunately, I had a blue denim jumper that I used to replace it. I did not get another shirt until I arrived at Bilibid Prison in July. At O'Donnell my wardrobe consisted of one suit of underwear, one pair of pants, a blue denim jumper, one pair of shoes, and one pair of socks. I had no hat of any kind. As I recall, I wore my army helmet (vintage World War I) through the Death March to San Fernando, but at some time before or after my arrival at O'Donnell I either lost or discarded it. Many POWs discarded their helmets early on because they were so hot and heavy. But all of us had to be alert about shoes or socks. Those highly prized items, once removed, were quickly stolen from the careless.

Doing laundry at O'Donnell was difficult at best. The drinking water obtained at the communal faucet was far too precious to be used for laundry. The only other water in the camp was hauled from the creek for kitchen use. To make matters worse, no soap was available except on the black market or perhaps from a friend who happened to have a bar of the precious stuff from only God knew where. Even if I could get soap and water, thievery further complicated the problem. Once any clothing was removed for laundering, it was fair game. Some POWs took turns guarding small communal laundry projects. Objects hung out to dry were especially vulnerable. The whole nerve-racking procedure was a little like getting horses through Comanche country in the old West.

If doing laundry was difficult, taking a bath was practically out of the question. Occasionally, I could get hold of enough creek water to wipe my body with a rag—if I had a rag. As with laundry, soap for bathing was extremely scarce or even nonexistent for those who could not pay the price demanded on the black market. As Sgt. Forrest Knox told Donald Knox in 1980, "The odor in the camp gradually increased. I thought it was me smelling—no water to wash or bathe." [17]

Those of us on the burial or latrine detail were exposed to serious sanitation problems. On the burial detail we had to handle corpses badly soiled with fecal matter; on the latrine detail we were also constantly exposed to large quantities of human waste infected with dysentery germs. To make matters worse, we had no clean-up facilities after a day's work. As Lt. Fred Gifford, a member of a burial detail recalls, "We had no water to wash in. You'd climb through that dysentery, it was all over the place. You had it on your hands, your feet, in your hair. . . . You wiped it off the best you could." [18]

Intellectual deprivation at Camp O'Donnell made the horror of our lives inescapable. During my weeks there I saw only a part of one Manila newspaper, which my mind devoured hungrily even though I recognized the stilted writing as primarily Japanese propaganda. One demented veteran of Bataan had somehow picked up an elementary geography textbook with maps. I wanted to see the maps to get my bearings and to compare my mental geography with reality. I had tried in vain to imagine panoramic views of various countries and to picture in my mind their relative positions. But no amount of begging could persuade the crazed POW to lend me the book that apparently had no intrinsic value for him. He cherished it only because he derived a distorted pleasure from denying others the privilege of using it.

There were few people I could talk to about anything not related to daily survival. The conversation that passed spontaneously between prisoners more often than not focused on the crudest matters of bodily function. The firmness of bowel movements was a favorite subject. At O'Donnell men were admired for their solid stools much as Olympians are admired for their muscles or beauty contestants for their figures. I recall a perfect stranger, who had just been squatting immediately to my rear at the slit trench, approaching me to offer congratulations on my firm bowel discharge. He declared it a top priority of his to return to a solid state.

One physical function we never discussed was sex. By the time the veterans of Bataan (starved, browbeaten, and sick) had reached Camp O'Donnell, sex was the farthest thing from their minds. The POW experience had already taught them that the sex function is a product of proteins. Sex as a topic of conversation had declined greatly in the latter days of the Bataan campaign. Then, I often heard expressions like, "I'd turn down a naked Hollywood starlet for a piece of chocolate pie." Only two women were important in the minds of the American POWs at O'Donnell: mother and the Virgin Mary. Every day was Mother's Day at O'Donnell. In fact, the whole idea of sex had disappeared from the minds of those men, not to appear again until after V-J Day.

Few events during a typical day took our minds off our own bodies, but there were the bombers. Japanese bombers flew low over O'Donnell on their takeoffs to Corregidor with heavy bomb loads. That created mixed feelings in us: sadness because our fellow Americans on Corregidor were bearing the brunt of those bombs, but pride because the island fortress was still fighting back like a noble old warrior. Time was not on the side of the Americans, and few of us believed that Corregidor could hold out much longer.

It may seem incredible, given the horror of O'Donnell, but there was no talk of escape. Donald Knox interviewed an American ex-POW who did describe his escape from O'Donnell,[19] but I was never aware of anyone escaping while I was there. It was a subject that never came up as far as I was concerned. Everyone around me was too absorbed with just staying alive to formulate escape plans.

To place O'Donnell in its proper context, one must see our imprisonment in that hellhole as an extension of the Bataan Death March. O'Donnell was not a place for recuperation from the Death March; rather, it was a place of punishment the Japanese devised for those with the insolent grit to survive the March. Though what lay ahead was in many ways worse than O'Donnell, the tragically high death toll there, very nearly including me, mounted because of the rigors of the March. It is important to understand that during our struggles at O'Donnell we were all merely freshmen in the Japanese school of survival. Our minds and bodies had not yet adjusted to the Japanese military's disregard for human life.

About three weeks after my arrival, the Japanese began to speed up the sending of small work details to various places in the Philippines. I did not feel confident about surviving at O'Donnell and decided to volunteer for one at the first opportunity. I probably had been at O'Donnell less than a month when I was accepted for a work detail. Unfortunately, I was not too lucky in the work-detail lottery. Mine was destined to be one of the most notorious of all—the infamous Tayabas Project. Donald Knox, in his chapter entitled "Details," overlooked the gruesome Tayabas affair.[20] That is equivalent to discussing baseball without mentioning the New York Yankees.

I would soon be among three hundred O'Donnell survivors glad to get away from that stinking death trap. What lay ahead for our group, however, was a test of endurance and survival as deadly as O'Donnell's brand of hell. We would be leaving O'Donnell, but we would be entering a hostile jungle full of lush growth and human death.

8

From O'Donnell to Tayabas: Journey to a Green Hell

By the time the exodus of Bataan veterans to O'Donnell had ended, the Japanese were already sending out American POWs in small work details to various parts of the Philippines, mostly to perform short-term tasks. At first the details were confined largely to southern Luzon. The majority of the early work projects were the notorious details dispatched to the recent battlefields and former American military installations on Bataan for salvage work. Eventually, some two thousand American POWs spent time on work details during imprisonment at O'Donnell.[1] Most of the ex-POWs interviewed by Donald Knox concerning those details had worked on Bataan or elsewhere in southern Luzon.[2] Eventually, however, the Japanese dispatched POWs to the far corners of the Philippine archipelago—to Baguio, the Visayan Islands, and Mindanao.

In June 1942, following the fall of Corregidor, the Japanese authorities established a new central concentration camp for American POWs at Cabanatuan, the capital of Nueva Ecija Province about forty miles east of O'Donnell. They soon began the transfer of American POWs from O'Donnell to Cabanatuan. From that point on, Cabanatuan was the home base for the majority of American POWs, but for some inexplicable reason Bilibid Prison in Manila became the primary distribution point. POW groups being sent out of Cabanatuan first went through Bilibid before being dispatched to the work sites; returning, work details headed for Cabanatuan were frequently routed through Bilibid. What purpose the Japanese authorities had in using Bilibid in that way was never clear to me, but the procedure had a favorable effect on American POW morale because the prison became a collection and dissemination point for news among POWs all over the Philippines. Prisoners could exchange information about members of their respective companies and other comrades because of the crisscrossing of paths at Bilibid.

At O'Donnell the method of recruiting work details was informal and haphazard. A Japanese soldier would enter the American sector and tell a prisoner that he wanted a certain number of men. The POW would call out the information, and the volunteers would grab their scanty possessions and fall in line. That was the method of recruitment at O'Donnell in the early days and, indeed, was the way I was recruited.

At first, prisoners were reluctant to volunteer for work details because there was some sensitivity to the charge of collaboration. But after a hesitant start, there was no problem finding volunteers. Everyone with the energy was eager to get away from that hellish death trap. In 1980 Donald Knox interviewed an American, Fred Gifford, who was a second lieutenant in MacArthur's Philippine Army. Gifford told Knox that

when I run out and volunteered to go on a detail, because I was an officer, they called me a collaborator. I figured, well, forget that Philippine Army commission, dump it down the drain. I didn't want to be charged with collaboration, if I ever made it through. I just quit it right there in O'Donnell. I also didn't figure I was collaborating. I was going to help myself, because I was ready to take one of them sixteen places in the burial hole and I didn't want that.[3]

That was one of the first details, but Gifford did, in fact, volunteer, and "when some saw that I'd volunteered, they joined up, too."

I happened to be at the water line when I was recruited for a work detail and had just filled my bamboo joint. When the first call came, I picked up my makeshift canteen and hurriedly got in line. Soon the recruiting was over; the required three hundred bodies had been obtained. Since the recruitment took place at the water line, the available group was a cross section of the prison population, and officers as well as enlisted men were among the volunteers. We were not permitted to return to our barracks, but that was no problem because none of us wanted to. Most of us carried our possessions with us wherever we went and were ready and willing to go. We quickly loaded onto the trucks waiting for us just inside O'Donnell's main gate. Without further fanfare or farewell, three hundred Americans, a stinking conglomerate of enlisted men and officers, never looking back, gladly hit the trail on an unknown journey. The Japanese did not bother to inform us about the location of our project.

As the small convoy of trucks pulled out, I had a pleasant emotional experience for the first time since my arrival at O'Donnell. My spirits rose high enough to respond to the striking beauty presented by the blue, hazy outline of the Zambales Mountains to the west. It was mid-afternoon, and the steamy humidity, together with the thunderheads over the Zambales, was telling us that the rains would be coming soon.

At Capas, where I had escaped the grave of a sealed boxcar a few weeks earlier, we turned south onto the main road toward Manila. Before long we could see the craggy face of Mt. Arayat, an isolated mountain made all the more impressive by the surrounding level plain of central Luzon. The mountain brought a feeling of nostalgia, for it reminded me of Black Butte between Bend and Sisters, Oregon. As the convoy hummed down the Manila Road, we soon reached San Fernando, a city whose holding pen will always remain for me a dark and indelible memory. We had speculated that we were probably being sent back to Bataan for salvage work, but when we reached the crucial road junction, we did not turn to the southwest toward Bataan but continued to the southeast on the Manila Road. Once we passed over the Pampanga River on the Calumpit Bridge, the scene of the most important fighting during the withdrawal to Bataan, we knew we were headed for Manila.

My return to Manila, even under those circumstances, lifted my spirits. A surge of memories of good times with good friends in that fabulous oriental city gave me new life. Our truck convoy headed toward the heart of the city. As we approached the old walled city of Intramuros, we veered to the left at the Pasig River and came to a forbidding stone wall and ancient iron gate—Bilibid Prison. For generations before World War II, Bilibid had served as the central penitentiary for the Philippines. Some years before the war a new penitentiary was constructed outside Manila, and Bilibid was converted to headquarters for the Philippines postal system. During the two years I was an inmate in Bilibid, I often read Bureau of Post brochures out of sheer boredom and intellectual deprivation.

We found Bilibid occupied by U.S. Navy prisoners of war. On December 10, 1941, the Navy suffered heavy casualties during the Japanese bombing of the Cavite Naval Base. When General MacArthur withdrew all American military forces in Luzon to Bataan during late December 1941, most of the naval medical personnel were left behind at the Navy's Canacao Hospital at Cavite to take care of the large number of wounded. In taking over the Manila area, the Japanese moved the captured naval medical personnel to Bilibid.

Soon after our arrival at Bilibid, the Japanese informed us that we would be spending only a couple of days at the ancient prison before moving to the site of the work detail. We found that the Japanese interfered little with the internal administration and that the Navy's performance was excellent. The Navy's medical personnel and patients, most of whom had recovered, wore clean clothing, and the prison compound was spick-and-span. The POWs, though pale and underweight, appeared to be relatively healthy. Bilibid and O'Donnell were radically different environments, yet we could not help comparing the Navy's outstanding accomplishments at Bilibid with the Army's apparent failure at O'Donnell.

The brief respite at Bilibid gave us an opportunity to look over the personnel in our work detail. We had left O'Donnell in such haste and confusion that none of the three hundred knew who else was in the group, except for fellow passengers in each truck. I knew hardly anyone in my truck, but I was delighted to learn that some other members of my old Company, as well as friends from other companies in the Little Baguio Signal Detachment, were in the work detail. People from the 409th whom I remember seeing at Bilibid this time included Bryan Beard and Irwin McVay (California), Louis Bailey (Texas), Fred Bright (Arkansas), one of the Iby brothers (Oregon), Paul Inzer (Tennessee), Glenn Rial and Garland Smith (Mississippi), and Lloyd Ridings (Montana). Also, there were a few other people I knew including my good friend Glenn Tilley, a cook in our Signal Detachment at Little Baguio, Bataan. Before long, we gathered into small groups of company comrades and other friends. I formed a loose association with Tilley and Carl Batey, a member of the Little Baguio signal detachment.[4]

At Bilibid, conditions were far from ideal, but compared to O'Donnell they were downright comfortable. The accommodations were much appreciated, but we suddenly found ourselves pestered by mosquitoes. If there were mosquitoes at O'Donnell I did not notice. I had been far too occupied just staying alive to bother with the pesky insects. The Navy had mosquito nets, but they did not offer to share them. Bilibid had plenty of latrines and cold showers. Though the latrines were the straddle type, they were kept clean by running water. They also were located under roofs so that they could be used comfortably during a rain. The showers meant that for the first time since the fall of Bataan, we were able to take baths. Though we slept on a concrete floor and swatted mosquitoes, no Hilton Hotel ever provided a more luxurious life-style, relatively speaking, than we enjoyed those two nights in that old prison.

The Navy had established a commissary in Bilibid that offered food and clothing items for sale. The medium of exchange was American dollars or prewar Philippine pesos backed by American dollars. When I arrived at Bilibid, I possessed the princely sum of five pesos. Neither one of my two buddies, Tilley and Batey, had as much as one centavo. Tilley wanted to use my five pesos to purchase a new pair of khaki pants. His pants were in bad shape, but so were mine and Batey's and those of everyone else on the work detail. Our old uniforms by now were tattered ensigns of a dead army.

In a heated discussion during which Tilley and Batey favored the pants purchase, I argued that food was more important to us than clothing. I pointed out the extreme skimpiness of our first two meals at Bilibid and said that I was hungry. Abruptly terminating the debate, I rejected out of hand Tilley's request and declared that my five pesos would go for food. Tilley viewed my decision as inhumane and a violation of our Bataan-tested friendship. Batey agreed with Tilley. Leaving my two buddies to sulk, I went grocery shopping at the Navy commissary. The prices were high. After looking around for the best food bargain, I settled on some skinny camotes (Philippine sweet potatoes). For the five pesos I received about a half gallon of the tuberous tidbits.

Carrying my precious cargo, I returned to the yard outside where the members of our work detail were resting, bathing, shaving, cutting each other's hair, etc. There my buddies, still angry, were waiting for me. We went over to the Navy's quawn, a place where people could cook their own food or have the food cooked for them. The quawnmaster exacted a portion of the cooked food as payment.[5] I was in luck; I did not have to pay anything because the personnel operating the quawn had no appetite for stringy sweet potatoes. The Navy's cuisine at Bilibid was far more appetizing than we had been used to at O'Donnell. The Bilibid regulars permitted us to watch them eat, but they never invited us to dinner. Our own ration, which consisted entirely of roughly hulled rice, was microscopic. We could have caught more rice than our Bilibid ration at an average American wedding.

At the quawn, Tilley instinctively assumed responsibility for cooking our emaciated tubers. He certainly was one of the best Army cooks in the Philippines. His talent for concocting tasty meals from scarce supplies was legend among Bataan troops. With the cooking completed, Tilley divided the meal into three equal portions. We thoroughly enjoyed the camotes and even talked a little while we were eating. At meal's end, Tilley and Batey made it clear that they were still angry with me, but at least all of us knew one another and continued to stick together.

The two days we spent at Bilibid provided the first period of relaxation for most of us since the fall of Bataan. Though my two comrades were giving me the silent treatment, I, along with most of the other members of the work detail, milled around, swapping information and rumors about the fate of friends in other companies. The small talk was confined entirely to the subject of survival and food—no mention of sex or alcohol. Talk about home was dominated by stories about mom's or grandmother's big, delicious meals. All in all, there was optimism about the future. Anything had to be better than Camp O'Donnell.

On the afternoon following the second night at Bilibid, the Japanese loaded us on trucks, and we bade farewell to Bilibid. I had a feeling that the Navy was glad to see us go. The scummy invaders from O'Donnell had posed a distinct threat to the social order of the clean-cut lads of the Pacific Fleet.

Our departure from Bilibid Prison did not signal an immediate exit from the Manila area as we had assumed. Instead, our Japanese overlords merely moved us across town to a schoolhouse south of Libertad Street in Pasay. After a couple of miserable and almost foodless days in the Pasay schoolhouse, we shoved off southward down the Parañaque Road past Nichols Field and Barrio Baclaran into the boondocks of Cavite Province.

Soon after passing the Cavite junction, we entered coconut country—mile after mile of great coconut plantations along our route through Cavite and Laguna Provinces. Somehow they reminded me of the orange groves in central Florida where I lived as a child. We frequently passed huge mounds of coconut husks where the Filipinos had been harvesting copra, dried coconut kernels from which coconut oil is extracted.

Somewhere in northern Laguna the convoy stopped for *benjo* (Japanese word meaning to go to the toilet). Since we were only loosely guarded, some of us began a hurried search of the adjacent area for anything to eat. We invaded a Filipino residence, a palm-leaf-covered shack, and pleaded for food. The frightened Filipino couple declared they had nothing, and after a quick search I saw they were telling the truth. They apparently did not have a single scrap of food, and I cannot imagine how they survived. Just outside the house was the usual pile of coconut husks, but all the coconuts had been processed. No one was finding anything to eat. When the call came to board the trucks, we began running back empty-handed. Along the way I got lucky: near the road bank I stumbled on a big coconut. It was partially covered with debris and apparently had been overlooked by the copra harvesters. Fortunately, the Japanese guards did not see me, and I was able to board the truck with my precious booty.

My having a coconut on our truck brought an immediate change in the attitude and demeanor of my two buddies. As the convoy chugged down the road, Tilley and Batey began trying to restore diplomatic relations with me. Both of them not only offered suggestions about how to remove the husk; both volunteered to do it. I spurned their offers of help and attempts at reconciliation and doggedly continued the laborious task of removing the tough husk, using a mess kit handle. When I succeeded in removing the husk, the fat coconut sparked a glint of anticipation in their eyes.

I proceeded calmly to play with the coconut for a moment. Then I got out my canteen cup (I finally acquired a canteen at Bilibid) and set it in front of me before punching out an eye of the coconut. Every man in the truck, each as hungry as I was, watched my every move. Tension was mounting, and when I started to tap the milk, the situation became dangerous. Like Tilley and Batey, the others began frantically offering advice and help. I feared that if I showed any willingness to share, the mob would lunge for my entire coconut. I resolved to bluff it out by pretending the others did not exst. As for Batey and Tilley, I merely wished to bait them a little as punishment for their treatment of me. Using my mess kit handle, I poked and grunted until I succeeded in punching a hole in the coconut.

It was a dramatic moment when I poured a little milk from the coconut into my canteen cup, raised the cup to my lips, and savored the sweet liquid. Looking directly at Tilley and Batey so that I could enjoy their predicament, I pronounced the milk of the highest quality. After a moment's hesitation, I invited them to put out their cups. They complied in a flash. After a three-way division of the milk, we began eating the coconut meat. I had intended to save most of the meat for a future, private meal, but the pressure from the other passengers was too great. I eventually shared the remainder of the coconut meat with all of them, not out of compassion but out of fear.

Early in the afternoon our convoy brought us to an abandoned lime kiln near San Pablo in the south of Laguna Province. After dumping us with a couple of guards, the trucks pulled away and left us at the evil-looking place. The situation depressed us. We guessed that our work project was to break up rock for the kiln. A small contingent of Japanese military was encamped at the entrance, and we assumed they were probably army engineers who would be operating the kiln. They appeared not to notice the American POWs, and our only contact with them was indirect: we raided their garbage for food.

At the lime kiln my partnership with Tilley and Batey was either dissolved or disrupted; here my memory fails me. Anyway, I soon met an officer (New Mexico National Guard) who also had been having buddy trouble and was looking for a new partner. After commiserating with each other, we decided to become partners, agreeing to share and share alike. During the two nights at the kiln, the two of us had our own campfire.

The Philippine monsoon blew its wet breath on us for the first time that season while we were at the kiln. We had dry shelter in the old kiln building, but it was a spooky, dirty place to stay. Still, we continued to believe that the kiln was to be our work detail until we were moved out.

The lime kiln was located on the main line of the Manila-South Railroad, which linked Manila and the mainland of Luzon with Legaspi at the end of the Bicol Peninsula. On the morning of the second day, we were ordered out of the kiln area and told to stand by the railroad. Meanwhile, a group of Filipino civilians came by selling various food items. Since I had no money, I could not take advantage of that attractive mobile market, but my new partner purchased a whole chicken, fried in pieces and wrapped in banana leaves. Oh, what a delicious odor! As my mouth began to water in anticipation of sharing in the chicken feast, we heard the train coming. Shortly, we were all seated on flatcars, and the train pulled out to some place known only to God and the Japanese.

When I asked for a piece of chicken, I instantly sensed by the defensive expression on the officer's face that he was becoming a reluctant buddy. He slowly fished through his chicken container and finally gave me a neck or a wing. As soon as I had eaten my skinny portion, I asked for another piece. He then announced the dissolution of the partnership. I complained about his timing, but he ignored me and continued to gorge himself. The event depressed me, not because of a lost partner but because of the lost chicken.

The journey on the Manila-South Railroad was a short one. A few miles below San Pablo the railroad curved to the east, and soon we entered Tayabas (now Quezon) Province. Just past the village of Pagbilao the train stopped and we were put off. Our unloading point was on the western end of Tayabas Isthmus very near Tayabas Bay—the point where the Manila-South Railroad crossed Highway No. 1.

We were herded into a nearby area enclosed by a fence. We soon discovered that a large group of people had been camping there recently. The evidence was human excrement so thick we could hardly find a place to sit down. After a relatively short wait there, the Japanese guards started us walking eastward on Highway No. 1.

We walked for a long time. Our weak condition tended to inflate our estimates of the distance, but the consensus was that we walked about twenty-five miles. It was probably only about fifteen. We walked all the way across the Tayabas Isthmus from Tayabas Bay to Lopez Bay, although we did not see either body of water. The Japanese guards were relentless, but they were not as brutal as those on the Bataan Death March. Nevertheless, they forced us to walk at a relatively rapid pace, and we were not permitted to rest. The rugged terrain made walking difficult. The formidable eastern cordillera, with its steep inclines and slopes, formed the backbone of the narrow Tayabas Isthmus, and exhaustion seemed to wait near the top of every hill. Fortunately, we were somewhat inured to such hardships by now; not a single POW fell out on the march.

We finished the Tayabas march proper when we came to the end of the completed road, near the village of Atimonan. There we were given a

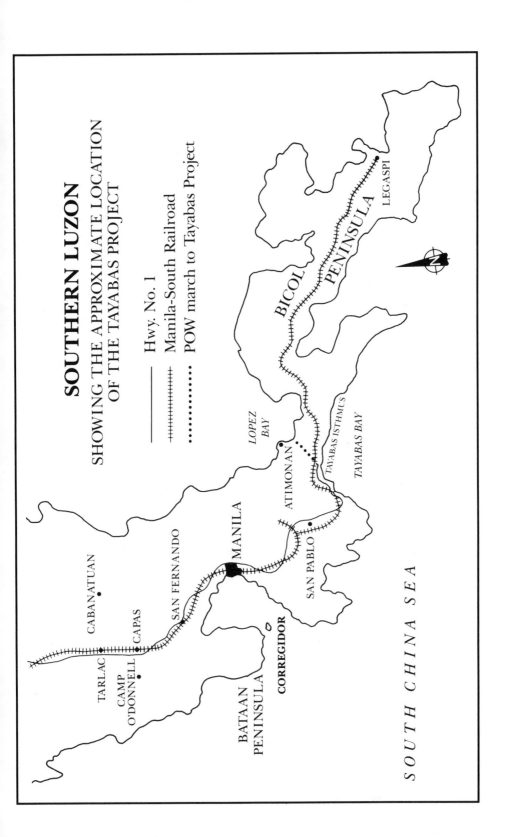

SOUTHERN LUZON

SHOWING THE APPROXIMATE LOCATION
OF THE TAYABAS PROJECT

——— Hwy. No. 1
+++++ Manila-South Railroad
·········· POW march to Tayabas Project

TARLAC

CAMP
O'DONNELL

CABANATUAN

CAPAS

SAN FERNANDO

BATAAN
PENINSULA

CORREGIDOR

MANILA

SAN PABLO

ATIMONAN

*LOPEZ
BAY*

TAYABAS ISTHMUS

TAYABAS BAY

BICOL

PENINSULA

LEGASPI

S O U T H   C H I N A   S E A

break at the camp of a small group of Japanese troops engaged in road construction. After a while the guards had us on the move again. In single file we passed by a supply dump where they issued us shovels and other road maintenance tools. They ordered us to move down the incomplete roadbed and fill potholes with loose gravel we scooped up along the road or found dumped in piles. Vehicles were already using that part of the road, but since it was the dry season, there was not a great deal for us to do.

After about three miles, we came to the end of the partially completed roadbed and to a larger encampment of Japanese troops. That camp included a large supply dump containing a wealth of U.S. Army canned food. We exchanged our tools for boxes of supplies that they forced us to carry down a jungle trail. The trail ended a mile or two further on to the east at a small river, the site of an even larger Japanese encampment. Japanese Army engineers were just beginning the construction of a bridge across the river. We deposited the supplies brought over the jungle trail at the Japanese camp on the west bank of the river. We were then sent across the river on a makeshift footbridge of planks. There, on a rocky sandbar in a bend of the river, we made our camp. Though the Philippine rainy season was just beginning, no provision was made for shelter. For the next two months we would live in the open, completely exposed to the Philippine monsoon.

Reaching our river-flanked campsite on the Tayabas Isthmus, we finally learned the identification and nature of our work project. We were to help complete the construction of Highway No. 1 across the Tayabas Isthmus in order to link the Bicol Peninsula (i.e., Legaspi and the tail of Luzon) with the Luzon mainland. The Japanese never finished the road. It was finally completed by the Philippine government after the war.[6]

On the Tayabas Project, the Japanese used our detail to work on a portion of the road about a mile east of the river, deep in the jungle. The American camp on the sandbar was located across the river and slightly downstream from the Japanese camp. The river ran through the general camp area, and water rights were established according to the following priorities, beginning upstream: (1) water for Japanese drinking and cooking; (2) a place for Japanese bathing; (3) a place for watering and bathing Japanese cavalry horses; (4) water for American drinking and cooking; (5) a place for American bathing.

The only shelter in the American camp was a thatched roof (about five feet by ten feet), which sat on four poles covering the kitchen. The kitchen equipment consisted of a few metal utensils, a wooden paddle for stirring the rice, a metal wheelbarrow, and an oil drum. The rice was cooked in the wheelbarrow and eggplants in the oil drum. Rice and eggplants constituted the staple diet, except for occasional American canned goods the Japanese would not eat.[7]

We kept our food supply covered in a small pen constructed from bamboo and banana leaves. Captain Pierce, the officer most respected by the POWs and the one trying valiantly to establish some measure of internal administration, found that someone was slipping into the food pen at night and stealing the canned goods. One night the Captain hid in the pen. About midnight a figure entered the facility and began picking up canned goods. Pierce lunged through the darkness, tackling the intruder. The culprit was another officer who had been staying in camp during the day, ostensibly to aid with administrative matters. As punishment, Captain Pierce sent the thieving officer out on the road detail.

Requiring the Americans to use a wheelbarrow as a cookstove could have been considered a demonstration of Japanese technological know-how, but the Japanese themselves did not use such advanced culinary equipment in their own kitchen. The mobility of our little kitchen on wheels was the one advantage we enjoyed over the Japanese.

Though there was enough rice and eggplant to go around, it was bland and unappetizing. American POWs who had money or valuables to trade could enrich their meals with foods from the local Filipinos. Because the Japanese were negligent in guarding the prisoners—in fact ignoring us when we were in camp—trade with native Filipinos, who came with goods to the edge of the jungle in the early morning and evening, was relatively easy. The chief barrier to POW-Filipino commerce at Tayabas was the Americans' lack of money or tradable goods. Fortunately, I would soon find a remedy for my personal poverty.

Meanwhile, in our camp the buddy system was in full bloom. In the evening each group of buddies had a campfire going, lighting up the sandbar like a county fair. There was plenty of wood for fires, and our Japanese hosts did not give a damn if we stayed up all night. In fact, it was obvious that in the Japanese camp across the river, which apparently had no officers, there was much rollicking around the saki bottle during the evening. The Japanese gave us some bags of green Brazilian coffee they did not want, so during the evenings on our side of the river the smell of roasting coffee filled the air.

When we settled into our new camp, Tilley, Batey, and I reestablished our partnership. But ours was not a happy campfire. None of us had anything to contribute to the central pot, although Tilley's skill in roasting coffee was unsurpassed. The newly revived partnership was already foundering when Tilley got a job in the kitchen. That did it. He joined the kitchen staff's campfire and was permitted to carry Batey with him. I already knew that members of the kitchen staff had sugar for their coffee and other goods acquired in trade with the Filipinos while the rest of us were out working. I was suddenly alone, but being lonely did not bother me as much as being hungry. Soon I would be glad that my partners had deserted me.

About the time our partnership dissolved, just a few days after we arrived, the Japanese placed me on a special work detail consisting of four or five Americans. We were to carry cases of U.S. Army type C rations from the supply dump at the other end of the jungle trail to the Japanese camp on the river. Though we had to carry a load only one way, the cases of food were heavy, and it was a tough job. We made four round trips each day. At the supply dump, many of the rations cases were open. Since the guards tended to ignore us, it was easy for me to slip the cans of rations into my pockets, which were partially concealed by my denim jumper. Around ten in the morning and two in the afternoon, the guard who accompanied us over the trail always permitted us a few minutes to cross the river to urinate in the POW latrine area. At those times I deposited my canned goods in a well-hidden cache among the rocks at my campfire. In addition, at lunchtime and at the end of the last trip in the afternoon, I carried my loot with me as I walked out of the Japanese camp.

The food-carrying detail lasted only a few days. By then the Japanese had scratched a road for trucks through the jungle. It was lucky for me that the detail came to an end when it did. If it had continued, I probably would have been caught and shot. In that brief time, I piled up considerable wealth—over a bushel of C rations. Other members of the detail stole the rations, too, but nothing on the scale of my thievery.

One evening soon after the detail ended, I wandered over to the kitchen staff's campfire where Tilley and his friends were eating supper. Batey was still with them. They greeted me with silence and cold contempt. I sat down at their fire, but no one would speak to me. I deliberately acted as if I thought I was welcome. Through their trading with the Filipinos using foods probably stolen from our common rations, they had quite a store of groceries. They, of course, did not invite me to eat with them. I thanked them anyway as if they had offered to share but politely refused on the grounds that I had my own supply of premium groceries. I then took from my pocket a can of dry C rations containing sugar, chocolate, coffee, and biscuits. The entire kitchen staff reacted as if they had been struck by lightning. They could not imagine how anyone in camp could come up with a can of C rations, much less dry rations.

I slowly removed the items from the can, savoring each one. As I consumed the rations, members of the kitchen staff campfire began to warm up to me, soon becoming downright friendly. Naturally, they asked me where I got the can of rations and whether I had others. I refused to answer directly but hinted that there were many more where that one came from. The kitchen group not only invited but urged me to become a permanent member of their campfire. Having had my little revenge against Tilley and Batey, I declined and withdrew to my own fire, which by now had grown cold. The truth is that my newly acquired wealth had brought out my own greed: I really did not want to share with partners.

For the next several days, I lived high on the hog. I did not consume many of my stolen C rations; rather, I traded with the Filipinos. Early most mornings I went to the edge of the jungle to meet the traders. The Filipinos had a keen appetite for the C's. I was able to trade for quantities of fried chicken, cooked pork, various rice dishes, eggs, and fruits (bananas, mangoes, papayas). I was doing so much trading with the Filipinos that a sergeant, who himself was trading, warned me that my activities were flagrant enough to attract the attention of the Japanese.

Of course when my C rations were all gone, I had the considerable problem of readjusting to poverty. My precious cache dwindled all the more rapidly after Batey, without invitation, rejoined my campfire. I suspected that Tilley also would have liked to renew his relationship with me but was too proud to do so without invitation. I was never close to Tilley again, but I shall always value the friendship we shared on Bataan.

I had another opportunity to supplement my larder during the project on Tayabas. One day about the time my supply of C rations had run out, I happened to be working on a special detail along the jungle trail that was being turned into a road. I was using a Philippine machete to clear brush. On the way back to camp that afternoon, I noticed a large banana tree alongside the partially completed roadbed that still contained a sizable bunch of bananas. I immediately attempted to climb the banana tree, but it was a difficult process, something like climbing a greased pole. Finally I was able to cut off the bunch of bananas with the machete. As soon as the bananas hit the ground, another POW picked them up, claiming half ownership on the grounds that he had saved them for me. When I rejected his claim, he seemed prepared to fight over possession of the bananas. Fortunately, he backed down, not knowing that if he had not I would have.

The bananas, which I had to share with Batey, served me well. I was beginning to suffer from malaria, and I could always eat bananas when I had fever. Within the camp area I also found tiny hot peppers growing wild that made my rice ration palatable when I had fever.

For the most part, American POWs on the Tayabas Project worked on the road about a mile east of our camp. There our task was to dig a roadbed through the top of a large hill and use the dirt for fill across the valley. For that task we were provided with three types of tools—picks, shovels, and wheelbarrows. We had only one main guard supervising the work; consequently, we learned to adapt to his personality. On the whole our relations with him were good. Though occasionally he would kick or slap goldbricks, he did not drive us particularly hard, a fact that saved many of us. Actually, he was lazy and seemed not to be particularly imbued with the spirit of the Co-Prosperity Sphere of Greater East Asia. He spent much of his time out of sight of the workers in a little shack in the woods at the top of the hill. There he talked with other Japanese personnel who drifted by, or he took short naps. We had some POWs who would not work while the guard was away but who would make the dirt fly when he returned. I had the feeling the guard was not fooled, and he granted them no special consideration.

During the noon hour, the workers gathered at the hilltop shack where the guard issued us lunch—generally rice and eggplant. After the guard had finished eating his lunch, he often engaged in some activity with POWs. Sometimes he would ask questions about life-styles in America. Occasionally, he boasted about the conquests of Japan. I remember his drawing on the ground a rough map of Malaya and Singapore. He pointed to Singapore and repeated several times, "Singapora! Boom! Boom!" At times he challenged and forced American POWs to wrestle. Most of the Americans were too weak for such strenuous activity, but one lad from the Kentucky mountains provided vigorous competition. For a while the guard seemed determined to hurt the Kentuckian, and we were afraid for him. But the guard soon lost interest and let the boy alone.

One day at lunch, I massaged the neck, shoulders, and back of a POW who was suffering from a severe headache. The guard decided that he, too, needed a massage. In the beginning I was afraid to touch him, and I pressed very gently. The guard complained threateningly, demanding that I get rough with him. I then physically hurt him, almost tearing his flesh from his bones. He moaned and groaned but loved it. For a while every day at lunch, I was required to give him a massage. Being the guard's private masseur brought me no special advantages on the work detail, but I thought it promoted better treatment for the group as a whole.

The Japanese guards' treatment of prisoners frequently seemed racially based. All of our work-detail guards, and especially our principal guard, took in stride the presence of POWs they considered Americans. They were neither especially brutal nor noticeably lenient so long as the prisoners were Caucasian in appearance. However, we had in our group a sizable number of Hispanics, some of whom had dark complexions. The Japanese were especially nasty toward them. They thought they were not Americans but Filipinos posing as Americans. The Japanese had great disdain for Filipinos. Though we had no blacks on the project, I noticed later at Bilibid that the Japanese showed special contempt for the few American blacks there.

On the journey to Tayabas and while the work detail was in process, the Japanese were amazingly lax in their guarding procedures. Escape was easy. Then again, if someone were to escape, he would immediately face the problems of where to go and how to live. We had one escape at Tayabas, and originally I was involved. In retrospect, I cannot understand how I rationalized my participation in that crazy scheme. Nevertheless, I joined six people, including my old friend Louis Bailey, with whom I had argued so vehemently over directions during the morning of the fall of Bataan. Others included Irwin McVay and Glenn Rial. As I recall, all of the planned-escape party were members of the 409th Signal except for a fellow named Rooney, who was a member of a signal company in our detachment on Bataan.

The escape party elected Louis Bailey as its leader, and a date was set. Meanwhile, I became engaged in a heated argument with Bailey, who was planning to lead the party northward to Lopez Bay, there find a boat, and begin island hopping until we reached Australia. I tried to explain to him that he was plotting a course in the wrong direction. His route would force us to navigate around the northern and northeastern side of the Bicol Peninsula, probably five hundred miles out of the way. I explained that we should go south across the rugged backbone of the Tayabas Isthmus to Tayabas Bay. There we would be in a better geographical position for island hopping through the Visayan Islands than after the long haul around the Bicol Peninsula.

Tired of arguing with me, Bailey, without informing me, rounded up the other would-be escapees and left early without me. Presumably all of them died. At least two, one of whom apparently was Irwin McVay, reportedly were caught and executed by the Japanese, the others dying of exposure. The escape created a dangerous situation for the remaining Americans in the camp. On some other work details, the Japanese followed a policy of executing innocent POWs when escapes occurred.[8] Apparently, the Japanese in charge of our detail did not notice the event, which was not surprising. They never required a head count and did not have a guard in our camp. Furthermore, since the number of working POWs was constantly declining because of deaths and the increasing number of acutely ill, any effort short of a well-organized, thorough, and frequently taken census would have produced little more than confusion. The group's escape, like their lives, went unnoticed by the Japanese.

The declining health of POW laborers was the principal reason the Tayabas Project became a horrible nightmare, although the causes of disease were different from those at O'Donnell. Our main camp area was cleaner than our O'Donnell facilities had been. Fortunately, we were better able to segregate the latrines and hospital from the main camp. Though our water for drinking and cooking was polluted to some extent, the flow of the river helped to ease that problem. As a result of those differences, dysentery was not nearly as bad at Tayabas as at O'Donnell.

What attacked all prisoners on the project, leaving them vulnerable to killing diseases, was exposure to the weather. We arrived at Tayabas at the beginning of the rainy season and were never able to take cover.[9] Some of our people, reacting suddenly to the exposure, died quickly of pneumonia, but larger numbers survived long enough to fall victim to malaria. We had no protection from mosquitoes. Those of us with malaria suffered a cycle of symptoms that, if unbroken, finally led to death from exhaustion. Generally, the repeating cycle included anemia, teeth-chattering chills, feverish sweating, severe aching, muscle cramps, and a concluding period of exhaustion. Most of those who died went through two stages: first came weakness from exposure, then any one or a combination of diseases, such as pneumonia or dysentery followed by malaria or blackwater fever. In the absence of medical care, those killers ravaged our numbers.

By the end of June 1942, the Tayabas work detail was virtually devastated by illness and death. The numbers of POWs in the hospital—located under the big trees at the edge of the jungle—and in the nearby cemetery were growing rapidly. By that time we were having burials almost daily. For some strange reason, I was appointed acting chaplain. I was not a member of any religious faith and was agnostic rather than pious. My favorite charity was myself. Furthermore, I had no idea how a funeral should be conducted. But I was chosen and did what I could.

I developed a set procedure for funerals. After we placed the deceased in his shallow grave, I read my favorite passage from the Bible, the Twenty-third Psalm. That scripture had a soothing effect on me and on those who attended the funerals. Though our souls may not have been restored, the words of the Psalm were appropriate for the occasion, for we surely had been walking "through the valley of the shadow of death."

The health problem was so bad that around July 1 the Japanese brought in two U.S. Army physicians who had been interned at Bilibid Prison in Manila. Without decent facilities or supplies, even they could not stem the tide of death; in fact, one of the doctors almost died.[10]

July 4, 1942, was a black day at Tayabas. The aura of death and sickness was everywhere. Nearly all of us were ill, including those still working. The event that made that day memorable for me was the bizarre behavior of an old sergeant who lost his mind, apparently because of fever. He packed his few belongings and started walking out of our camp toward the Japanese camp, declaring that he was going home. We were afraid the Japanese would shoot him, and it took a mighty effort of some of his friends to put him down.

About the middle of July 1942, the Japanese brought to an end the POW project at Tayabas, probably because few members of the detail were still able to work. By that time the road from the west to the river had been completed, and the Japanese had finished construction of a wooden bridge. Now the trucks were driven right into our camp, which was fortunate because some of our people had to be carried to the trucks.

On the morning we left Tayabas, our departure was delayed briefly while we waited for some of the severely ill POWs to die and be buried. We understood that one of the Army doctors, Capt. Paul Ashton, gave some of the most severely ill, comatose POWs overdose shots of a medication. At that time and for many years after, I assumed that Dr. Ashton decided on euthanasia because he thought the men would surely die if moved.

As I recall, some of the gravely ill, who were at best only semi-conscious, were put on the trucks anyway and carried back to Manila. For example, my future close friend Jack Garcia, whom I did not know by name at Tayabas, recently stated in a letter to me, "I don't remember too much about Tayabas. I know I was there, then I was in Bilibid, but I can't remember how I got back to Bilibid."[11] Garcia was unconscious, or very nearly so, when we arrived at Bilibid and remained in a coma for many weeks. No one expected him to live. At the time I, too, was severely ill with malaria, making the events of that last day hazy in my mind.

In his book, Dr. Ashton states that the reason for euthanasia was that the Japanese guard gave orders to abandon a group of seven men who were comatose and near death. Ashton, according to his own account, asked the guard for a few minutes' delay in our departure in order to administer the drug to the men and bury them. All were given lethal shots of morphine, and they died as their shallow graves were being dug. The doctor notes that he and two Army corpsmen who helped him felt emotional relief after administering the morphine; the unfortunate men at least would not be left alone, alive but unconscious, their bodies subject to the laws of the jungle.[12]

We were eager to get on the road because most of us were suffering from malaria or dysentery, or both. After what seemed an interminable wait, we boarded the trucks. This time the Japanese informed us of our destination—Bilibid Prison in Manila. As I recall, some of our people died on the way to Bilibid, and others succumbed soon afterward. The final death toll of the Tayabas Project was around 180 out of 300 Americans, or 60 percent.[13] In spite of the tragic fact that we were leaving many of our group molding in their shallow graves, we were glad to be leaving the green hell of Tayabas, relieved to be heading back to Bilibid, thankful to have survived the grueling work detail. Those of us who lived have carried scars from Tayabas in our bodies and in our minds ever since.

9

Bilibid: A Refuge from Death

The arrival of the Tayabas survivors at Bilibid in late July 1942 was a happy occasion for me, for I considered that old Spanish prison a haven in the storm. However, Dr. Charles Brown, one of the two Army physicians the Japanese brought to the disease-ridden Tayabas Project just before its abandonment, saw Bilibid in a different light. Brown, who was extremely ill when we arrived at Bilibid, admitted that "the walls [of Bilibid] somehow or other looked even inviting after weeks of torment in the jungle [Tayabas], where death had awaited us on all sides." But he added,

As I shuffled along in the rain, I felt that surely this would be the end. The jungle had been horrible enough, but at least it had been alive. Bilibid Prison was dead! The odor of death clung to it like the fungus on the walls, and the maddening fall of each raindrop in my face seemed to accentuate the prison stench. The sickening odor was seared into my nostrils, where it seemingly will remain forever.[1]

Our different views of Bilibid do not indicate essentially contrasting judgments. Rather, they demonstrate that even in Hell everything is relative. Compared to the Tayabas jungle, Bilibid was an improvement, and compared to Dr. Brown's physical condition mine was good—good enough, at least, for me to see Bilibid Prison as a refuge.

To the inmates of Bilibid, we must have been a gruesome sight. Even when our detail passed through on our way from O'Donnell to Tayabas, we were in grimy contrast to the conditions at Bilibid, but our return appearance horrified our Navy hosts. Comdr. Thomas Hayes, who kept a secret diary during his imprisonment, witnessed our arrival and reflected the impression we made on the prison population:

Late yesterday we were notified that more than a hundred "heavy sick" were to arrive from Tayabas. Eight truckloads showed up this afternoon. . . . Two men died moments before they left and one was dead when we unloaded the trucks.

Plate 5. Bilibid Prison, aerial view. *Photo courtesy of A. B. Feuer* 1. Front gate and administration area   2. Central guardhouse   3. Cellblocks   4. L-shaped buildings   5. Main hospital and north compound

Plate 6. Bilibid Prison, garden plots in front of the execution chamber. *Photo courtesy of Dr. Paul Ashton*

Two more prisoners lasted long enough to be laid out on stretchers, where they immediately expired. Another dozen men, nearly dead were placed on the ground until the Japanese released them to us. The others were horrible walking creatures, like living dead—dirty, bewhiskered, hollow chested—struggling to carry their few remaining belongings in small bundles.[2]

The principal reason I was glad to be back in Bilibid was the cleanliness and sanitation that the Navy medics maintained there. The longer I remained at Bilibid the more I appreciated the American Commandant (under the Japanese, of course). He was Capt. L. B. Sartin, Medical Corps, United States Navy. For the first three and a half months of my imprisonment, I had lived in an environment permeated by the stench of human excrement and by my own and my comrades' sickening body odors. Now, at least, I could feel clean again.

Bilibid Prison was completed by the Spanish colonial government in 1865 to serve as the central penitentiary for the Philippines. The prison occupied seventeen acres fronting on Calle Azcarraga near Rizal Avenue about a half-mile from the old walled city of Intramuros. The prison proper formed a square surrounded by a formidable stone wall twenty feet high with guard towers at regular intervals. In its exact center was a large circular guard tower. With a few exceptions, the cellblocks were identical and radiated from the guard tower like spokes from a wheel. The exceptions included four L-shaped cellblocks in the corners of the central compound and a specially shaped cellblock housing the execution chamber. The high walls prevented inmates from seeing outside the prison except from the top floors of the main hospital building, located on the north side of the compound between the cellblocks and the wall.

When I had come through Bilibid in early May, only the hospital building was being used for prisoners of war. When we returned to Bilibid from Tayabas, however, the Navy personnel had moved to a cellblock area and set up their hospital in the L-shaped building in the northwest corner of the central compound. They also maintained a sparsely supplied pharmacy and surgical facilities in part of a cellblock in the Navy personnel area. The main hospital building was being used largely to house transient American and a few Filipino POWs.

At Bilibid the Japanese military exercised absolute control though they delegated much authority to Captain Sartin. They largely left the internal administration, including most routine inspections, to the Navy Medical Corps. During my two years at Bilibid, the Japanese never subjected us to a numbers count-off, a security procedure rigorously applied later in Japan. When Japanese guards did come through, we had to be alert and quick with the proper responses of respect: failure to bow, for instance, could get us a fist in the face or an order to stand at attention for hours. Language problems often inadvertently led to serious friction. On one occasion, I was slapped by a Japanese guard apparently because he thought I was mocking him. He had asked a question in Japanese, ending with the verbal question mark, *ka*. My response was to repeat his question in an effort to test my understanding of his request, but I incorrectly included the word *ka*. I thought it was a polite form of ending a sentence. The incident was an excellent if unpleasant learning experience for me.

The Navy personnel certainly did a first-rate administrative job of running Bilibid. All areas of prison life from food distribution to pest control seemed well organized. Navy doctors, pharmacist's mates, corpsmen, as well as recovered Navy patients (who had been wounded in the bombing of Cavite Naval Base), were all assigned to various internal work details necessary for an efficient operation of the Navy's mission there. In short, the Navy ran a taut ship at Bilibid.

It appeared to me that Navy medics at Bilibid were scrupulously fair (as between officers and men and Army and Navy) in the use and distribution of scarce resources. I do not recall hearing a single Army man complain of Navy discrimination. The meager food rations were prepared in the central galley and distributed under close supervision to minimize stealing or unfairness on the part of Navy personnel. Nor was I ever aware of any black market traffic in drugs. Amazingly, the entire Navy medical staff (doctors, pharmacist's mates, and corpsmen) seemed as dedicated to Navy service as if they were on regular duty and not POWs.

No doubt the Navy's superior organization and administration of their imprisonment was in large measure due to the conditions they enjoyed at Bilibid, conditions infinitely better than those suffered by Army POWs from Bataan and Corregidor. For one thing, the prisoners at Bilibid had money, or access to money. The Japanese had permitted Navy personnel to retain a considerable amount of cash and to establish sources of income and goods outside the prison, permission never granted the Bataan and Corregidor veterans. As a result, Navy medical personnel could purchase food at the commissary, which, added to gifts from the outside, provided a diet that seemed almost luxurious to us Army POWs. This extra food was evident at the quawn operated by recovered Navy patients in their residential area. But the Navy medics refrained from flaunting their wealth before the poverty-stricken survivors of Bataan and Corregidor, a chest-puffing exercise they seemed to enjoy when I passed through Bilibid the previous May. Furthermore, some of us were destined to share that wealth in various ways.

When we arrived at Bilibid from Tayabas, the first act of the Navy's administration was to separate the officers from the enlisted men. I understood that they assigned the officers to the old execution chamber near the entrance to the north compound. The rest of us were led (or carried by stretcher) to a cellblock in the north compound just inside the gate. There they classified us according to how sick we were. Those deemed well enough to travel were put on hold and placed in the hospital building for transfer to Cabanatuan. The rest of us were moved into a cellblock in the north compound and placed under quarantine. We heard that the Japanese Commandant of the prison quarantined us because he feared that the sick Tayabas survivors posed a health threat to the Japanese military staff. We would remain in quarantine for seven months. How long or how many, if any, of the officers housed in the execution chamber were quarantined I never found out.

We entered quarantine in late July 1942 during the monsoon season. Masonry walls separated the cells from each other, but there were no outside walls, only bars. Wide eaves kept out most of the rain, but in the soggy atmosphere the cells tended to stay rather damp whether it was raining or not. In early October a typhoon hit Manila, reaching its greatest intensity on my birthday (October 5). We got soaked. By then, given the experiences we had survived as POWs, being partially exposed to the torrential blasts of a Pacific typhoon seemed little more than inconvenience. In the long run, the open design of the cells was a blessing. During the dry season the trade winds brought a soothing flow of air. We were also fortunate that mango and breadfruit trees shaded the area.

At first we were all crowded into one of the two cellblocks in the quarantine area, in some cases the critically ill and dying being placed in the same cells with those making a good recovery. After a short while, the other cellblock was opened, giving us more room and permitting the Navy corpsmen to segregate and separately care for the seriously ill. Sadly, additional space also became available with the deaths of many of those desperately sick men.

For the men in quarantine, there were two broad categories of problems: survival of diseases contracted in Tayabas and, for the more healthy, boredom. The first three months, many of the sick died. Among the dangerously ill at this time was Jack Garcia of Santa Maria, California, who would become my best friend during the war. I had seen Jack on the Tayabas detail and was aware that he was one of the dying brought back to Bilibid. But he and I were little more than nodding acquaintances when we arrived at the prison. For a while in the quarantine section, Jack hovered close to death, and even after many weeks of improving health he was a living skeleton. By the time of our release from quarantine, he seemed to be well again, having regained some weight as well as his handsome Hispanic features. But Jack has suffered much since the war; he has never fully recovered from his bout with death at Tayabas and Bilibid.

In the quarantine area, time went by at a dreadfully slow pace for those of us recovering from our ills. There were few contacts even with other Americans in Bilibid; I felt completely isolated from the rest of the world. A Navy corpsman was in charge of sick call each morning, and a Navy doctor made the rounds once or twice a day. We had the same doctor during the entire seven months, and he did a superb job despite the lack of medicines. His high professional standards and his obvious concern for our welfare were important morale factors for us. He was also gifted in individual counseling. He often helped us cope with the smaller problems that loom so large in unoccupied minds. I recall one occasion when I had become the unwilling host of a magnificent crop of crab lice. I could not sleep because I had slightly burned myself with a strong mercury ointment given me by the corpsman. The doctor explained the action of the ointment, assured me that the burn was not serious, and convinced me that the pain was temporary. After that session, I slept like a log and my pain disappeared. The ointment eliminated the crab lice, and I remained vermin-free during the rest of my days in the Philippines.

One incident that relieved the boredom was the arrival of an American POW who had renounced his American citizenship and tried to enlist in the Japanese Army. The Japanese, to whom allegiance to country was complete and without qualification, could not comprehend such an act. They considered the American traitor mentally incompetent and committed him to the quarantine area. There the rapscallion, who probably was mentally disturbed, loudly continued his obnoxious praise of the Japanese military. Because we considered him more comical than insulting, no one tried to hurt him; we just had great fun taunting him.

During those long days, the sounds of a piano greatly boosted my morale. About four o'clock on most afternoons, a Navy doctor came to play a piano that had been left in a room at the west end of the hospital building adjacent to the quarantine area. I was starved for music, and the doctor played the tunes I loved—beautiful big band and light classical numbers. His performances were therapy for me.

Jack and I discovered each other in the quarantine area after his recovery. We were both poorly educated peasants with a great deal of intellectual curiosity. When I obtained reading materials, I shared them with Jack and we discussed them. We enjoyed our discussions for the pure pleasure of the mental stimulation, but under those circumstances our comrades found our behavior more than a little peculiar. Several were convinced that we both had gone soft in the head.

The sanitation facilities in the quarantine area were good. We had the same type of latrine as elsewhere in Bilibid, an aboveground gravity flow system that was self-cleaning with running water. Also, we had an outdoor cold shower, and we could take baths anytime we wanted, except when the doctor was making his rounds. I was able to shave daily but with cold water. The first couple of months I was in quarantine, getting pieces of soap for shaving or bathing was difficult. I had lost all of my toilet articles at Mariveles at the beginning of the Death March. At O'Donnell I had been able to pick up a razor and some blades on the black market, but by the time I arrived at Bilibid from Tayabas my blades had become instruments of torture.

Until shipped to Japan, I remained in Bilibid where clean water was available for bathing and washing clothes and where sanitation facilities complemented fairly decent housing. Those necessities were not generally available to other prisoners of war in the Philippines. Our concerns for hygiene focused primarily on vermin. In addition to the problem of crab lice in the quarantine cells, the chief threats from insects in Bilibid came from bedbugs, cockroaches, and mosquitoes. We fought the bedbugs with paper torches, and except for a short time following my discharge from quarantine, I had mosquito nets. We just learned to live with the cockroaches, but the Navy's insistence on a high standard of cleanliness in the prison helped keep them down.

My social status was painfully low the first two or three months I was confined to the Tayabas survivors' quarantine section. One reason for this was that early on I violated security regulations and put everyone in danger of Japanese retribution. Since our quarantine cells were located in the northwest corner of the north compound, we were enclosed on two sides by the main wall of Bilibid—the great stone wall. Oddly enough, during my seven-month sojourn in quarantine no guard ever occupied the guard tower at the northwest corner, although there generally were guards in the other towers. In the west wall in our area was a circular hole around a pipe eight inches in diameter. Some of the men found it possible to communicate with Filipinos on the street through the pipe, and limited trade ensued. I decided to try my hand. Just as I had made contact with a prospective client, Captain Sartin walked into the quarantine section, catching me red-handed. Though the Commandant did not speak to me directly, he raised hell with the Navy corpsmen assigned to the area. Had the Japanese caught us at the hole in the wall, mass punishment probably would have been meted out throughout Bilibid. I was the goat of the peephole affair.

From the beginning of quarantine, the fever I had brought from Tayabas curbed my appetite. At first, there were relatively liberal rations of rice and soup since many of the patients were too sick to eat very much, producing a surplus for the well ones. But within a few weeks, almost everyone who survived shed his Tayabas fever and dysentery and developed a strong appetite. The Japanese supplied the prison with food on some basis other than demand. As survivors recovered and regained their appetites, food became more and more scarce, and hunger haunted the compound. The daily distribution of food soon became the dominant activity and was especially important to those of us who were extremely weak and undernourished because of the Tayabas illnesses.

The central galley sent food to our quarters where the Navy corpsman assigned the food to two permanent chow men, who distributed it cell by cell under the theoretical supervision of the corpsman. There was a general feeling that the two Army chow men were strafing the pot for some of the more solid food in the soupy stuff that generally accompanied our rice ration. In American POW camps, some food distributors became highly skilled in the art of strafing. Our two chow men adhered to the first principle of food distribution in American POW camps under the Japanese—they served themselves first just in case the ration had to be reduced or diluted to make the food go around.

To make matters worse, the physical weakness of the sicker patients stimulated the chow men's sadistic tendencies. Many POWs, especially those suffering from extreme malnutrition, made a practice of brownnosing the food distributors because they felt that odious practice necessary to get a fair portion of food. In addition to flattering the chow men, the brownnosers, in the presence of the chow men, frequently denounced the weak ones who had been unsuccessful in ingratiating themselves with the distributors. I was a member of that unfortunate group. For example, an old career sergeant made a point of denouncing me when we were in earshot of the chow men or the Navy corpsmen. He and some of those same detractors, however, were friendly toward me when the chow men were not around.

That type of social activity was the survival instinct at work. The ghost of Charles Darwin may well have approved such behavior, but it was no fun to be a social outcast even among POWs. Fortunately, the men who continued to be weak from illness had the special protection of the Navy corpsmen, who, with only one exception, ignored and were unaffected by the brownnosing.

About the end of the third month (October 1942), my fortunes began to rise. At that time my name luckily came to the attention of a Navy pharmacist's mate who had not had duties involving the Tayabas survivors. His name was Neal Gallaher, and he was from my hometown, Lawrenceburg, Tennessee. Neal was two years ahead of me in Lawrence County High School. He came to see me right away and made many follow-up visits while I was in quarantine. On some occasions he brought his friends to meet me.

My social standing in the quarantine area immediately improved. Just the visits by the pharmacist's mates were enough to turn the tide in my favor. My fellow patients as well as on-duty corpsmen were greatly impressed. By then Neal and his friends had initiated a flow of precious supplies to me—American and Philippine cigarettes, cigarillos, shredded tobacco, and foods such as Philippine sweets and native brown sugar. Even more important, they sent me a stream of reading materials—books and old magazines—from their personal collections.

By Christmas 1942, I was king of the quarantine compound. Everyone lionized me, treating me as if I had become the soul of truth and wisdom. Because of Neal Gallaher's great influence in Bilibid's Navy Medical Corps, the on-duty corpsmen treated me with noticeable deference. With the help of the corpsmen, I began to arrange and sponsor quiz programs (popular on radio in the States before the war) and other activities to entertain my comrades. I even put up some of my windfall wealth as prizes. About that time Jack Garcia became well enough to join in with his fellow patients, and he and I immediately became good friends and collaborators against the common enemy, boredom. By the end of my stay in quarantine, I was a much respected person who had developed a better opinion of himself.

The materials I received from Neal Gallaher and his friends made a substantial contribution to morale in the quarantine area. At the time Neal discovered me, life was becoming a battle with hunger, scarcity of tobacco, and boredom. The surplus food rations of the early days had vanished; by now everyone had recovered from fever and dysentery and was driven by hunger. Though I did not receive enough extra food from Neal and friends to share substantially with many of my comrades, I spread the tobacco products around and offered the books and magazines to anyone who enjoyed reading.

At Christmas we received a few warmly welcomed Red Cross items (food and cigarettes), but we later learned that the Japanese had expropriated most of the Red Cross packages. The Japanese Commandant's office actually had the gall to justify the theft by declaring that it would have been unfair to give Red Cross packages to American POWs and deny them to the more deserving Japanese soldiers. Rumors circulated among the POWs that the Japanese had filled a large warehouse in Manila with stolen materials and had seized whole shipments of Red

Cross packages. What I know for certain is that no more Red Cross items were distributed in Bilibid while I was there.

When we arrived at Bilibid from Tayabas, our clothing was not only rancid with bacteria but rotten and literally falling off our bodies. When we were quarantined, most of our old clothing was burned, and we were issued Navy hospital pajamas. From time to time, Navy corpsmen brought items of used clothing into our compound. Eventually, a few people had one or more extra garments, but for most the hospital pajamas were the uniform of the day. Those of us who were strong enough washed our clothes at the water faucets using occasional bits of soap provided by the corpsmen. When we were released from quarantine, no clothing was provided to replace our pajamas, which by that time were little more than thin rags.

Our shoes were worn out and rotten by the time we reached Bilibid. Most of us removed and saved what was left of them and wore home-made clogs during our stint in quarantine. We made the clogs ourselves. The Navy corpsmen brought us a hammer, a handsaw, and pieces of nail-filled lumber from an abandoned construction site just outside the quarantine compound—everything required to make a pair of clogs. Of course, we needed a piece of leather, cloth, or wire for straps. Even though I acquired a good pair of shoes later, I wore clogs exclusively while I was at Bilibid.

We Tayabas survivors were finally released from quarantine in February 1943. Once out, we were housed on the second floor of the main hospital building. That imposing edifice was no longer being used as a hospital; it served primarily as a holding depot for transient POW work details. We were issued mosquito nets but no beds or bedding. We slept on a concrete floor. We were inhumanly crowded, but our sleeping area was reasonably well ventilated—high ceilings and big open windows barred only with slanted wooden shutters to keep out the rain as well as sunshine. Though there were far too many of us for comfort, compared to O'Donnell and Tayabas our living quarters seemed magnificent. I knew, of course, that we were slated for transfer to Cabanatuan, which already had a reputation only slightly better than O'Donnell's. I hated the idea of having to leave Bilibid.

Soon after my release from quarantine, I went to see Neal Gallaher primarily to thank him for all he had done for me. He was incensed that we were not issued clothing. He managed to scrounge an outfit for me and a good pair of shoes. The next day Neal introduced me to another Navy man from Tennessee, a chief petty officer in charge of the wood-cutting detail that provided firewood for the central galley near the hospital building. The wood-cutting detail was composed entirely of recovered sailors and marines, including the Chief. The Chief greeted me warmly and immediately invited me to become a member of the detail. I was ecstatic. I was now a member of the Bilibid permanent party and would not have to take my chances at Cabanatuan or some other place in the boondocks. I quickly accepted the offer and asked the Chief if I could bring my friend Jack Garcia with me. He readily agreed. The Chief's generous act made me even happier. He told me that we could move into our new quarters at any time. I ran to get my few possessions and give the good news to Jack. We both knew that we were two lucky men and that Neal Gallaher had paved the way for our good fortune. Being named to the Bilibid permanent party was an honor accorded few Army men. My debt to Neal was enormous. It was not the kind of debt that is ever payable, but what joy it would have been to try. Neal Gallaher—as well as most of the doctors, corpsmen, and pharmacist's mates I came to know at Bilibid—was destined to die on one of the notorious Hell Ships sunk by an American submarine in late 1944.

As members of the permanent party, Jack and I were billeted in a dormitory room in the east wing of the administration building, a large two-story wooden structure that housed a number of administrative offices including that of the Japanese Commandant. In our new quarters I met another POW from Tennessee. He was pilfering gasoline from trucks parked just outside. He and others were drinking the gasoline because the Japanese were mixing sugar alcohol with it. Guards were constantly on duty in the area, which was also just outside the Japanese Commandant's office. They maintained a precisely timed march across the lot, permitting the Tennessean a few seconds on each round to dash out unseen and draw out a gallon of the fuel. Fortunately, he was never caught. I had to try some of the horrible stuff just once. It was much worse than the charcoal-treated Kreml hair tonic that was briefly a popular drink on Bataan.

The wood-cutting detail carried on its operations in the north compound close to the central galley. Most of the work involved using two-men crosscut saws to cut logs into short pieces, many of which then had to be split with ax and wedge. Much of the wood was just limbs of various sizes that we cut with an ax. The timber, which was fuel for the kitchen, consisted largely of varieties of Philippine mahogany. The scraps provided a side business for some members of the detail who worked the wood into various ornamental pieces and utensils. The most popular items produced by those ambitious entrepreneurs were mahogany pipes, just right for smoking Philippine shredded tobacco. To make a pipe, the artisan began by choosing the right size limb with a smaller branch running off at a suitable angle. The body of the limb became the bowl, the small branch the stem. The bowl was hollowed out with a hot wire as was the air tunnel in the stem. These artisan-industrialists used the fires of the central kitchen for heat. Some of the Bilibid-made pipes, as well as other mahogany pieces, were strikingly beautiful.

The members of the wood-cutting detail received an extra ration of food because of the hard work required. At the noon meal we went by the galley to obtain our extra ration, which we then carried back to our living quarters where we also received the regular Bilibid ration. The added ration was entirely a policy of the Navy's administration and had not been approved by the Japanese. We were frequently warned not to pass in front of the guard stations flaunting the additional food while returning to our quarters, but to go the back way where we were not likely to see any guards. Consequently, all members of the wood-cutting crew scrupulously avoided the central guardhouse when carrying the special portions. Several weeks after Jack and I began our new work, an unruly and loud-mouthed corpsman joined the crew. He was specifically warned to avoid the guardhouse. The headstrong corpsman laughed at the warning and deliberately strutted in front of groups of guards while carrying his second helping. After he had made a few trips, the guards stopped him to investigate. The result was no more extra food. The corpsman's popularity with the wood-cutting detail dropped sharply with that incident. Even so, I can remember him only with fondness; he died in the hold of a sunken Japanese Hell Ship in the fall of 1944.

Whenever I had to go from the north compound to the administration building or Navy personnel living areas on the south side, I generally took the longer circular route around the west side of the central compound. I took that route to avoid passing in front of the central guardhouse because I hated to have to bow to the Japanese guards. One day I was in a hurry and took the direct route. Unfortunately, I absent-mindedly failed to bow to the on-duty guard. He stopped me and ordered me to stand at attention in front of him as punishment for not bowing. I was frantic. I knew that I would probably have to stand all day, or possibly be put to death if I collapsed. My mind began to search for an idea to spring on the guard. Suddenly I realized that I had not reached the 90° point on the right angle in front of the guard when he stopped me. I asked for permission to explain. He agreed, so I got down on my knees and drew a right angle, explaining (and lying) that I had intended to bow at the 90° point. I swore that U.S. Army regulations required that. The guard began to laugh and finally told me to go. Fortunately for me, he had a sense of humor.

One Navy man on the wood-cutting detail I was not fond of was a POW from Chicago with the personality of a warthog. Because I was a

Southerner, he tried to bait me about race relations. On the one hand, he denounced all Southerners for allegedly mistreating blacks; on the other, he poked fun at me for allegedly having Negro blood. He derisively declared that all Southern whites had Negro blood. My response to him was that he could not have it both ways: if he really maintained the moral and ethical standards he claimed, then he could not consider my having Negro blood such a bad thing. Otherwise, he would be guilty of hypocrisy. He was too obtuse to get the point.

It would not be fair, however, to suggest that the Chicago sailor was alone or even unusual in the expression of racial slurs. In fact, I was not innocent of racial and ethnic prejudice, and not just because I was a son of the rural South. About that time I had a spat with Jack Garcia, the only incident that ever marred relations between us. As Jack and I lay on our bunks reading, I read about the Mexican government's expropriation in the 1930s of foreign-owned oil properties in Mexico. I turned to Jack and sneeringly condemned the action, expecting him to confirm my opinion. His response was cautiously defensive. I turned away and angrily cast an ethnic slur against the Mexican people: "Those damn Greasers." Jack instantly sat up, his face beet red, his fists clenched. My world was suddenly shattered. With a stupid remark, I had probably destroyed a friendship that had become precious to me. Without another word, we both lay back on our pillows and stared at the ceiling.

As I lay there, I remembered how painful I had found slurs against Southern white people when, after July 1939, I first traveled and lived outside the South. The more I thought, the more I felt emotionally and spiritually devastated. A few minutes later, however, Jack sat up and began talking and laughing about some other subject as if the unhappy incident had not occurred. I had never been happier despite my profound shame. Jack's words and manner brought an end to our impasse, and I knew I was forgiven. Somehow that incident strengthened our friendship.

Ironically, after the war I came strongly to support the 1930s expropriation of foreign oil properties in Mexico as well as the superbly humane way President Roosevelt and Ambassador Josephus Daniels subsequently handled the issue. I also came to admire President Lázaro Cárdenas, who had seized the oil properties.[3]

Jack and I were soon thoroughly occupied again with day-to-day survival. When I went through Bilibid in May 1942, the sailors operated a small quawn just outside the hospital building. When I returned to Bilibid from Tayabas, they were operating a much larger one near their living quarters in the southwest cellblock area. It was the only quawn permitted in Bilibid, and it served not only the Navy regulars but also the

many POWs passing through. We had no cooking facilities in the quarantine area and did not have access to the official quawn. Then again, we
had little use for one while in quarantine; in fact, it was several months
after my release from quarantine before I had any money or tradable
goods to spend on the cooking services of that private kitchen. After a
while, Jack and I occasionally purchased some mung beans or a few
camotes from the Navy commissary and had them cooked at the quawn.

The commissary, a private enterprise operated under the supervision
of the Navy administration, was also much larger when I returned to
Bilibid in July and had been moved to the sailors' living area adjacent to
the quawn. Some naval personnel, particularly the officers and petty
officers, were allowed to keep money when they became prisoners. Also,
many of them received money from relatives, friends, or business
sources. The income came either from Santo Tomás, a Catholic school in
Manila where American civilians were interned, or from Filipinos outside. Some wealthy American civilians were interned in Bilibid, businessmen who had been with the military when Bataan and Corregidor
fell and who had financial connections outside the prison. One such
person owned, or was a principal owner of, the Manila Bus System. They
were the regular customers of the commissary. How they got their money
into Bilibid and why the Japanese tolerated the operation of a commissary remain a mystery to me. Equally mysterious was how the operators
of the commissary purchased goods from the Manila markets on the
outside.

The Navy commissary from time to time had American cigarettes for
sale. A few of those delicate nicotine delights began circulating in Bilibid
following the limited issue of Red Cross materials at Christmastime 1942,
and a few people actually received packets from home that always contained cigarettes. By early 1944, when it was generally assumed that
there were no more American cigarettes in Bilibid, they began to appear
again. The reason was the "Great Kotex Caper." About that time, Captain Sartin made a special appeal to the Japanese Commandant for drugs
for the pharmacy. The Commandant's response was to dispatch a party
of Japanese troops to raid a Manila drugstore. According to a report
circulating in Bilibid, the troops completely emptied the drugstore of its
contents, all of which were brought to the Navy pharmacy. Though the
loot contained hardly any valuable drugs, there were large quantities of
Kotex and aspirin. Navy doctors used the Kotex for bandages, and
doctors and corpsmen issued liberal quantities of aspirin to hospital
patients and Bilibid personnel.

The aspirin, oddly enough, was the source of the new flood of
cigarettes. By this time venereal disease had become a serious threat to

the Japanese Army in Manila. Japanese soldiers and sailors, who faced much more stringent punishment for contracting VD than did their American counterparts, had heard about the American miracle drug sulfathiazole and had been able to acquire some of it. Japanese soldiers frequently traded American cigarettes, stolen from Red Cross and POW packages, for the drug. News of the demand for sulfathiazole and the large quantity of aspirin from the looted drugstore arrived about the same time. Since an unlimited supply of aspirin was now available, Bilibid entrepreneurs set about to meet the demand. The Japanese identified the drug by a telltale groove on the tablet. Bilibid craftsmen began converting the handles of Army mess kits into delicate aluminum chisels for cutting the required groove in the aspirin. The Japanese soldiers eagerly purchased the false sulfa pills, using stolen American cigarettes as currency. For a while the commissary had a fairly good supply of Lucky Strikes, Camels, and Chesterfields. By the time I left for Japan, however, Japanese "Joes" apparently were losing faith in the Bilibid brand of the miracle drug, and the trade had largely disappeared.

A few people in Bilibid received packages from home, but no one I knew received more than one. There were not enough such packages to have any significant effect on the supply of goods appearing in the Bilibid market and commissary. We believed that the Japanese stole most of our packages from home. After the war, we learned that relatives of American POWs, under the auspices of the International Red Cross, had regularly sent packages, but few were ever received. Obviously, the Japanese confiscated them along with the official Red Cross packages. I received one package that contained no food, only toilet articles and a Bible. I complained loudly about my parents' sending me a Bible and no food.

In the Navy's living area, I was pleasantly surprised to find a library containing a small but delightful collection of books. The librarian was a pharmacist's mate who was a good friend of Neal Gallaher. The books were from the library at Canacao (Cavite) Naval Hospital and from Santa Scholastica Convent, where the Cavite wounded had spent a brief period before coming to Bilibid.[4] Of the many books from those shelves that I devoured, the one I remember most clearly, perhaps because its subject was so far removed from our circumstances, was a historical novel about the English settlement of Australia entitled *The Timeless Land*, by Eleanor Dark.

After several weeks of living in the east wing of the administration building, Jack and I were moved to the little screened-in garden house in a corner of the north compound, near the central galley. The one-room building, sitting on a slab of concrete, was filled with double bunks so that it could house about twenty people permanently located at Bilibid but not members of the Bilibid permanent party. They were largely older or handicapped persons, some of them civilians who had been caught with the American military, including two Europeans.

Jack and I were transferred to the garden house to serve as food distributors there. We still had duties, although reduced, on the wood-cutting detail as well. As usual, the basic food ration consisted of lugao (a thin rice porridge) for breakfast and steamed rice and a soupy substance for lunch and supper. Our rice, which was cooked in the central galley in large cauldrons, was unpolished and contained a lot of chaff. That type of rice was eaten by poor Filipinos and, in fact, was the reason the Japanese issued it to us. The Japanese ate polished rice, but the joke was on them. We now know that the unpolished rice contained vital nutrients (such as vitamin B) that were removed by polishing in the rice mills.

The watery substance served twice a day might consist only of a vegetable soup made with camote vines or bits of celery or spinach. Often the Japanese gave us a wretched soup made from a vegetable resembling ragweed. We contemptuously referred to it as "weed soup." Occasionally the ration was fish soup made with fresh or semifresh catches from Manila Bay, where the Japanese fished with hand grenades. Japanese soldiers threw the grenades; Filipino forced labor scooped up the catch. When one of us found a fish head in his soup, it was a rare, highly valued prize because it was the biggest piece of fish he was likely to get. Sometimes the fare was camote soup containing small pieces of sweet potato if the food distributors had not strafed the pot. Strafing was always a threat when solid pieces of food—meat or vegetables—appeared in the soup.

When we began our jobs as chow men in the garden house, Jack and I resolved to run an honest, aboveboard operation. The Navy had been good to us, and we felt obligated to distribute the food honestly and fairly. We believed we did, and during our tenure of over a year as chow men, we had only one complaint. It came from a little Texan most of whose mouth was blown away by shrapnel during the Japanese conquest of Corregidor. He had barely survived, and at Bilibid he had become a pet of the Navy Medical Corps. By the time he was sent to the garden house, he had learned how to eat his food. His teeth on the extreme sides of his mouth had been saved, and our food seldom required serious chewing. Otherwise, he constantly had to wear a gauze mask to cover the hole in his face. The Navy, of course, did not have the facilities at Bilibid to deal properly with the problem; he would have to wait until the end of the war for further treatment. The Navy petting had given him a vile temper, and he frequently threw tantrums. He accused Jack and me of discriminating against him in distributing the food, and he physically assaulted me. I could not bring myself to hit him. Since he was smaller and weaker than I, I just grabbed his hands and held him until he cooled off. Jack and I were cleared of wrongdoing by the supervising corpsman and by the Navy doctor assigned to that area. They praised us for the way we handled the situation and were even apologetic that we had to put up with the little fellow's venomous disposition. As a matter of fact, I worked on relations with him until we became friends. Later, he would help Jack and me in our garden project.

A Navy doctor from Wisconsin was assigned to the garden house. We were all fond of him, and he treated us as if we were members of his own family. Though he had not known Jack and me before we moved to the garden house project, he grew close to us and depended on us to keep him informed about health or other problems among the inmates.

The two Europeans who lived in the garden house were unforgettable characters. One was a big Swede, an elderly but handsome giant from the Swedish Merchant Marine who was popular with everyone, kept especially clean, and never complained. He spent most of his days playing cards. The other was a Russian. He was thoroughly irascible, complained constantly, wore dirty clothes, and had objectionable sanitary habits. I constantly nagged at him in the mornings for coughing and spitting on the hydrant we all had to use. Both the Swede and the Russian just happened to be caught with the American troops when Corregidor fell.

The most unforgettable character of all was an old American merchant marine named Seymour. Seymour the Sailor had a mean temper, but at times he could be quite pleasant, particularly when he had an audience to listen to his tall tales. His body was covered with tattoos, allegedly inscribed by tattoo artists in various ports around the world. He never tired of bragging about some of those works of skin art, which were mildly pornographic. Seymour claimed to have a legal wife (and a daughter) somewhere in the States but also to have married a Moro woman while he was working for the U.S. Navy at Zamboanga in Mindanao. According to Seymour, she had borne him several children. He swore that he would return to his Moro wife in Mindanao rather than to his American wife after the war, though he expressed the hope that he would be able to see his daughter again before he died. He never saw either family again. When I returned to Manila from Japan in September 1945, I learned that Seymour had died about a month before Bilibid POWs were liberated by General Krueger's Sixth Army. Ever since the end of World War II, the word *Mindanao* has evoked in me a feeling of sadness for Seymour the Sailor, who never returned to his Moro wife and Moro-American children.

Another interesting person I met during that period was an ex-Navy man who had been working for many years as a civilian employee at the Olongapo (Subic Bay) Naval Base. He was from Tennessee and had attended Maryville College. Before World War I, he had joined the Navy and eventually was stationed in the Philippines, a country he grew to love. He married a Filipino woman and on retirement from the Navy bought a small ranch a short distance south of Olongapo and raised such exotic things as small deer, bananas, papayas, and mangoes. I had many conversations with him, and he often expressed anxiety about the fate of his wife and children and what the Japanese were doing to his ranch. He was a good example of many Americans I met who had fallen in love with the Philippines and had adopted those beautiful islands as home.

The ex-Navy man from Olongapo illustrated an important fact about Navy policy at Bilibid. Since he was "pure Navy" and was permanently located at Bilibid, he did not live in the garden house but, instead, in another building nearby in the north compound where permanently placed ex-Navy civilians were segregated from the Army riffraff. Though the Navy at Bilibid was scrupulously fair, it did not fail to recognize its social superiority over the Army.

Something that always bothered us at the garden house was its close proximity to the Bilibid cemetery, which lay along the great wall between us and the hospital building. Because of the water table, the dead were buried shallow, sometimes naked or wrapped only in a blanket. During the year or so I lived in that part of the prison, I do not recall seeing any funeral services. The corpses were just dumped unceremoniously into crude graves. But the corpses made us remember them. Always there was the awful smell of death. Human corpses, at least in the tropics, smell like no other. It was an odor of cloying, overripe sweetness. It stuck like syrup in the nostrils. I never got used to the sweet smell of death.

After Jack and I moved to the garden house, we continued our food distributing and other duties for some time. Then a big change in main jobs came when the Japanese ordered all lawns, parks, and other non-agricultural lands in Manila plowed up and planted in food crops. A chief petty officer named Crews, who was in charge of the central galley, was placed in charge of the crash agricultural program in Bilibid as well. Chief Crews was from Tennessee, and I cultivated his friendship. We found that I had gone to high school with some of his nieces and nephews. As soon as he was put in charge of the new project, the Chief dumped it on me, appointing me head gardener of Bilibid and naming Jack Garcia, at my request, assistant gardener. Jack and I felt we had it made. Surely that assignment would nail down our permanent status at Bilibid.

As the official Bilibid gardeners, Jack and I did not have to work particularly hard, most of the manual labor being performed by transient POWs drafted by the Navy administration. Using pick and shovel, the transients broke all the land we used, and they did most of the planting. When it came to harvest, however, Jack and I were selective about who labored in the fields.

We had good success in growing okra and a delicious Philippine variety of spinach. But our camote crop was largely a failure, producing primarily vines with few edible tubers. The vines were used by the central kitchen to make soup, camote-vine soup ranking next to ragweed soup in unpopularity with the men. A major reason for the failure of the camote crop was that Jack and I "strafed" the seed camotes, depositing the larger ones to our own account. We reasoned that the smaller camotes, some hardly more than roots, would produce more than enough slips to set out on the available land. Consequently, we put the inferior tubers in the seed bed, which, sure enough, produced more slips than we could use. However, they tended to produce inferior camotes also. Jack and I felt some guilt about the matter, but we confessed only to ourselves.

Theoretically, all produce from the Bilibid gardens was to be turned over to the central galley. The galley in turn would issue a part of the produce to the Bilibid hospital for patients suffering from acute nutritional problems and put the balance in regular rations. Jack and I often bypassed the system by removing some of the best produce before sending it to the galley. We personally delivered the hijacked high-grade foodstuffs to certain favored people, especially our favorite doctors, pharmacist's mates, and corpsmen. We justified that bit of skulduggery on the grounds that we were contributing to the good health of those whose services were essential to the welfare of everyone at Bilibid. Should our efforts reward us politically, so much the better. And we were rewarded: by accepting those gifts, our favorites caused Jack and me to feel that our positions at Bilibid were growing more secure and that the chances of being sent out on another detail or to Cabanatuan were increasingly remote.

Except for the seed camotes, Jack and I did not actually steal (i.e., appropriate for our own use or sale) any produce from the Bilibid garden project. We had our own garden. By taking in as our partner a Navy cook in the galley, we were able to acquire some land between the galley and the garden house as a private plot, our Navy partner getting one-third of the produce. Our specialty was hot pepper, but we grew a few other vegetables, especially Philippine spinach. Alongside the garden house, Jack and I planted a private patch of garlic, which did quite well. We sold and traded some of the produce from our private garden, we gave some of it to the others living in the garden house, but we gave most of it to members of the Navy administration we knew personally in hopes of further securing our permanent status at Bilibid.

Because of the mind-stifling boredom, nothing was more precious to us than some form of amusement or diversion. Other than reading materials from the library, entertainment was rare unless we invented it ourselves. The Japanese prohibited radios under the penalty of death. In spite of their prohibition against current Manila newspapers, some were smuggled in from time to time, but they were so full of Japanese propaganda we could hardly tell how the war was going. Worse still, we were not permitted to write. Writing of any kind by POWs, even in a diary, could lead to solitary confinement or execution.

Occasionally, our hosts showed a Japanese movie on an outdoor screen. At one showing, the movie was interrupted by shouting Japanese guards charging the audience with rifles, causing the POWs to bolt like a herd of wildebeest. We thought the guards intended to kill us all. As it turned out, an escape alarm near the front gate had been set off, apparently by accident. No one was hurt, but everyone on both sides was terrified.

I discovered, surprisingly, that the Japanese made some good movies. During the 1930s, cheap Japanese movies were competing with cheap Hollywood and European movies in the Far East. One of the Japanese films shown at Bilibid had an enormous impact. It was based on the Japanese Navy's preparation for the attack on Pearl Harbor. Most of the Bilibid audience assumed that the scenes of the bombing of Pearl Harbor were the product of studio imagination. At that time (ca. 1943), we still did not know or suspect that the Navy had sustained so much damage at Pearl. After the movie, veteran sailors in Bilibid who had served at Pearl Harbor began to spread the alarm: they believed that the scenes were actual footage shot by the Japanese in the attack on Pearl Harbor.

We also were permitted to create our own live entertainment. The theater was a large room in the west wing of the hospital building. The thespians were POWs. No full plays were performed, just variety skits. I was enthusiastic about Bilibid theater and helped write some of the sketches. Alas, my theatrical writing career came to an end one evening when an Army officer rose from the audience and stopped cold a Bataan sketch I had written poking a little fun at MacArthur and Wainwright. I was in disgrace in Bilibid's theatrical circles and was never invited to participate again.

Another entertainment venture of mine also ended in offense. At the garden house, I, assisted by Jack Garcia, initiated what was intended to be a series of discussions on a variety of subjects. I found that the first subject, socialism, attracted so much attention from the men that I never got to another. Exploiting the surprising interest in the subject, I drew up a plan for a socialistic society that surely would have had the approval of Marx and Lenin. The plan called for a complete redistribution of wealth and equality of income. Most of the garden house crowd liked the plan, at least as a topic of discussion, except for a few malcontents including one cynical Darwinist. Soon our nearest neighbors, the ex-Navy civilians, joined the discussion and the debate heated up. A Navy pharmacist's mate whom I knew and respected was sent to inform me that, in effect, my socialist plan was un-American and that I should cease and desist. That was the end of the discussions series.

One source of diversion never pursued at Bilibid was sex, not because the absence of women prevented it but because nobody wanted it. A long-term shortage of proteins is a powerful suppressant of sexual urges. In Bilibid I saw no evidence of either homosexuality or masturbation. In the midst of starvation sex seems silly.

A form of diversion everyone would have delighted in was news about the outside world, particularly about the war. In Bilibid we received most of our news from American civilians interned at Santo Tomás University in Manila. The news from that source was not reliable, however, and we remained pretty much in the dark regarding the battlefront and all other subjects that might have been of interest.

Most of the contact between Santo Tomás and Bilibid involved shipments of food and clothing from the civilians at the university. Those imported goods were not designated for general consumption but were sent to specific persons (mostly officers and petty officers in the Navy) by civilian dependents. Little or no help for Army enlisted men came from Santo Tomás.

I managed to remain in Bilibid for two years as a member of the permanent party. Had the Tayabas detail lasted a month longer, I think I would have died in the jungle. As news began to filter into Bilibid from the transient work parties, I realized that my survival probably depended on being able to remain at Bilibid. The work details reported not only terrible health problems but also brutality such as we had known on the Death March: violent beatings, grotesque physical and psychological torture, and the execution of POW hostages.

According to our information, Cabanatuan, the main POW camp in the Philippines, was a death trap. Though I learned that conditions there were better than those at O'Donnell and far better than on most of the work details, it was clear that dysentery was ravaging the population at Cabanatuan. My information and instinct told me to hang on to Bilibid as long as possible.

The fall of Saipan in June 1944 led the Japanese to speed up sending American POWs to the homeland. In early July, most of Bilibid's outside work detail was sent to Japan. Suddenly, Jack and I and other members of the Bilibid permanent party were selected to replace them. When we arrived at our new quarters, we were informed that we would be shipping out within a few days. Two weeks later the call came, and Jack and I were on our way to Japan.

10

Nissyo Maru:
The Hell Ship

During the two years I spent in Bilibid (July 1942 to July 1944), the days and months dragged by with little news from the outside world. In Bilibid, most news of the war came to American POWs in the form of rumors, some of which turned out to be true, some partially true, but most totally false. Since radios were forbidden and newspapers heavily censored if available, the Philippine press was of little use to us in locating major war fronts, much less in finding out how the war was going.

Though news came on a regular basis from our connections with Santo Tomás University, it was often neither current nor accurate. As late as June 1944, American POWs at Bilibid had little inkling of the development of the war, either in the Pacific or in Europe. We did not know about the Battles of the Coral Sea and Midway, we were completely ignorant of the decisive action on Guadalcanal, and we had no knowledge of General MacArthur's victorious campaign in New Guinea. Our most solid news before the Battle of Saipan consisted of vague reports of American naval victories in the Solomons, but we never got any specific facts about the campaign. The news of Saipan came like a bolt from the sky—a total surprise.

I distinctly remember the excitement I felt on hearing the rumor in late June that Americans had captured Saipan. All over Bilibid, Americans excitedly and jubilantly talked about the Saipan story. We all sensed a rising hope for survival. A report that Americans had captured over a million bags of rice on Saipan was of special interest to us in our starving condition, and we made jokes about what we could do with all that rice. We used the rice report as a basis for all sorts of comic bits, including a flow of grotesque rice recipes from our nutritionally starved imaginations, as a way of expressing and releasing our excitement.

With the Saipan story came rumors that the Japanese were planning to speed up the transfer of American POWs from the Philippines to

Japan, presumably as a result of the alleged defeat in the Marianas (Saipan, etc.). In fact, the rumors were true. Following the defeat at Saipan, the Japanese almost frantically rushed the process. Donald Knox suggests that as the Japanese hurried to transport their human cargo they also lowered the standard of treatment for American POWs on prison ships. According to that view, before the midsummer crisis the movement of American POWs to Japan "took place relatively without incident." Knox supposes that only in late 1944, as a consequence of the desperate Japanese attempt "to get the American prisoners to Japan before they could be liberated," did chaos develop:

Without a sufficient number of available freighters, the Japanese authorities tried to make do with what they had. Consequently, . . . too many prisoners were put on too few ships. The resulting treatment aboard, coupled with the prisoners' physical and mental condition, earned these freighters the name 'Hell Ships.'[1]

Knox's train of thought seems reasonable but must be incorrect. It seems clear to me that the treatment of American POWs on the Japanese ships did not get noticeably worse after the midsummer crisis because the standard was already so low it could hardly have sunk lower. For example, Col. E. B. Miller's *Bataan Uncensored* (1949) and John S. Coleman's *Bataan and Beyond* (1978) give accounts of their voyage from Manila to Japan in 1942 on the *Nagato Maru*. Both accounts indicate that treatment on the ships was about the same in 1942 as in 1944. Miller did not call the *Nagato Maru* a "Hell Ship" without reason.[2]

The fact is that there was a terrible consistency in Japanese treatment of prisoners of war. Even though the effects of that treatment varied with the surrounding conditions, the standard did not change. An obvious example stands out when the Tayabas Project is compared with Bilibid. The higher death rate in the jungle indicates only a difference in physical conditions, not in the standard of Japanese treatment of prisoners. Japanese atrocities on the Hell Ships cannot be explained as a part of some defensive strategy made necessary by their defeat in the Marianas or MacArthur's advance toward the Philippines. All of my experiences as a prisoner indicate that Japanese treatment of POWs issued from an attitude unaltered by time, place, or strategy. From the first day of the Death March until the moment of liberation, the brutality suffered by prisoners was rooted in the moral and ethical standards of the Japanese military.

When Jack and I were drafted into Bilibid's outside work detail in early July, we understood that we should prepare ourselves for a quick exit on short notice to slave labor camps in the fatherland. Under normal circumstances, being transferred to the outside working party was not the worst fate that could befall a POW in Bilibid. Far better to be a member of that group than to be shipped to one of the terrible work projects, or up country to that great hellhole Cabanatuan. In fact, for some time a measure of admiration for the outside work detail had been developing throughout Bilibid. Members of that crew had spread stories of their derring-do as thieves and smugglers, which fostered an image of semiheroic proportions—one documented by the considerable quantity of goods they were bringing into Bilibid despite the vigilance of Japanese guards.

But these were not normal times. I could not develop much enthusiasm for the project, even though it had fringe benefits, because I knew that we would probably be on the detail only a few days or weeks. Jack and I were no longer members of Bilibid's permanent party, and the shock was like that of a college professor or civil professional losing tenure, except that our stakes involved survival, not just a job. In fact, within two weeks we would be boarding a ship for Japan.

In spite of my concern for the future, my first day on the Bilibid outside work detail was extremely exciting. It was the first time I had been outside the walls in two years. Except for one brief glance from the top floor of the tallest building in Bilibid, I had not even seen the outside world for two years. During that time, my ability to remember what the real world looked like diminished so much that only by conscious effort could I imagine any scene beyond Bilibid's grim walls. The sights, sounds, and smells of Manila Port Area, especially the ships and great waters of Manila Bay, triggered a host of memories and sensations. As I looked across the bay and saw on the horizon the blue, smoky mountains of Bataan, I was filled with conflicting emotions. One moment I wanted to sing; the next I wanted to cry.

I made the most of my time on the outside work detail by taking advantage of the many opportunities for trading with the Filipinos and even some of the guards. Each day we were trucked to a central assignment area just south of the Pasig River about a mile from Bilibid. There the members of the detail were deposited in an outdoor holding pen from which small groups of POWs were dispatched to specific jobs as ordered by Japanese authorities.

The abundance of goods available for bartering or theft was in dramatic contrast to the shortages we would soon face in Japan. Filipino agriculture was still wonderfully productive; besides, many Filipinos had hoarded vast quantities of American canned goods. Little cash was available and no standard of exchange prevailed, a condition producing a haphazard and uncertain price system. But the system of buying and bartering with the Filipinos, and even some of the guards, provided additional and much-needed food. Many Filipinos with access to food gave freely to American prisoners, even at the risk of beatings by their Japanese masters. Also, the Japanese, who had captured an enormous quantity of goods from the American Army and Navy and from Filipinos, had a large surplus of canned foods they would not eat because of cultural bias. Prisoners became skilled at stealing and even more skilled at smuggling those goods into the prison in spite of the risk of serious punishment. Those caught smuggling were badly beaten. Provided they did not have to exert a great deal of energy in doing the detective work, the bored and depraved Japanese guards looked forward to turning an American POW into an ugly, bloody pulp.

While mingling with the local people during this assignment, I discovered that the Filipinos were in dire straits, living and working in conditions no better than slavery. Most of them were suffering from malnutrition that was becoming alarmingly apparent in the children. They informed us that the Japanese in the Philippines (like the Nazis in France) were confiscating the bulk of the country's food, leaving the ordinary Filipino family little to live on. Disease and infection were also taking their toll.

Many of the Filipino laborers I met were suffering from repulsive tropical sores that were going untreated, particularly foot sores since by then most of the workers were barefooted. I saw one poor Filipino, worked hard by the Japanese, who seemed to have leprosy. But never once during my stay on the Bilibid work detail did I hear Filipinos blame Uncle Sam for their troubles. They still appeared to view themselves as loyal American nationals.

When Jack Garcia and I were informed that the new members of the outside work detail would be included in the next draft for Japan, we were not surprised. There had been rumors for a year or more that most of us would likely end up in Japan. In anticipation of Japanese residence, some of us began to lay away items in a kind of hope chest. My homemade clogs, which I repaired or replaced from time to time, sufficed as footwear in Bilibid, so the shoes I had recently acquired and begun to wear on the work project were nearly new. I had come by an additional garment occasionally, and I was able to add two or three items to my wardrobe from the used clothing distributed by a Manila charitable organization. I could not, of course, store food items in my hope chest, but I was gradually accumulating packages of shredded Philippine tobacco. By the time I was tapped for Japan, I must have owned a half-dozen or more of those bags of delightful and surprisingly mild cigar tobacco, shredded for pipe or roll-your-own cigarettes. I also had a few toilet articles and other miscellaneous items in my hope chest, a large duffel bag given to me by a Navy friend in Bilibid.

When the call came for our departure to Japan, I was ready. Our trip from Bilibid to Manila Port Area was uneventful. We were loaded on trucks and within a few minutes deposited at the pierside, ready for embarkation. It was soon evident that the Bilibid outside work detail constituted only a fraction of the POWs to make the trip. In fact, approximately sixteen hundred prisoners were brought to the famous Pier Seven for boarding the same ship to Japan that afternoon.

Fortunately, we were spared the brutal ritual that accompanied the departure of some other groups of American POWs, before and after the day we sailed. Those groups were forced to march from the railway station (if they came from Cabanatuan) or from Bilibid to the Port Area in cruel parades witnessed by large numbers of Manila's citizens.[3] The purpose was to humiliate the Americans in order to intimidate the Filipinos. Apparently, that Japanese program of dehumanization backfired because many of the spectators lining the streets demonstrated in various subtle ways their pro-American sympathy and feeling of loyalty.[4] I do not know why our group was spared the brutality of the parade. Perhaps it was just another inscrutable Japanese mystery, or perhaps it was an unintended blessing of the inefficiency and oversight so much a part of all military organizations. The Japanese Army, like Japan's industry in those days, was a formidable force not because of organizational and operational precision but because of a ruthless tenacity in carrying out orders without regard for reason or creative alternatives. Those of us who left for Japan that day had no knowledge of the ritual parades and would not know about them until after the war.

We arrived at the Port Area in the steaming heat of July 17, 1944. At another time, the Japanese held a group of Japan-bound POWs overnight in the hot pier warehouse before allowing them to board their ship.[5] Members of my group, however, were put into the line for boarding as soon as we arrived. I was in the single-file line for about an hour. As the line crept toward the gangway, everyone was in a good mood. We had been anticipating the trip to Japan for weeks, and now that time had arrived. To a man, the expectation of better treatment ran high; hope predominated. John Coleman reports in *Bataan and Beyond* that when his group at Cabanatuan was slated to leave for Japan, the expectation of better treatment was so high that some POWs not scheduled for travel begged to trade places with someone on the list. Coleman states,

I thought surely we would get better treatment and more food if we were in the Japanese homeland. I did not believe that the Japanese people would sanction the kind of treatment we were being subjected to if they knew about it.[6]

In *Bataan Uncensored*, Colonel Miller, who also expected better treatment in Japan, tells of an old Japanese colonel at Cabanatuan who assured Miller's group that once they reached Japan they "would receive better treatment and lots of food."[7] Like Miller's Japanese colonel, various guards at Bilibid told us emphatically that we would receive better treatment in Japan. Almost invariably when a Bilibid guard learned that we were being transferred to Japan, his face brightened as he told us how wonderful Japan was, assuring us that we would like it. The reason for that reaction from people who otherwise were treating us with great inhumanity was that most Japanese soldiers suffered from a serious form of homesickness. The war was not going well, the seas were increasingly controlled by the Americans, and all in all, a Japanese soldier's future in the Philippines must have seemed bleak. Conversation with prisoners slated to go to Japan permitted a Japanese soldier a brief vicarious return to a homeland that, in all probability, he never expected to see again. Though the hope generated in POWs by the wistful memories of Japanese soldiers was false, it helped to maintain a life wish in those who survived the dark holds of the Hell Ships.

In a state of euphoria and weighed down with baggage, I walked up the gangway of the *Nissyo Maru*, a rusty, decrepit freighter that looked as if it had been retrieved from a maritime junkyard. As I reached and then walked across the main deck, I still had no inkling of the most brutal shock of my life. I followed the line of POWs to a stairway descending into a dark hold where hot, stagnant air enveloped me. At the bottom of the stairway Japanese guards were directing traffic. A plank had been lifted from the floor of the hold, and a guard was forcing everyone to drop into the hole all baggage, shoes, belts, and other paraphernalia. They permitted us to keep only our canteens, cups, and mess kits. As each man dropped his possessions, the guards drove him into the swelling mass of alarmed prisoners. As I was shoved further back into the black dungeon, I found myself in a writhing tangle of sweating humanity. By that time I had begun to panic because of the lack of air and mobility. A few seconds earlier I had resented the loss of my beloved hope chest, but suddenly all thought of it was displaced by a fight to live.

Soon the crowding required the guards to close the hole in the floor to provide additional space, and then they continued packing the hold with prisoners. Within a few minutes we were wedged against each other so tightly that our arms were pinned to our sides. Movement occurred only in mass waves, like jelly in slow motion. Colonel Miller described a similar situation when he boarded the *Nagato Maru* in November 1942:

The prisoners were herded down into the hold like a flock of stumbling sheep and were packed in as tightly as they could be jammed. Finally, the Japanese themselves had to admit that not even the Imperial Mind could possibly cram 600 human bodies into the space. However, between 550 and 560 were jammed in.[8]

Almost two years later, the Japanese were trying to squeeze approximately six hundred POWs into a small hold that could have housed comfortably only about fifty and in which one hundred would have violated all standards of human decency. The Japanese planned to put six hundred in the midship hold and the remaining POWs (nearly one thousand) in an aft hold. But before they could finish packing the first six hundred, the overloaded facility began regurgitating its contents. Precisely how that happened I cannot say because by that time I was incoherent.

When the open area near the stairway filled and my arms were pinned to my sides, I panicked. The stifling, foul air had become virtually unbreathable. I was suffocating. Suddenly, I was overcome by memories of the sealed boxcar I had barely endured in April 1942. All around me men were screaming—some praying, some cursing. I lost consciousness. A little later as I regained semiconsciousness, I was vaguely aware of being passed up the stairway and laid out on the deck. The deck had been extremely hot, but fortunately the Philippine monsoon season was under way. The daily afternoon shower came just in the nick of time. Under a cloud cover that masked the broiling Philippine sun, the cool raindrops and breezes from Manila Bay revived me.

Looking around, I could see that the deck was littered with POWs belched from the hold. A Japanese guard was walking among the scattered bodies, kicking each one to determine who was dead or alive. I thought he might be trying to rouse us for another go at the black hold. I was determined to stay out of that place if at all possible. It seemed to me that reentry would mean certain death, so I decided to play dead for the time being. When the guard came by me, he gave me a bruising kick in the ribs. My acting was superb, and he passed on to others. Meanwhile, I heard voices, and looking up, I saw Japanese personnel conferring. Soon the word was passed around that they would not force us back into the midship hold, and within minutes we were marching to alternate quarters. I could see that some of my comrades on the deck were still lying there, apparently unconscious or dead. I never knew what happened to them.

Those of us who had been ejected from the midship hold were

transferred to a larger one, where the other nine-hundred-plus POWs were quartered. That was an improvement, but conditions were far from rosy. Colonel Miller's accommodations on the *Nagato Maru* in 1942 were similar: "There was just barely room to sit down, with the knees drawn up tightly under the chin. The heat was almost unbearable. . . . It was almost unbelievable that such a thing could be happening in our age."[9] Colonel Miller's group apparently had more space than we did. There was room for most of us to sit in the fashion he described, but some two hundred had to stand at all times. Two chaplains attempted to develop a fair system of rotation, but they were notably unsuccessful. Only the removal of the dead in days to come had any permanent effect on overcrowding. The problem of rotation was finally solved by the natural course of events: the strong standees evicted the weak sitters; the weak standees seized the places of the sitters who went to *benjo* (the latrine); some standees bribed the sitters with water; and some standees collapsed on sitters, who then had the problem of removing the unconscious, draping bodies by whatever means possible. I do not recall seeing any deaths caused by the standee-sitter conflict, but there were some bloody fights.

The hold's internal administration tried to cope with the situation but could not. Administrative authority was vague and inconstant at best. The last of approximately two hundred POWs to enter the hold were required at first to stand in a designated corner. The general idea was that all standing would take place in that corner and that the men standing, when relieved, would take the places of those providing relief. The system failed, of course, because few volunteered relief or obeyed orders to stand. The tightly packed POWs became a slowly but constantly moving human swarm. Many of the men picked their way or climbed over bodies to get into lines for the hold's slop bucket or for the latrine on deck. Some were on the move to steal water, food, or other goods—but mostly water. All of that varied motion was so widespread that standing could not be limited to one spot. At times standing and motion in the hold were so general as to permit accommodation of all those who wanted to sit.

Enduring the heat in our hold was a trial by torture, especially while we were anchored in Manila Bay. Late in the afternoon of our boarding, the *Nissyo Maru* moved from the pier a short distance out into Manila Bay, where she dropped anchor. There she lay for five full days, trapping the heat from the Philippine sun. Though the long, narrow hatch above our hold—a side-to-side slice of the deck—had been removed, there was no circulation of air. The building heat would have been unbearable during the long wait had our minds not been fully absorbed by the constant and conscious effort to breathe. About midmorning on the sixth day, the *Nissyo Maru* began to move. Those permitted to go up to the deck latrine (which was located shipside close to the ladder) could see that the *Nissyo Maru* was but one of several ships congregating near the harbor. Then we knew why we had been sitting in Manila Bay: our ship had been waiting for the formation of a convoy.

As the convoy sailed out of Manila Bay, passing near Corregidor and in sight of Bataan, the sea breezes lowered the temperature in our hold, but it was still as hot as hell. A few daring souls discovered that some relief could be had by climbing down into the hold below us. Getting to the lower hold required lifting a small but heavy metal hatch under which a long ladder led to the bottom of the large, empty chamber. Though the lower hold was a forbidding place, the air in it was much better than in ours. It at least provided the illusion of escape from the cramped and desperate life above. Also, if a prisoner was lucky enough to have a cigarette, he might get a few drags of nicotine without risk of punishment by the Japanese. There were some problems, however. The feces, urine, blood, and vomit that covered the floor of the POW hold seeped through small cracks in the floor, which was the main hatch of the great bottom hold. Consequently, while we tried to find a little rest and relaxation below, we had to endure a constant rain of excrement. As repulsive as that sounds, it was no worse than sitting in the cesspool of the upper hold.

Another problem was getting in and out of the lower hold. Normally, men were sitting on the small hatch. If someone wanted to open the hatch to go down, he had to persuade them to move. On the return trip, those resting in the area had to be persuaded not only to move from the hatch but also to lift it up. That was not an easy process. The returning POW had to climb the long ladder, knock on the hatch, and wait until bodies moved and the hatch lifted. Eventually, access to the lower hold was cut off when we reached Formosa, where the cavernous compartment was filled with sugar.

As we sailed beyond Formosa into the waters of the East China Sea, the *Nissyo Maru* ran into several squalls. Though the pitching of the ship made many POWs seasick, the accompanying wind and rain helped to cool our hold. We had learned in the Philippines that soaking a dehydrated body with rain can partially quench thirst. Though the August heat was still with us, the climate of the East China Sea seemed slightly cooler than that of the South China Sea. But the problem of heat, with its attendant evils of suffocation and dehydration, was never solved until we disembarked at Moji, Japan.

Strangely enough, cigarette smoking was not even a minor contributor to air pollution in our hold on the *Nissyo Maru*. From the beginning, Japanese guards informed us that smoking in the holds was prohibited. But the edict was hardly enforced, never by the guards and only sporadically by the feeble internal administration. The two principal factors limiting smoking were the scarcity of tobacco and the effect of dehydration. The general confiscation of goods when we entered the holds stripped us of most of our tobacco, matches, and cigarette lighters. If one had a cigarette and wanted to smoke it, finding a light took time and patience. An even more important deterrent to smoking was the hold's suffocating heat and the resulting dehydration suffered by the men. During most of my imprisonment, I found that despite the most devastating food shortages, cigarettes were of greater value than food to large numbers of POWs. Many starved themselves to death by trading food for cigarettes. But cigarettes could not compete with thirst. Extreme dehydration discourages the nicotine habit. Most of the POWs in our hold did not want to smoke because of their unrelenting thirst, nor did they not want those around them to smoke. In short, the Japanese did not have to enforce their no-smoking ban; it was largely self-enforcing.

Food distribution was chaotic. Theoretically, we were fed once a day, the menu consisting of a scoop of steamed barley, euphemistically referred to as rice. The Japanese brought the barley to the hold in wooden tubs and lowered it by ropes. The food was received by those ostensibly appointed official chow men, although no one else seemed aware of the appointment. In the absence of any obvious authority inside or outside the hold, we concluded that the chow men had assumed their own authority.

The haphazardness of distribution was in part due to the great difficulty the chow men had maneuvering through the packed mass of humanity. It was impossible to distribute the food to a moving line, so the chow men somehow had to move through the hold. Eventually, they learned to travel an elliptical path around the center of the hold, relying on the men to help pass the food. The process was cumbersome and confusing because it often involved passing forward the empty mess kits of those on the outside edge. The kits often got mixed up, and fights ensued over ownership. Some who lost their mess kits and canteen cups had to resort to other makeshift containers, including their bare hands. At times the chow men were able to work through the crowd to get nearer the recipients, but the result of this hit-or-miss mess system was the failure to serve food to some POWs on each go-round, though most of those missed were too sick to protest.

Knox's record of Captain Lawton's experience on the *Oryoku Maru* in December 1944 indicates some similarities and differences:

The distribution in my hold was not easy and probably not equal. Some men got a lot, some none at all. The stronger fellers controlled the distribution. Nothing prevented the healthy from going back more than once, and no one aided the sick and weak in getting their share.[10]

In our case, there was no going back because there was no line. The chow men continued to distribute until they ran out of food, having earlier taken care of their own requirements. Every day on our ship some POWs tried to feed their sick buddies, though some of the sick had no friends to depend on.

Apparently, the most common ration on the Hell Ships was a steamed grain (like rice, millet, or barley, or a mixture of the three) and a thin soup. According to Manny Lawton, seaweed soup was served on the *Oryoku Maru*, but "most of the soup was spilled."[11] I do not recall any soup being served on the *Nissyo Maru*. We certainly would have welcomed soup because of its liquid content—and Japanese soups for POWS were almost exclusively liquid.

Strangely, there was more interest in food during the first meal (which occurred in the late afternoon of the boarding day) than during the subsequent days of the voyage. On that first afternoon the rains and cloudy skies had cooled the ship somewhat. Though our hold was hot and uncomfortable when the boarding was completed, it was not nearly as hot as it would be in the future. Thus, most people ate all of their ration of steamed barley that first day and wanted more. The next day under a cloudless sky, our hold became extremely hot, and we began to suffer the agony of dehydration. At chowdown in the afternoon, the steamed barley was dry in our mouths. What we wanted was more water. For the remainder of the voyage, most of the men who regularly ate all of their barley ration did not want more, many regularly did not eat all of their ration, and some of the ill hardly ate at all. After that first meal, there was plenty of barley for those who wanted it. On the whole, we ate so little during the succeeding two weeks of the voyage it seems a miracle that anyone survived, especially the sick. For the most part, life during those weeks would be like living continuously in a hot, filthy Turkish bath.

What we needed to cope with the environment of our hold on the *Nissyo Maru* was water—and lots of it. But the Japanese gave us precious little. The daily ration of half a canteen cup per person was distributed by the chow men. There was no assurance of fair distribution of even that meager ration. Because of personal connections and a clumsy system allowing spillage, some got more than others, and many times some, especially the ill, got none at all.

Despite the various forms of hands-on physical torture—including outright murder—that the Japanese inflicted on their captives during World War II, the greatest crime they committed was denying helpless prisoners of war adequate drinking water. Lack of water had caused enormous suffering on the Death March, at O'Donnell, and at other places in the Philippines. Denying prisoners water became the trademark of the Japanese. On the *Nissyo Maru*, the guards played a game on the deck above our hold. They brought out containers of water, some of which they drank to show that it was pure, washed their feet, and flung the rinsings into the hold. Then they laughed uproariously. How awful it is that one man's game can be another's exquisite torture.

Under normal conditions GIs talked mostly about women and sex. As I have pointed out earlier, sex had been driven from the prison camps in the Philippines by a starvation diet lacking in protein. Instead, food dominated polite and impolite conversation. On the *Nissyo Maru* thirst assumed the throne, surpassing hunger. From the second day to the last on the ship, all that the men talked about was water. Daily, dozens of cool-water anecdotes were spun, replacing food recipes. Those old country swimming holes became prominent. Many of the involuntary passengers on the *Nissyo Maru* even went so far as to renounce the idea of becoming a chef after the war in favor of operating a swimming pool. Sgt. Forrest Knox, reminiscing about the water problem on his particular Hell Ship, remembered

a kid from Arizona or New Mexico. . . . That sonovabitch irritated me to the point where I almost killed him. . . . He kept talking about water, about how he'd go up to the mountains where the water bubbled out of the ground in cold clear streams. . . . Endlessly he talked about this cold water.[12]

Captain Lawton reported that as the *Oryoku Maru* sailed out of Manila Bay, the heat in his hold was so great that the POWs "began to yell and beg for water." They loudly chanted, "Water! Water! Air! Water!" As punishment, the Japanese guard officer closed the hatch cover, but "the cry for water continued" until the officer threatened, "If you do not shut up, I will order the guards to shoot into the hold!"[13] Sergeant Knox recalled a POW, crazed by dehydration, who for hours tried to scratch through the ship's steel bulkhead to get to the water outside. And Pfc. Lee Davis remembered that he saw American POWs "scrape sweat off the steel sides of the ship and try to drink it."[14]

For lack of water, many of the men on the *Nissyo Maru* and other Hell Ships went mad. Frantic victims of dehydration fought each other over water, stole or attempted to steal each other's water, and pitifully begged for water. So far as I know, no one in my hold resorted to vampirism as has been reported by survivors of other Hell Ships. Captain Lawton relates a story about two men who used their canteens as weapons to kill a "bloodsucker" attempting to ravage another prisoner.[15] Pfc. Lee Davis told Donald Knox that "one person near me cut another person's throat and was holding his canteen so he could catch the blood."[16] Stories that desperate POWs on the *Nissyo Maru* were drinking urine circulated widely. I did not see this, and I vividly recall that I was determined not to see it. I was still suffering from the trauma caused by witnessing a Filipino POW in Bilibid urinate into his mess kit containing his rice ration, which he then consumed wolfishly. Captain Lawton also reports that some thirst-crazed creatures on the *Oryoku Maru* drank urine.[17] There is little a man will not do to quench thirst in its final stages.

As bad as the problem of thirst was aboard the *Nissyo Maru* my dreams are disturbed even more by the images of men living in each other's excremental filth. Many of the POWs being transferred to Japan had some form of dysentery, either active or dormant, when they boarded the Hell Ships. The filthy conditions in the holds led to the rapid infection of most of those who had been free of dysentery. In turn, the growing epidemic further compounded the sanitation problems.

In my hold, two latrines were available for the approximately one thousand men assigned to it. A large wooden tub (the "slop bucket") had been placed near the foot of the ladder as a urinal. When the tub was full, an appointed crew of POWs was supposed to draw the urinal tub up to the deck by ropes and pour the contents over the ship's side. A second latrine had been constructed on the deck near the top of the ladder, its rear side slightly protruding overboard. That facility was to be used for defecation. The actual use of those facilities, however, did not proceed as originally intended.

Fewer men took advantage of the deck latrine than one might have anticipated. Most of the hold passengers had some form of dysentery and opted to use the urinal tub instead. To reach the deck, those of us with the strength had to get in line at the foot of the ladder and wait our turn. The Japanese, always nervous about having prisoners on deck, permitted only a couple of people to use the latrine simultaneously, even though there was plenty of space for more. Consequently, use of the deck latrine was an ordeal.

I was one of the fortunate few on the *Nissyo Maru* who did not have dysentery. For some strange reason I had avoided a recurrence of that devouring disease since nearly dying at O'Donnell in April 1942. All of us without dysentery used the topside latrine, but not often. Not only did the difficult passage discourage us, but most of us were constipated. After all, we were eating just enough to sustain life, and the small ration of water we received was largely lost to perspiration. On the *Nissyo Maru*, bowel movements were either very loose or very hard.

As I recall, during the seventeen days of the voyage I used the deck latrine three times. In that facility, excrement was caught in a box below the hole where the user sat; as the box filled, the feces oozed out through a large opening into the sea. On one of my trips to the deck latrine, I accidentally dropped my precious canteen (with cup) into that pit of septic slime. Luckily the canteen did not topple into the sea but instead partially sank into the collection box. I pulled it out and lovingly wiped it off with my hands as best I could.

As it turned out, large numbers of sick POWs, most of whom were suffering from acute dysentery, were too weak to wait in line and then climb up the ladder to the deck latrine. And when the demon dysentery made the guts growl, there was no time for waiting and climbing before the feces and blood began to flow. Dysentery, like time and tide, waits for no man. Those wretched victims of rotting bowels were forced to use the urinal tub when possible. Frequently, they could not get to the tub in time because they were too weak to work their way through the crowd. Sergeant Knox's description of the situation on his Hell Ship is depressingly similar:

The honey bucket was in one corner, so guys with dysentery real bad would get up and run for it. Some wouldn't make it all the way and they'd begin to squirt as they ran. Fellers lying down would wipe the shit off themselves and roll over. You got used to being shit on.[18]

Colonel Miller also records a comparable scene on the *Nagato Maru* in 1942:

To reach the latrine, you had to actually walk on other men's bodies. You simply stepped on a human form as you picked your way. We procured two tubs which were placed at the bottom of the steps in our hold. These were for the worst dysentery cases.[19]

Many victims of dysentery gave up trying to go anywhere or became too weak to move, having their bowel movements in their pants where they lay.

One of the most pitiable of the dysentery-ridden groups consisted of those who decided to camp by the urinal tub because of the increasing frequency of bowel movements. Those poor devils, when not trying to use the tub, lay on their sides in the filth with knees and head drawn together in fetal position, their pants either down or missing altogether. Eventually, the time would come when most of them would not try again to reach the tub. For them the war was over. The dead would lie there for two or three days, some so close to the tub they became thoroughly coated with urine and feces, until the Japanese would permit a burial. The same ritual taking place around the urinal tub was also occurring at other places around the hold.

During most of the voyage, one to two inches of semi-fluid excrement coated the floor of the hold, producing the most nightmarish aspect of our tortured existence on the *Nissyo Maru* The foul liquid consisted primarily of feces and urine mixed with vomit and rainwater. It looked like a thick beige soup. The feces itself contributed to the soupy condition because practically all of it had been produced by POWs infected with dysentery whose stools were watery and frequently bloody. The blood gave the flux more color. Because some of the sewage leaked through to the hold below, the depth of the filth was limited. Our hold was fairly well drained at Takao, Formosa, when the Japanese removed a large part of the center of the floor that served as the loading hatch for the hold below. However, as soon as they loaded the sugar and replaced the hatch, our hold began accumulating the foul and disease-laden waste again. In fact, beyond Formosa the pollution got worse. Sea squalls brought more rainwater and more seasickness, which produced more vomit. Also, the rougher seas beyond Formosa caused the feces and urine in the great slop bucket to slosh out onto the floor.

The slop bucket dominated the hold like some evil monster. The prisoners were supposed to empty the bucket regularly, but generally it was full to the brim and running over long before removal. The disposal procedure only made matters worse. The men were weak and clumsy, nearly always spilling half the contents in the process. Furthermore, there was no disposal at night, constant use meant the bucket was soon running over, and invariably that scene greeted us in the morning. On some days, delirious and deranged from heat and dehydration, I had hallucinations about that tub of soupy excrement—the awful thing seemed to grow until it appeared to be as big as a backyard swimming pool. That great wooden slop bucket has haunted my nights for the last forty years. I still see the emaciated bodies of what once had been men lying dead and dying around that grotesque slop bucket while the sloshing contents wash over them.

The pollution on the floor of our hold on the *Nissyo Maru* infected every detail of our lives. I vividly recall, for instance, the effect on my clothes. For most of our days on the ship, our clothing was soaked with putrid, foul sewage. In my dreams I can still feel my soaked socks, the one pair permitted us after the guards relieved us of our shoes. Just the idea of those filthy, squishy socks makes me shiver in revulsion.

Apparently, Mother Nature provides some protection for people undergoing traumatic experiences like ours. For example, from the time I first entered the *Nissyo Maru*'s hold, I did not smell the terrible odor that obviously was rising from it. Near the end of the voyage, the Japanese permitted small groups on deck for a few minutes to get air. On the only occasion I had that opportunity, I smelled normal things like the sea and cooking odors from the ship's galley, but I did not smell the odors from the hold. When I returned, my nose continued to ignore the stench. The guards, however, could not stand the smell. To deal with the problem, they addressed the symptom: they put on masks.

On Colonel Miller's voyage on the *Nagato Maru* in 1942, American POWs were permitted to set up a sick bay on the main deck. He writes,

No medicine was aboard the ship. We were allowed to set up a so-called sick bay on the open deck, in the midst of coiled ropes and other paraphernalia. In reality there was nothing we could do. . . . A number of deaths occurred.[20]

On the *Nissyo Maru* there was no sick bay on deck—or anywhere. Prisoners became ill and often died in the holds, where they sat with faces propped on folded knees. They died alone, without medical attention, without even enough space to lie down. Those filthy creatures, often infested with vermin and maggots, had become nonentities. They not only suffered the horror of death by torture; they were deprived of their humanity as well.

One aspect of death seems to have been common to most of the Hell Ships: there had to be an accumulation of dead bodies before burials were permitted.[21] Only after several POWs were pronounced dead would the guards allow the bodies to be removed. The Japanese did not generally permit prisoners to attend the funerals. Only those involved with handling the bodies or helping the chaplains could participate. Because I was in one of the small groups permitted on deck near the end of the voyage, I was able to observe a funeral. On burial days, the bodies were hauled from the hold to the main deck by rope. They were then placed on wooden litters that were carried to a side of the deck near the rail. Dirty white shrouds were placed over the bodies, converting the litters into biers, and the chaplains were then permitted to conduct a brief common funeral. Following the grim rites, the work crew placed the foot end of each litter on the ship's rail and raised the head end until the body slipped out from under the shroud and tumbled into the China Sea. Coleman saw the Japanese putting weights on the dead so that they would sink quickly, thus leaving no sign of the convoy for the U.S. Navy.[22] I do not recall such weights being used in the burial of the *Nissyo Maru's* dead.

Leadership in the holds during our hellish ordeal was practically nonexistent. Perhaps on earlier voyages, as in the case of Colonel Miller's group in 1942, officers effectively took charge, but on the later ones leadership appears to have been little if any better than that on the *Nissyo Maru.* The most effective leaders in my hold were the two chaplains, one Catholic and one Protestant. I do not remember the name of the Protestant chaplain because he and I were assigned to different camps in Japan. I vaguely recall that he had served at Nichols Field before the war. I had not seen the Catholic chaplain before we boarded the *Nissyo Maru,* but I came to know him well because he and I were sent to the same Japanese camp. He was Father Stanley Reilly from San Francisco. The two chaplains worked tirelessly to bring some small measure of comfort and hope to the sick and dying; they appealed for fair distribution of water; and they promoted systems of seating rotation so that the standees could be relieved. I tended to take the work of the chaplains for granted until the incident of the American submarine attack.

The month of July 1944 was the beginning of the great U.S. naval submarine campaign in the China Seas. The American conquest of the Marianas beginning with Saipan had made those waters more accessible to the Navy's rapidly growing submarine fleet. Between September and December, thousands of American POWs on Japanese Hell Ships, badly weakened because of Japanese brutality, died in ships sunk by American torpedoes and bombs. Fortunately for me, the Navy's stepped-up campaign was just beginning in July and August. Consequently, our convoy had only one major incident during the voyage, but the Japanese remained on the alert for submarine attack by constantly scanning the seas with binoculars.

When our convoy made up outside Manila Bay, the *Nissyo Maru* assumed a position just to the starboard and almost in the shadow of a large tanker. We maintained that position even when we zigzagged. We concluded that the *Nissyo Maru* was deliberately being used as a shield for the tanker. One night soon after we had emerged from the Formosa Strait into the East China Sea, an American submarine put a torpedo into the tanker's side. Given our position in the convoy, it is clear that the torpedo had swished by our ship by the narrowest of margins. At the time, we thought we had been hit. Apparently, the pilots of one or both of the ships had panicked, nearly colliding with each other. The burning tanker came so close to the *Nissyo Maru* that for a moment flames appeared to be coming from our stern. Smoke was pouring across our deck, some of it coming into our hold. Word spread that our ship was on fire.

When the smoke and flames from the tanker swept across the deck of the *Nissyo Maru*, hysteria broke out in our tightly packed hold. When some of the men began struggling toward the ladder, the guards set up machine guns on both sides of the hold's hatch opening and prepared to start shooting. At that time I was sitting beside a fellow from Texas whom I had known either at Nichols Field or on Bataan. Tex, a large and muscular man, suggested that we attempt to work our way to the center of the hold, where there would be greater safety. He assumed that each Japanese machine gunner would shoot to the side of the hold opposite him. Tex and I began moving toward our destination. We discovered that the best way to move was under the packed standing bodies of the men because the floor, covered by a couple of inches of soupy excrement, was quite slick. It took all of Tex's strength to slither under the bodies and pull me along with him until we reached the center of the floor. I will never know what mysterious force saved us from suffocation.

When it appeared that the Japanese would start shooting into the hold, Father Reilly, his hands slick with sewage, climbed a steel pole near the forward end of the hold and attempted to calm the panic-stricken multitude. That he was able to hold himself up on the pole was, if not a miracle, at least remarkable. Occasionally, he would slide down for a brief rest, but soon he was back clinging to his post. Though the Japanese machine guns and threats to use them played the major role in calming the wild crowd, Father Reilly's voice made an important contribution. He continued to try to soothe the frightened men until he was completely exhausted. Over and over he repeated the "Hail Mary"—at first loudly and then more and more quietly. Even though I long had been a hardened agnostic from a Protestant background, I profoundly appreciated Father Reilly's renditions of the prayer:

> Hail Mary, full of grace,
> The Lord is with thee;
> Blessed art thou among women,
> And blessed is the fruit of thy womb, Jesus.
> Holy Mary, Mother of God,
> Pray for us sinners,
> Now and at the hour of our death, Amen.

Sometime in August, after seventeen days and nights of pure hell, the *Nissyo Maru* arrived at her destination—Moji (now Kitakyushu), Japan. With flying colors, she had qualified as one of the notorious Japanese Hell Ships. Our disembarkation from that evil vessel was the happiest moment of my life. As we stepped onto the pier, a Japanese soldier halfheartedly sprayed us for vermin. Two years before, Colonel Miller had gone through the same process when disembarking at Moji:

As we stepped off the boat, two Japanese, with tanks and spray guns, disinfected our exteriors. Whether they believed this would kill the germs inside of our clothing and on our bodies, was another sixty-four dollar question. That's the way the Nip does things.[23]

When we arrived at Moji, we hoped we would be able to retrieve our possessions confiscated by the Japanese as we entered the holds of the *Nissyo Maru* in Manila, but they returned nothing except shoes. The shoes were piled on the pier, and we were permitted to hunt for a pair that fit. My hope chest had gone with the kamikaze (divine wind).

Manny Lawton asserts that the Hell Ships were "by far" the "worst experience" he suffered as a POW under the Japanese, including the Death March.[24] And so it was for me. Earlier episodes of brutal treatment actually produced higher tolls of death and despair than the Hell Ships. The larger numbers, however, do not mean that those events were somehow more dreadful than the experience of the prison ships. The long-term trauma produced by the Death March and the sealed boxcars perhaps was greater than that produced by the Hell Ships, but at the time of the Death March I was not an experienced, hardened product of Japanese torture. Excluding those killed by American planes and submarines, the death toll in the Hell Ships was not as high as that of the Death March. But the POWs of the Hell Ships were torture-tested survivors, whereas many of the victims of the Death March died from the initial shock of the consistent brutality of the Japanese military. Actually, O'Donnell and early Cabanatuan largely completed the weeding-out process. The graduates of those two great universities of survival were much better equipped psychologically to endure Japanese atrocities; nevertheless, a considerable number of the alumni could not complete their voyages on the Hell Ships.

After the war, the horror of the Hell Ships was underestimated only by those whose knowledge of them was secondhand. In a 1945 press conference following his liberation, Gen. W. E. Brougher, who was captured on Bataan, charged Japan "with 'criminal cold-bloodedness' in suffocating men on prison ships."[25] On the other hand, in a series of articles in the *New York Times* in September 1945, Gen. Edward King, who surrendered Bataan, spoke of the Death March as the worst event of prison life under the Japanese. But General King admitted that he and General Wainwright received much better treatment than the other

POWs on their voyage to Formosa.[26] The fact is that General King never realized just how bad the Hell Ships were.

Until recently in the historiography of the American war with Japan, the Hell Ships have been neglected. The Death March was much easier to describe and visualize. Some movies about the Death March have been made (though none with any sophistication), but so far as I know no one has attempted to make a movie about the Japanese Hell Ships. This may tell us as much about art as about history. Every novel, painting, or movie needs points of contrast, moments of relief, scenes that permit differing viewpoints. But the Hell Ships do not lend themselves to varied viewpoints or contrasting scenes. The damned, dark world of the Hell Ships lies buried beyond the reach of memory or imagination. It was a world providing only scenes and experiences unrelieved by humor or light, unvaried in routine and setting, unfathomable for reader or viewer. Such a movie or novel or painting, like the astronomer's black hole, would only collapse into itself, shedding no light, yielding no understanding.

In the history of the Japanese military's treatment of prisoners during World War II, the gem of all contrived evil was the Hell Ships. Only the sealed boxcars in San Fernando produced the same sick panic, and that endured for less than a day for each group. But it may be that the Hell Ships represent a kind of depravity, a supremely pure form of evil, beyond the scope of history, beyond the creative imaginations even of those who survived. As survivors attempt to tell the story of that hideous experience, their minds frequently recoil in horror and refuse to believe what they know happened. Even more than the attack on Pearl Harbor, the Japanese Hell Ships deserve to "live in infamy." Unfortunately, they will probably vanish from the thoughts of mankind when the last survivor has gone to his grave.

Plate 7. *Nissyo Maru*, apparently the only Hell Ship to survive the war. It plied the seas as one of Japan's commercial fleet for several years following the war, the world ignorant of its history. *Photo courtesy of Paul H. Silverstone*

11

Nagoya: Slavery, Starvation, and Death

The survivors vomited from the bowels of the *Nissyo Maru* on the docks of Moji, northern Kyushu, Japan, in August 1944 were completely dehumanized. Huddled on the waterfront, we were the remnants of beings whom the Japanese had debased, degraded, disgraced, and dishonored as far as possible this side of death. We were also dispossessed—having been deprived of virtually all personal possessions when we boarded ship. We were permitted only to scramble and fight for a pair of shoes from a soggy, filthy pile of footwear Japanese stevedores had thrown helter-skelter from the ship's hold onto the docks.

The port area of Moji, where the *Nissyo Maru* had tied up, apparently served as a Japanese Army overseas depot. As I recall, the *Nissyo Maru* was the only ship at berth. The port seemed strangely idle except for a small horse cavalry group just arriving, apparently to board ship for overseas service. I surmised that the functions of that military port facility were similar to the combined overseas operations of Ft. McDowell on Angel Island and Ft. Mason in San Francisco. In my imagination, I saw General Homma's Army of Bataan sailing from this port to unknown adventures in the South Seas, and also General Yamashita's Army setting out to conquer Singapore. Japanese troops embarking at those docks could just as well have gone to Korea and Manchuria. The famous old seaport of Moji had unquestionably played a significant role in Japan's attempt to spread its empire.

We disembarked from the *Nissyo Maru* about 9:00 A.M., and everyone was dehydrated, almost insane with thirst. Someone soon found a hydrant nearby, and like thirsty dumb animals we rushed to the smell of water. Alerted by the mass movement, the Japanese guards soon brought us to a halt. For a while the guards prohibited drinking the water because they said it was contaminated. They were probably telling the truth; we soon learned that practically all water in Japan was contaminated. The Japanese did not drink water—except in the form of a weak tea steeped

165

from green tea leaves. It soon became obvious both to us and to the guards that they could not restrain us indefinitely, and before long they gave up trying. We all eventually filled our bellies since it was evident that the Japanese were not going to provide us with water or tea. Except in a most perfunctory way, the guards had absolutely no compassion or sense of responsibility for their barbarian prisoners.

Quenching our thirst triggered acute hunger, except among those too ill to eat. As usual, a rumor that the Japanese were preparing to feed us spread like a brushfire through our ranks. Such rumors generally circulated as one POW told a second POW that a third POW knew someone who had talked to a Japanese guard who had stated that something was going to happen, in this case that the POWs were going to be fed. Someone probably had a garbled conversation with a Japanese guard. Some guards tended to respond affirmatively to questions from POWs without knowing what had been asked and perhaps without caring. All such rumors grew from the fertile soil of wishful thinking.

The Japanese had no intention of feeding us. As the day wore on, that fact became apparent to even the most optimistic prisoners. By that point we had become somewhat inured to such cultural arrogance. The Japanese saw themselves as a superior people with no obligation to show compassion for Americans or any others considered inferior; to do so would indicate weakness. That kind of arrogance was explained graphically in a movie I saw at Bilibid. The setting placed the Japanese Army in China. A private innocently praised the fighting qualities of some Chinese soldiers they had just killed. He was sharply reprimanded: a Japanese who praised inferior people insulted the Emperor.

Fortunately, from time to time we came across Japanese civilians who did not adhere to that racial code. But for the most part, even kindly Japanese found it difficult to treat barbarians as human beings. That all non-Japanese people were impure, weak, or intellectually inferior was deeply ingrained in the Japanese psyche.

Once it was generally accepted that the Japanese did not intend to feed us, we turned our attention to finding our old buddies. From the time we boarded the *Nissyo Maru* in Manila, the Japanese made no attempt to keep specific personnel units intact. We were placed in the ship on a first come, first placed basis: the guards filled the first open hold and then went on to the second. In short, we were treated like two-legged cattle. That laissez-faire policy continued on the docks of Moji where we milled around aimlessly, a motley crew with no specific unit assignments. Slowly, we gathered into small groups of company or prison acquaintances. My Company (the 409th Signal) had too few representatives to establish a separate group, and none of us present had any great affection for the others. Thus, we of the 409th Signal either were loners or joined other groups. Fortunately, Jack Garcia, whom I had not seen since boarding the *Nissyo Maru*, found me and was included in my group. Talking with Jack raised my spirits and kindled my burning hope for survival.

By midafternoon our group of two hundred men was formed, and we marched, or stumbled, out of the area to a nearby ferry terminal. We were on our way north to a prison camp near Nagoya, some to survive and some to die. Other similar groups were sent to various camps all over Japan. Soon we were aboard a ferry bound for the historic city of Shimonoseki. The crossing was a brief one of about three miles, a connection now made via under-sea tunnel. Landing on the north shore, we walked a short distance to the railway station, one of the most attractive buildings we would see in Japan. Shimonoseki impressed me as being much cleaner and more colorful than the industrially polluted Moji area. It was a beautiful, clear day, and the brilliant late afternoon sun hanging above the Korea Strait glinted brightly off the city's beige stucco buildings and their red-tiled roofs. Shimonoseki also had more trees, shrubbery, and grass than the Moji area. Though Shimonoseki and its environs gave a false impression of the real Japan, for the moment that historic gateway to a mysterious land served to boost our morale in spite of our raging hunger.

About five o'clock that afternoon, we boarded American-style railroad passenger cars, which seemed luxurious to us. That we were permitted to ride two to a seat in passenger cars, rather than in freight cars as in the Philippines, seemed a good omen. As the train steamed out of Shimonoseki station, we had some cause to be optimistic. Though we were extremely weak and hungry, the prospect of the unknown excited us as we rolled through the mountain shadows falling across the rocky shores of the Inland Sea. Through the evening hours the train snaked along the southwestern coast of Honshu and then north to Hiroshima, though at night we could see little of the city soon to be immortal.

As we passed through the country west of Kobe the next morning, I came to appreciate the importance of the Japanese mountain system. I had known that Japan had mountains—most Americans have heard of Fujiyama—but I was not aware of the many other peaks and ranges so much a part of Japanese geography, economics, and culture. As the train moved along between sea and mountains, a new impression of Japan's geography took shape in my mind. My mental picture of Japan had been drawn by my notions of its agriculture—dainty gardens, rice paddies, cherry trees. But I soon realized that the mountains occupied much of the country, extending almost to the sea and leaving little tillable land.

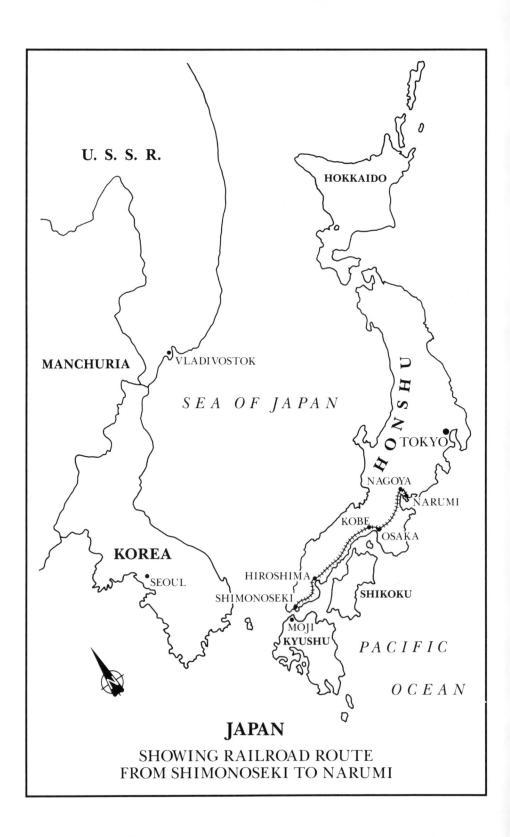

U. S. S. R.

HOKKAIDO

MANCHURIA
VLADIVOSTOK

SEA OF JAPAN

H O N S H U

TOKYO

NAGOYA

NARUMI

KOBE

OSAKA

KOREA

SEOUL

HIROSHIMA

SHIKOKU

SHIMONOSEKI

MOJI

KYUSHU

PACIFIC

OCEAN

JAPAN

SHOWING RAILROAD ROUTE
FROM SHIMONOSEKI TO NARUMI

Most of the narrow but level and fertile mountain valleys were given over to the cultivation of rice. Around the edge of the rice-occupied plains was a narrow upland on which terraces had been constructed. When we arrived, vegetables were growing on terraces from which the farmers had recently harvested a crop of millet or barley, both of which would appear regularly in the POW diet.

Normally, the autumn months in southern Honshu are warm and humid, making it possible to grow the vegetable crops on the terraces following the grain harvests. The most important vegetable produced in the fall was the famous daikon, a white radish. Fertilized by human feces, the plant grew quickly and unbelievably large. The radishes were cut up and pickled in brine in barrels similar to Tennessee tobacco hogsheads. During the spring, when the cherry blossoms were in bloom and the farmers were fertilizing with the human "honey," the daikon barrels were cleaned out, thus adding another pungent aroma to the Japanese countryside.

By noon we reached Kobe, the industrial heartland's greatest port. The city appeared to be essentially a long, narrow industrial area squeezed by the port facilities on one side and the mountains on the other. In the middle were numerous large smokestacks. Several ships were in the harbor, but it was clear that Japan's shipping had already been reduced by Allied action. I imagined the great swell of commercial and naval activity that went on in Kobe Harbor in 1942-43 when the newly expanded Japanese Empire was at its height.

In the early afternoon we arrived in Japan's second city and the capital of the industrial heartland, Osaka. The city, located on a fairly level plain, covered an enormous area. Osaka is the Chicago of Japan. Though Kobe was dotted with large smokestacks, Osaka was a crowded forest of ugly, dirty brick-and-mortar trunks, and they seemed mostly to be downtown rather than in suburban areas as in America. For me, the skyline of Kobe, and especially Osaka, came to represent the look of the great industrial cities of Japan: low gray wooden buildings surrounded by towering smokestacks lazily emitting swirls of lethal-looking smoke. All of the smokestacks in the world seemed to have been moved to Kobe and Osaka.

While our train was sitting in the Osaka railroad station, we were served the most delicious meal of our lives. We had not eaten for two whole days, not since the last night on the *Nissyo Maru*. Each POW received a wonderful lunch packed in a little wooden box, along with a cup of hot tea. As I recall after more than forty years, the lunch box contained a packet of gummy Japanese rice (I am still hooked on it to this day) sprinkled with a few soybeans, a small piece of pickled fish, a slice of daikon, and a wad of seaweed. I became addicted to the seaweed and still like it on the rare occasions I can get it. Perhaps there were other items that I cannot recall.

While eating our box lunches, we saw Japanese pedestrians passing through the busy area. Though they obviously saw us, they pretended not to see us. There was a deliberate, almost studied refusal to admit that we existed. Their response to us was a product not only of historical isolation but also of more recent racial and cultural propaganda. Surprisingly enough, Japanese civilians demonstrated little, if any, explicit hostility toward us. The presence of another cohort of American POWs would not have seemed unusual to them since they still expected to win the war and no doubt associated groups of foreign prisoners with military victories. They had not yet felt the hot breath of General LeMay. We had long looked forward to being received by civilians in Japan. It had been an article of faith with us that once we reached Japan, the civilians would not permit the continuation of the brutal treatment we were receiving from the sadistic military. But POWs must have looked and smelled like animals in a zoo—socially offensive to a superior people.

There in Osaka station, my comrades and I had a revival of the feeling that better days were on their way, despite the cool reception given us by Japanese civilians. The box lunch, so neatly and efficiently packed, led us to think that we had reentered civilization. Like the rumors at dockside, our hope that we would receive better treatment in Japan was hard to suppress. Within two weeks, however, we would see that illusion permanently dashed. The flame of hope for decent treatment flickered for the last time in Osaka.

Leaving Osaka in midafternoon, we made good time in covering the eighty or ninety miles to Nagoya. On the way we saw more arable land than we had seen west of Kobe. The more cultivated open land we passed, the more we noticed the effects of the 1944 drought that left the landscape a parched brown. Though there was less forest greenery on the route to Nagoya, we saw many sawmills and other evidence of a lumber industry. I suddenly realized that the huge, forest-covered mountain ranges made Japan a major producer of lumber and other forest products. I had never thought of Japan in that light. I offer these reflections as an indication of my state of mind at the time. I was a starving POW in the homeland of unjust captors; yet, despite overwhelming fatigue and concern for our immediate future, I was fascinated by the sights and activities of a strange country.

When we arrived in downtown Nagoya in late afternoon, we transferred to a station where, after a short wait, we were hustled aboard an electric interurban train. Though we did not know it at the time, that particular train would provide our daily transportation to and from work as slave laborers for the next twelve months. The availability of uphol-stered seats for everyone and the orderly, unhurried boarding were deceptive. If we had been more observant, we would have noticed a prophetic, more stressful scene in the same interurban station: Japanese "stickmen" loading civilian passengers going home from work.

The interurban train took us to Narumi, a suburb of Nagoya in the foothills about ten miles southeast of downtown. The Narumi railway station was located two or three miles inland from Ise Wan, the shallow bay that provided limited ocean access for the city of Nagoya. The village houses built into the neatly landscaped hillside were varied in design and color, unlike the rural villages on the Honshu coast west of Kobe with their gray, medieval appearance.

From Narumi station, the center of the older part of the village, we walked for over a mile, uphill most of the way, through an area of housing projects mixed with terraced agricultural land. There at the end of the road was our prisoner of war camp, perched atop a hill overlook-ing Narumi station. To the east, extending up to the edge of a pine forest, were terraced fields where late vegetable crops (especially daikon) were being cultivated. It was an undeniably beautiful, peaceful country setting almost in the shadows of the great smokestacks of Nagoya. I knew the scene before me was one of beauty, but there was no joy in the seeing. As hopeless POWs, we suffered the sadness of soul that permits aware-ness of beauty but denies any response. We were too weak, hungry, and depressed to enjoy anything.

The Narumi prison camp on the edge of Nagoya was composed of four barracks, a small clinic, a kitchen, and a long headquarters building containing the Commandant's office and a food storage area. Attached to the rear of the headquarters building was a facility that would be used later as an isolation cell for some of the Air Force personnel shot down in the air raids on Nagoya. The headquarters building also contained a room designated as a post store, where POWs could theoretically pur-chase items with the wages from their work. Since the Japanese never paid us for work, as required under the rules of the Geneva Convention, the store was used only once. When the camp was "inspected" by the International Red Cross, the "store" was filled with various items. But when the fat Swiss inspectors left, out went the goods. There was also a guards' shack at the main gate until B-29 bombers hit our camp in January 1945, obliterating the guards' shack as well as the guards.

Three of the barracks were used for prisoner of war lodging, the fourth by the Japanese for other purposes. The barracks we were as-signed to sat at the very top of the hill, exposed to the cold Siberian winds during the winter. The two barracks at the foot of the hill housed British POWs. The latrine for all POWs was located between the American and first British barracks. The facility was designed for maximum convenience for the "honey" man, a Japanese who periodically removed the excrement for fertilizer. No stigma was attached to the profession, and, ironically, the night soil was moved during daylight hours. By providing fertilizer for the crops of Japan, the POWs were making a distinct contribution to the war effort, but the Japanese showed no appreciation. The Americans reached the latrine via a set of wooden stairs set on the hillside and covered by a flimsy canopy. On cold nights in the coming winter, American POWs would have problems negotiating the stairway because of snow and ice. For those with dysentery, the problem was greatly complicated by their weakened condition. Often they could not reach the bottom of the stairs before losing control of their bowels; their bloody excretions glazed the steps and made it more difficult for everyone to use the stairway, especially in the winter.

The British POWs, already in residence at the Narumi camp when we arrived, had been captured at Hong Kong when it fell on Christmas Day 1941. Though the majority of the British were Europeans, there was a scattered representation from the far reaches of the empire: Indians, Hong Kong Chinese and Portuguese, Australians, New Zealanders, and others. On the whole, the British were courteous to us, but we did not reciprocate too well. The Americans were made generally uncomfortable by the "Limeys." To put it another way, the well-spoken and unflappable British made us Yanks feel a little inferior. Even so, in spite of the cultural barriers useful relationships were established between the British and the Americans. For example, among the British, who had no official Army chaplain, was a Chinese Anglican minister from Hong Kong who served as chaplain. The American chaplain, Father Reilly, was Catholic; the Americans had no Protestant minister. In a spirit of cooperation, the British minister held services for American Protestants, and Father Reilly provided services for British Catholics.

Out of those contacts initiated by the two clergymen some solid friendships were formed. Father Reilly's magnificent performance as spiritual counselor for both the Americans and the British did much to build good relations between the two groups. But it was not always smooth sailing. The severest test of the international friendship occurred in 1945 after the bombing began. The Japanese punished the Americans because of the bombing, and the resulting favoritism toward the British increasingly brought a strain to British-American relations.

When we first arrived at the Narumi camp, the British politely but firmly requested that Americans not attempt to smuggle Japanese newspapers into camp. Newspapers were strictly prohibited by the Japanese; in fact, they had decreed the death penalty for violators. What motivated the British was not concern for the Yanks' welfare but a desire to keep the paper coming. The British believed they had worked out a nearly fool-proof scheme for smuggling in newspapers and were afraid the inept Americans would foul up the system by getting caught.

Among the British POWs at Narumi was an Englishman who formerly had been a professor of Chinese literature in a Hong Kong school. He was the official translator of the Japanese newspapers. Because of the British smuggling system and the professor's linguistic skill, the war news we received was much more accurate than that available in the Philippines, even though the English translator had to wade through much propaganda to reach the approximate truth. The Japanese press at that time was a propaganda tool of Domei, the official wire service.[1] Domei covered the news under such thick layers of propaganda that we wondered why they cared if we read their newspapers. When the British completed each translating session, they sent a messenger with the news to the American barracks. They performed this service not only to satisfy our need to know but also to discourage Americans from going it alone. Actually, no one in the American group could have read a Japanese newspaper anyway, though some of our group had made great progress in speaking that baffling language.

Soon after we reached Narumi, we learned from our British source that Anglo-American forces had landed in Normandy, broken out, and were in rapid pursuit of the Germans hastily retreating across northern France. Though all of us were elated at the good news coming from the lower barracks, some of us had trouble believing it. Good news had so often proved to be rumor. But the steady stream of good news tended to make believers out of all of us. Then came the German counterattack and the Battle of the Bulge. Those events, when we learned of them in January, shook us badly. Again, we began to question the reliability of the news system.

After the Battle of the Bulge, for some unexplained reason the British were unable to keep on top of the war news as well as they had earlier. That was probably due to the increasing difficulty and risk in smuggling in newspapers. By the spring of 1945, however, we developed a supplementary source of news. The Japanese workers at the plant began to talk more freely with Allied POWs. They often divulged pieces of information for our rumor mills. By then it was evident that Japanese wartime propaganda was having little effect on the Japanese working class.

One of the most memorable pieces of news was the report of the death of President Roosevelt. It hit hard at the morale of all the American POWs. Most of us had grown up under the presidency of FDR and viewed him as a father figure. We simply could not imagine anyone else being president of the United States. The first news of Roosevelt's death came not from the British but from the Japanese themselves, who were glad to inform us. The death of the American leader temporarily boosted their spirits.

The Japanese did not know the name of the new American president, and none of us, including the British, knew who had been elected vice-president in 1944. In the absence of solid information from our British source, rumors sprang up daily about the identity of the new president. One day at our work site, I ran into Mickey Owen, a reporter for the Honolulu *Advertiser* captured during the fall of Bataan. As soon as Mickey saw me, he shouted, "Hey, Hubbard, guess who's president." I cannot recall my exact response, but Mickey exclaimed, "It's Rex Tugwell." Tugwell was a liberal New Deal Democrat, a former governor of Puerto Rico in the Roosevelt administration, and a political scientist-economist considerably to the left of Roosevelt and certainly of Truman. What the origin of Mickey's rumor was I cannot imagine, but I remember that I said something like, "Gosh, Roosevelt has sure gone radical." Later that evening, the British sent up a messenger with the question, "Does anyone know an important American politician named Trueman?" I had been an avid fan of national politics from 1928 until Pearl Harbor. Immediately it all came back to me. "Truman," I shouted. "He's a United States senator from Missouri." The news that Harry Truman was possibly our president surprised me because I vaguely remembered his being associated with, and tainted by, the Pendergast machine. We did not know for sure who the new president was until the war was over.

We were given a couple of days to settle in at the Narumi camp before being sent out to work. The American barracks, like the British barracks, was divided into four bays, fifty POWs to each bay. Each of us had an assigned space about the width of a man's body. We were able to enlarge our spaces only as members of our group died. We slept on the floor of the bay on rice-straw mats called tatamis. Thus, each man referred to his space as his tatami. In the absence of any official assignment of places in the barracks, the strong took what they wanted; the weak took what was left. Unfortunately, Jack and I became separated. My tatami space ended up near one end of the barracks, Jack's near the other end. Since we were also in different work groups, I rarely talked to Jack except on rest days. On workdays, body-racking fatigue killed everyone's desire for talk.

Since we had been forced to give up all of our surplus clothing aboard the *Nissyo Maru*, the clothes we were wearing were in tatters. The

Japanese issued each of us a light cotton outfit consisting of pants, a shirt, and a cap with our prison number on it. I can still see that cotton cap with my number 540. The cap fit, but the other two items were too large. In the late fall when the weather turned cold, we traded in our cottons for padded winter garments. The Japanese did not issue underwear or socks. To them that would have been like buying garments for a dog, an irrational and frivolous expenditure. Almost none of the POWs had any underwear or socks except what they were wearing when they arrived. Eventually, it became fashionable for the prisoners not to have those two items in their wardrobes.

In our prison camp, we received two regular meals a day, breakfast and supper. For both meals there was generally plenty of tea since the Japanese used only a few leaves in making their weak but delicate green tea. For breakfast, the one consistently important food issue was steamed barley, a product not highly valued as human food by the Japanese. Later, millet (Japanese chicken feed) would be mixed with or replace the barley. At noon we received a small loaf of bread and soup, but after the first few days the noon meal was issued at the factory where we worked. The evening meal consisted of steamed barley or millet, which we always referred to as rice, and soup. The soup was little more than hot water barely colored by tiny bits of the final residue of soybean processing, a product we called cardboard. On rare occasions Japanese generosity broke through: they would give us a rabbit to put in the soup pot—one rabbit for nearly six hundred men. When that happened, word that the soup contained small bits of rabbit meat produced a surging mob around the assistant chow man and the soup pot. Occasionally, we would get a little something extra for the evening meal, like a piece of salted fish. On a couple of rest days (*yasumi*), we each received a small piece of semifresh fish.

At breakfast and supper we ate our meals while sitting cross-legged on our tatamis. Eating in bed can be messy, but in our case not a speck of food soiled the mats. In consuming our meals, we were as efficient as ants. Occasionally, during the day while we were out at work, the British kitchen staff distributed small individual portions of salt and pickled daikon at our tatamis. It was always pleasant to return from work and find such treats at our places.

As far as the prisoners were concerned, the distribution of food was the most important activity in the camp. In the American barracks, each bay selected two chow men, a head and an assistant. At meal times, the chow men went to the central kitchen to be issued the food for each bay. Returning, the head chow man distributed the solid food, and the assistant doled out the soup and tea. In the beginning there were few guidelines for selecting chow men. The first ones in the American barracks were bullies who assumed office by the right of might. They then sought endorsement by one of the two American officers. When the head chow man issued the steamed barley for breakfast and supper, everyone in the bay watched with eagle eyes.

During the early days at Narumi, frequent controversy broke out in our bay about the food issue. Charges were made and rumors floated that the chow men favored their friends and also strafed the soup pot of all solid items. No one seemed to trust anyone. But after forcing a change of chow men a couple of times, my bay mates happily discovered a person they could trust. His name was Butler, a west Tennessean, who briefly attended the University of Tennessee at Martin. For some mysterious reason, the entire group had faith in Butler; they knew an honest man when they saw one. I can vouch for his honesty because my being a fellow Tennessean did not bring me one extra grain of barley, much to my disgust. In fact, I felt he possibly gave me a few grains less just to prove his integrity.

At Nagoya, the distribution of food by the POW administration was fairer and more efficient than in the Philippine camps because of the virtual absence of corruption. That was so for two principal reasons. First, the British managed and operated the Nagoya camp's central kitchen without American participation or intervention. The British personnel appeared to be so equitable and capable that the American POWs came to consider them more trustworthy than their American counterparts. Had the matter been put to a vote, most American prisoners undoubtedly would have chosen to continue with British administration of the kitchen. Americans at Nagoya came to feel that the sissy-accented Limeys, as well as the foul-mouthed Aussies, were innately fair.

The second factor promoting fairness was that there were no supplementary sources of food at Nagoya, so common in the Philippines. The official, pathetically small ration was the only food a prisoner was likely to get. As a result, most of the prisoners watched with keen interest all stages of food distribution to make sure they were getting their fair shares. Chow men worked under watchful eyes as they distributed food in the barracks and were under constant pressure to distribute equitably.

Another reason life was harder for us in Japan than in the Philippines was the attitude of the guards. Whereas in the Philippines the guards were generally careless, in our prison system in Japan they abided strictly by camp regulations. The best example of the guards' mindless adherence to regulated routine was their devotion to count-offs (*tenko* or *bango*) of prisoners. In the morning before breakfast we had to count off while sitting cross-legged on our tatamis. After breakfast we lined up in front of the Commandant's office for the *tenko* procedure, and when arriving at Narumi station we went through *tenko* again. We counted off yet again just after leaving the train at the downtown station, which was close to our factory workplace. When we reached the factory, we stumbled into line and again had *tenko*. Fortunately, we were not required to *bango* at lunchtime, but at the end of the workday we again went through the counting procedure. We did not count off before boarding the train for camp, but at times we had to *tenko* after leaving the train at Narumi station. Invariably, the *tenko* process was required when we arrived at camp, along with a search for smuggled goods. We did not have to *tenko* at supper, but the lights-out *tenko* (about 8:45) was one of the most important counts of the day. Except for the count-offs in our bay spaces, the exercise made no sense, for in all of the other counting events the guards did not know exactly how many people were supposed to be in the groups. They kept no records or notes. Had our count been short or long the guards probably would not have known the difference. *Tenko* (except for the evening tatami counts) was merely a routine of the Japanese military.

The *tenko* routine helped to maintain a kind of discipline. We had to say our numbers in Japanese, and except for the lights-out count-off in the evenings, our individual numbers were constantly changing. The numbers of the evening *tenko* changed only as a result of deaths or admissions to the clinic. Woe to the POW who did not utter the correct number! That man was a candidate for a broken jaw. The Japanese had an effective system of teaching language: a slap in the face, a fist to the nose, or a boot to the stomach created a more efficient learning environment than a home computer. For the first months of our internment at the Narumi camp, the evening *tenko* numbers in my bay remained more or less constant, and the sound of the person to one's right saying his number almost instinctively triggered the next person's number. For example, for a long time my bay number was thirty-four (*san-ju-shi* and my saying "shi" caused the next person, my blanketmate, to say his number, thirty-five (*san-ju-go*). But the Japanese have two words meaning *four*. One evening during *tenko*, when one of the meanest guards (we called him Joe Louis) was taking the count, I inadvertently gave the alternate number for four, i.e., *san-ju-yon* That, of course, caught my blanketmate napping. He began to stutter, "San-ju! . . . san-ju! . . . san-ju! . . ." That serious breakdown in the counting process immediately brought down the wrath of Joe Louis. He gave the stuttering POW sharp raps across each cheek with the flat side of his sword. To make things worse, Joe profusely praised me for my progress in learning the subtleties of the Japanese language. Joe made it clear to the guilty person that he should view me as a role model. As Joe Louis moved on to the next bay, my blanketmate mumbled threats that, if carried out, would have provided a little more living space in our bay.

Our first days in the Narumi camp were disillusioning. The chief disappointment was the scarcity of food. Our ration was so small and of such poor quality we realized that it would not supply enough calories to support life for long. The American barracks were clean compared to those in the Philippines, but we were too crowded and ventilation was poor in the hot weather of the early fall. We also realized that the barracks did not have proper insulation for the coming winter. The latrine was kept fairly clean, but its relative inaccessibility at night caused a problem. The Japanese authorities never overtly gave or denied permission for the prisoners to use the latrine after nightfall. Most guards did not interfere, but occasionally one would slap or severely beat a prisoner caught using the latrine at night. In contrast to the disappointments was one remaining hope—that we would get a good noon meal at the factory. Rumors based on statements allegedly made by the British helped to keep that hope alive.

With a great deal of anxiety and apprehension, we anticipated going to work much as children look forward to their first day of school. On that first day, immediately following a fast *tenko* we were herded downhill to the Narumi station. After the count-off there, our train, like all Japanese trains, arrived on time, and over five hundred prisoners were shoved into two railway passenger cars. From the first day, we learned that there were two main incentives to board the train as quickly as possible: (1) the early birds got the seats, (2) the late birds were beaten by railway stickmen.

The work train, the same vehicle that had brought us to Narumi from Nagoya, ran through four or five miles of villages interspersed among rice fields before reaching the main city of Nagoya. We then traveled about the same distance within the city to a large central railway terminal. Metropolitan Nagoya, like the other great Japanese cities, was a network of villages similar to Narumi connected by rail lines to large industrial and commercial establishments in a downtown center.[2] After detraining and *tenko*ing, we marched a short distance to our workplace. We learned that our new employer was the Japanese railway system and that we would be working at the railway manufacturing facility where most of the locomotives in Japan were made, along with other railway equipment and war materiel. At one time the plant had produced landing barges for the Japanese Army, but by that point in the war, the Japanese were no longer making landings. The barges we saw were rusty hulks surrounded by weeds, some of them being torched for scrap steel.

The principal war items being produced at the plant were kamikaze torpedo boats and bomb cases.

Arriving at a designated open space within the plant area, we had *tenko* and continued to stand at attention awaiting job assignments. We were all nervous because we knew that survival could well depend on the jobs assigned us. Various honchos showed up for the American labor draft, each requesting a given number of men. Whether their requests were filled completely or partially we were unable to determine. The honchos were not permitted to pick their men; each had to take his allotment consecutively down the line. Some jobs turned out to be exhausting, particularly those to which larger numbers of men were assigned—jobs like shoveling slag all day. By now, many of the POWs, including me, were physically weak—so weak, in fact, that only with great difficulty could they stumble through each day.

But I was lucky. I was picked for membership on a small (five-man) crew with the kind of assignment much more likely to permit survival. Our principal duty was to deliver supplies throughout the factory. The Japanese called our crew work *haikyu*, meaning distribution, allotment, or rationing of work. We corrupted the term slightly, calling it "High-Q." Periodically, we delivered axles and rims for the engine drive wheels to the assembly line; carbon sticks to the electric furnace where the inside portion of the drive wheels was poured; pipe to the boilermakers; and Chevrolet engines to the suicide boat plant. Less often we delivered completed locomotive cabs and other objects related to steam loco- motives. On one occasion we moved a large number of locomotive headlights from one warehouse to another. We moved them to and from our cart by lining up and tossing them down the line. Our honcho did not object to that method of handling the fragile objects, but a stickman came by and worked us over for negligence. The stickman's stick almost tore off my left ear. We got the not-so-subtle hint right away.

Japanese labor in that factory contrasted sharply with the modern image of the efficient, dedicated Japanese work force. Though the Japa- nese moved heavy objects and loads over the rails with a dinky steam engine, our *haikyu* crew and most of the Japanese moving crews delivered supplies by pushing small railway carts on the rails. The Japanese crews were twice the size of ours and extremely inefficient. Two or three men could have pushed one of the loaded carts rather easily if the plant track and turntable had been kept in good repair. It was commonly held among POWs, both in the Philippines and in Japan, that when it came to machinery the Japanese were contemptibly negligent. Everyone had his favorite anecdote to demonstrate the point. For example, there were stories in the Philippines about Japanese soldiers permitting truck engines to burn up simply by failing to add water or oil. In Japan we could see clearly that maintenance was poor.

Instead of servicing the carts and tracks regularly to reduce friction, the Japanese used big crews. Often the circular track at the turntables would be covered with dirt. Rather than keep the tracks clean, the Japanese cart crews would tug and grunt, chanting, "Ichi-ni, san shi! Ichi-ni, san shi!" We on the *haikyu* crew persuaded our honchos that greater efficiency lay in calling for the maintenance crew when we encountered a balky turntable or debris-laden tracks. The plant repair crew had a small crane mounted on a railway cart for the purpose of lifting the heavy steel covers from the turntables, and they responded fairly promptly but sullenly. They also cleaned debris from the tracks when our crew requested it. Otherwise, they apparently provided maintenance only when the whole system broke down; at least, the Japanese cart crews never requested help so far as we knew.

The major function of the *haikyu* crew was to move spindles, rims, and other heavy parts or components from the central steel yard to the locomotive assembly line. The central steel yard, about the width of a football field and twice as long, was a massive jumble of unorganized inventory. Heavy steel components delivered by incoming trains were piled haphazardly on top of each other. Riding on tracks set far apart, a huge crane straddling the yard could move easily from one end to the other. After receiving an order for a particular piece of steel, the crane would move to the area where it was located or believed to be located. Unless the piece was on top of the pile, tons of steel would have to be moved to get to it, and in many cases the moving was more like a random search. The inept management of the steel yard was further indication to us of Japanese inefficiency.

Two additional duties of the *haikyu* crew were transporting pipe from the central pipe racks to the boilermakers and delivering engines to the suicide boat house. On those two projects, particularly, the High-Q crew demonstrated, to the amazement of the Japanese, American ingenuity and know-how. One member of our crew was a half-Cherokee Indian from Oklahoma, William Ellis, who as a child had lived on a reservation. He had little formal education, but he was a mechanical genius. He was constantly figuring out ways for our crew to perform jobs with less effort, not to help the Japanese but to make it easier on the crew members who were weak from malnutrition. For example, when we loaded and unloaded pipe, Ellis set up a procedure whereby one person, using gravity, could actually load pipe onto or off the railroad cart more easily than a group of people, who tended to get in each other's way. The boilermakers were astounded by the *haikyu* crew's efficiency.

The Oklahoma Indian's greatest mechanical feat simplified the unloading at the boathouse of the 1934 Chevrolet engines used to power the suicide boats (*shinyo*). The boats were small plywood craft about eighteen feet long and powered by one or two Chevrolet engines. They were designed primarily for crashing into enemy ships at night. Most of them were deployed along the southern coasts of Japan to be used in case of an American invasion, but a number were used, apparently without success, in the Battle of Okinawa.[3] Each load of four engines (two in each box) was placed on our cart at the steel yard. The engines were not piled in the yard, but instead were loaded directly from a railway freight car. The first time we were sent to perform this job, we caught up with a large Japanese cart crew at the boathouse also unloading the Chevrolet engines. The Japanese crowded around each two-engine case and laboriously lifted it while they chanted, "Ichi-ni, san shi!" When the *haikyu* crew arrived, Ellis, after briefly observing the grunting and sweating Japanese, immediately prepared a setup permitting maximum use of leverage, something the Japanese workers had not yet discovered. With little effort, we moved the heavy cases onto the floor where Ellis had laid down a few short pipes. When the Chevy engines hit the pipes, two people, one pushing the engines and one moving the pipes, quickly scooted them to their designated place against the wall. The Japanese cart crew as well as the boathouse employees were amazed at that feat of Oklahoma Indian know-how.

I was surprised at the inefficiency, negligence, ineptness, and downright laziness of many Japanese workers. It is no wonder that stickmen patrolled the factory to keep them working. I later learned that Koreans, who made up much of the slave labor force, had to be worked in guarded groups to achieve any reasonable level of production, but I did not know at the time that many of the Japanese workers were probably prisoners. Some fifty thousand Japanese prisoners were assigned to the factories during World War II. In fact, there were more of them than Allied POWs (thirty thousand) in forced labor. We probably had some Chinese slave laborers in the plant as well since a considerable number were sent to Japan during the war.[4]

It was clear to me that the biggest labor problem facing the Japanese was the growing unwillingness of their own workers to work hard and effectively. An increasingly high absentee rate was reducing and confusing production. By 1944 the absentee rate for Japanese labor was 15 percent in 761 leading factories. As a result of the absenteeism and moonlighting, shoddy work was a chronic problem.[5] No doubt contributing to the poor morale and performance of the Japanese labor force was the fact that many of the common workers had been drafted for their jobs, just as others had been drafted into the military. The labor draft obviously accounted for a considerable amount of worker "reluctance."[6]

By 1944 males as young as ten were drafted for factory work, and some of them were working on the locomotive assembly line at our plant. I recall one Japanese boy, surely not more than ten, who was operating a metal lathe on the assembly line, preparing the heavy metal spindles to fit into the big drive wheels. His fittings were not the best—at some spots one could stick a finger between the two pieces of metal—but they apparently worked anyway.

The role of Japanese women in the work force and in society at large was strange to us Westerners. Though young unmarried women were required to register for the labor force in Japan during World War II, they were not drafted. Apparently, the government encouraged women to work but was reluctant to coerce them and thereby devalue their role as mothers and housewives.[7] At our plant in Nagoya, a group of women worked in a unit of the cold rolling mill. Every time we went there for steel plate, we saw them; during the hot weeks of the late summer of 1944, they worked topless. Ordinarily, that would have excited American servicemen, but our protein deficiency caused us to ignore them. The Japanese men also appeared to be less than titillated by the exposed breasts. In fact, Japanese men seemed not to interact at all with women in public. When we saw a Japanese couple at the railway station, the woman invariably walked behind the husband, who always permitted his wife to carry the packages, groceries, and children. In wartime Japan, women seemed almost nonentities in public. We saw them everywhere but did not really see them. Japanese men took women completely for granted. In the factory or at the railway station, I never saw women conversing with men. I never saw teenage males and females together in mixed pairs or groups. Japanese women seemed to be almost a separate race of people.

I recall one event, when I got permission from the honcho to *benjo* as we passed a latrine, that illustrates the cultural adjustment an American POW had to make in wartime Japan. Women workers at the railway plant used the same latrines as men. As I stood using the urinal that lined one side of the structure, a woman entered who was obviously in a hurry. She quickly opened the toilet doors one by one only to find all the stalls occupied by a squatting male. Each time, she grunted, "Ush!" loudly and impatiently. When she discovered that the last hole was also occupied, she rapidly pulled down her lower garments and backed over to the urinal beside me to do her business. That may have shocked me, but to the honey man it was all the same. Whatever the peculiar social arrangements at the latrine, the product made the daikon grow.

Though I had some feeling for the lot of women in Japan, my life depended on adjusting to other, more immediate problems in the factory. Inefficiency was apparent everywhere, but our real concern was the danger from the lack of safety regulations. The Japanese method of detecting cable flaws, for instance, was to use one until it snapped. Shortly before our arrival in Japan, the British prisoners who preceded us on the *haikyu* crew fell victim to that kind of negligence when a broken cable dropped a huge drive wheel rim, killing one and severely injuring a couple of others. Each time we took a cart full of heavy steel objects to the assembly line, we had to avoid being caught in the cable or being hit by a cart overturned by the careless Japanese crane operator. We came to believe that the operator was trying to injure us. Once the cable was attached, the crane operator generally started moving the crane before lifting the heavy load. He frequently dragged it off our cart before picking it up, flipping the cart and sending the lethal load swinging at a low level down the assembly line where the Japanese workers, some of them children, had to duck to keep from being hit. It seemed a miracle to us that anyone could survive in our factory for a long time.

One of the most miserable jobs the *haikyu* crew had to perform was delivering steel plates to the boiler factory. We picked up the plates from stacks after they had been processed in the cold steel presses. Not only were they heavy; their temperature created problems for us as well. In cold weather they froze our hands; in hot weather they burned, and we had to handle them without gloves.

The *haikyu* crew delivered its supplies by cart over the internal railway system, except for carbon fuel sticks used by the electric furnaces. The furnaces produced the molten metal for the solid insides of the drive wheels, as well as a few other components. Since there were no rails to the furnace, we used a rickety general-purpose pushcart instead. The cart's wheels wobbled badly on worn-out axles because the Japanese never greased them. For some unknown reason, the *haikyu* crew did not deliver any of the products of the electric furnaces to the locomotive assembly line.

The carbon sticks were about a foot in diameter and twelve feet long. They were partially covered with a loose burlap wrap, and they were difficult to handle because the carbon was so slick. We always dreaded that job. On one occasion we broke a carbon stick, and we as well as our honcho literally feared for our lives. We thought we might be shot. The workers at the electric furnaces apparently did not see the accident happen; no one reported us to the factory stickmen, some of whom were national police.

Occasionally the *haikyu* crew was dispatched to the executives' mess in the headquarters building to cut wood for the kitchen stoves. Our honcho would drop us off there, leaving us under the supervision of the cook, a middle-aged Japanese woman. She was an extremely kind person, and we looked forward to working for her. She always gave us a friendly greeting at the mess door and returned to her duties inside while we five POWs, unsupervised, fell to cutting wood with those strange Japanese wood-cutting tools. As important as Japan's timber industry was, their versions of the saw and ax seemed to us designed for maximum awkwardness. We did the best we could with what we had. After a while the cook always came outside and invited us into the kitchen. Our response was something like that of hungry dogs at feeding time. Every time we were assigned to the mess, she prepared us a dish of food neatly and delightfully arranged. At the bottom was a layer of green vegetables liberally doused with soybean oil. On the bed of greens she placed a large rice ball sprinkled with soybeans. Oh, what a meal! Even now, when I am especially hungry, I can conjure up some of the same thrill I experienced during stolen moments in the kitchen of the executives' mess hall.

While we joyfully ate the delicious treat, the cook stepped outside the door and stood guard. She knew that she (as well as we) would be severely beaten if the stickmen caught us eating the forbidden food. We wondered why she was willing to take such a risk for dirty, stinking prisoners of war. As a reward for her inexplicable tenderness and kindness, we viewed her as our personal Japanese saint—our Blessed Lady of the Executives' Mess. Many years later, I was reminded of her by Kenji Mizoguchi's magnificent movie *Ugetsu*, which I interpreted as a tribute to Japanese womanhood. The specific scene that brought our Nagoya lady to mind was the homecoming of the potter, after a fruitless journey in search of false values, to the devoted wife he had taken for granted. Though she prepares his tatami, tea, and food, she has been dead for some time. Only the next morning, when she has vanished back to the grave, does the potter understand that the true value in his life all along had been his loving and devoted wife.

The supervision of my work detail at the railway factory was strange indeed. Four honchos, each of whom appeared to be of vastly different rank and influence, took daily turns at the task. After more than forty years, I have forgotten their names, except for one. The head honcho I shall call Sourpuss; the next in rank was our favorite honcho whose name I do remember—Okadora. The next two down the line in social status were Scaredy-cat and Brownnose. Each of them bossed us every fourth day and in the exact order stated above. What they did on the other days we never knew, but we learned that they, along with other Japanese factory personnel, operated out of a *yasumi* (rest) shack where they maintained a locker and other personal possessions.

Sourpuss's strutting walk projected his arrogance. His influence in the factory was obvious as he made the rounds on his days with us. He was unafraid to express his contempt for the stickmen, and it appeared to us that those evil creatures actually avoided him. Sourpuss was a dedicated Japanese nationalist who hated not only Americans but other Asians as well. He treated Korean workers at the factory brutally, and when any of our crew mentioned the Philippines, he generally expressed utter scorn for the Filipinos. At first, Sourpuss was given to kicking prisoners and refrained from doing so only with difficulty. Almost invariably his kicks were aimed at the back of the leg inside the knee. As time passed, he began to take pride in our skills and came to enjoy showing us off to his colleagues. Because of pride in his possession, he gradually stopped abusing his skillful little crew of Americans. But he invariably exploded with anger if we talked to other POWs outside our crew. On those occasions he would run, screaming ferociously, to kick them. We learned to avoid all contact with our fellow POWs on the days we worked with Sourpuss.

In the early days, Sourpuss worked us hard, but as time passed, working conditions improved. Not only did he develop a better feeling for us, but much to our liking, he began to work less and loaf more. On many days we hardly hit a lick because Sourpuss was visiting and drinking tea with his friends in various offices around the factory. Of course, we waited outside like hitched horses, but in our weakened condition Sourpuss's socializing permitted us to conserve energy. On extremely hot or cold days, being "hitched" outside while Sourpuss carried on animated conversations with his friends could be extremely uncomfortable.

Of all the Japanese I encountered during World War II, my favorite was Okadora. It was, of course, impossible for me to determine what Okadora thought of himself, but I viewed him as a citizen of the world whose first loyalty was to the human race. Not only did he refrain completely from expressions of banzai nationalism; he frequently revealed a subtle but definite antiwar sentiment. Okadora's attire, which was completely non-Western, made him appear the most Japanese of our four honchos. As I recall, he looked like a medieval Japanese character plucked from a Kurosawa movie.

All the members of our crew looked forward to our day with Okadora. We knew that we would do very little work and that he would never push us when we did perform a job. After lunch, he usually took us to the honchos' *yasumi* shack where he invariably shared his food, cigarettes, and wine ration with us. But mostly he wanted to talk. He wanted to learn about our lives in America, what sort of environment we grew up in, what our families did for a living, and the like. None of our four honchos could speak English, but Okadora wanted to learn. Consequently, we spent some of our time hiding from work in the *yasumi* shack teaching Okadora English. One member of our crew was an absolute wizard with the Japanese language, thus making it easy for us to communicate with that gentle soul. I can see him now—that little Japanese man dressed in a lavender and purple blouse, black spider-leg pants, oxentoed cloth shoes, and wearing a great Japanese sombrero—sitting cross-legged on the floor growing excited by his conversation with us and frequently taking time-outs to reload his long-stemmed pipe with "hair" tobacco. Like Sourpuss, Okadora had contempt for the Japanese stickmen, and there seemed to be an understanding among those despicable creatures that crossing swords with him could be dangerous.

Okadora's larder appeared well stocked for a Japanese of his class at that stage of the war. It was obvious to us that food for Japanese civilians was scarce and getting scarcer. Though their rations were superior to ours, there was plenty of evidence suggesting serious hunger among the Japanese workers. Because of Okadora's plenty, we suspected that he was operating in the black market. Actually, we saw no other evidence of it, and I was greatly surprised to learn recently that an enormous black market existed in Japan during the later part of the war.[8]

Scaredy-cat was not so bad, but he was terrified of the stickmen. He had little social or professional prestige at the plant, and the stickmen knew it. They constantly hassled him. On our days with Scaredy-cat, we often had to work especially hard as a result of his attempt to appease those vultures. Scaredy-cat did not work us hard by resorting to direct force but by working hard himself, by using himself as a role model. He led the way in hard work. Yet, despite his great fear of the stickmen, he frequently hid us out for long periods of rest. On those occasions, he did not talk to us much but generally stood guard watching for the stickmen. Though he never carried us to the honchos' *yasumi* shack as Okadora did, we had some regard for Scaredy-cat. In spite of his painful submission to the savage stickmen, he showed at least primitive respect for our humanity.

The best thing I can say about Brownnose is that he was less brutal than some of my Japanese supervisors during World War II. By Western standards his moral and ethical values were stunted. He lacked all compassion for POWs; despite our weakened bodies, he was ready to work us to death to impress his superiors while avoiding work himself. Brownnose did not display much arrogance because he was too busy trying to promote himself with his betters. Though he feared the stickmen, he sought them out as if to demonstrate what a toady he was. All in all, Brownnose was thoroughly reprehensible.

I am thankful that, after forty years, I am able to recall the surnames of the other four members of my crew in the Nagoya railway factory. They were Ellis, the Oklahoma Indian to whom I have already referred; Oldaker, also from Oklahoma; Kennedy from North Carolina; and Morgan from Florida. I could not have had more compatible workmates than Ellis, Oldaker, and Kennedy, though Morgan and I had personality clashes. Oldaker frequently cheered us up by singing, "Away down yonder in the Indian nation," poking good-humored and well-received fun at Ellis. Kennedy, whose formal education was poor, had a great ear for the Japanese language. By the time we began work at the factory, he possessed by far the most sophisticated knowledge of Japanese of any American I knew. His understanding of the subtleties of the language played an essential part in our fruitful intellectual exchanges with Oka-dora. Yet Kennedy, a modest man, never used his superior linguistic ability to seek special favors from the Japanese. Despite my difficulties with Morgan, I enjoyed listening to him talk about the economic and social life of rural northern Florida.

In the Narumi camp, health conditions were considerably inferior to those in Bilibid. Though we were not subjected to tropical diseases as in the Philippines, we had to contend with the problems created by the cold weather. Poor heating in the barracks, inadequate winter clothing, and a deficient diet made exposure to the cold the greatest threat to our health. Yet our death rate was much less in Japan. The improvement in survival rates was due to two things: the absence of those two great killers, malaria and dysentery, and residual survivability. By the late summer of 1944, American POWs arriving in Japan had developed much greater endurance. It took more than a little abuse to kill them.

At the factory, threats to survival were constantly changing with the task or the overseer, but at the Narumi camp there was a dreadful sameness to the threats to life and health. Day after week after month, poor sanitation, parasites, disease, and starvation wasted our bodies, our minds, our numbers. On the one hand, sanitation in the Narumi camp was helped by the Japanese honey men keeping the latrines clean and by the relative cleanliness of our barracks. On the other hand, sanitation was undermined by inadequate body and bed clothing and other conditions that caused parasites to grow—especially crab lice, body lice, and fleas. When we arrived in August, we were issued one set of cotton clothing, later exchanged for padded winter garments. We had no change of clothing. Though we were permitted to take a bath on *yasumi* day, which occurred every two weeks, rarely were we permitted to wash our clothes. On *yasumi* days some POWs attempted to launder their clothes if they had access to a bucket, only a few of which were available. But there was no soap to be had, except for an occasional piece filched at the factory, and no hot water on a regular basis. Since we had lost our toiletries on the *Nissyo Maru*, razor blades were scarce. At Narumi, the Japanese issued razors and blades only once, in August 1944. That one issue constituted our shaving equipment for a year.

Soon after we arrived in Japan, we had an epidemic of crab lice and not long afterward an even greater epidemic of body lice. Our only method of fighting these vermin was steaming our body and bed clothing. We were permitted to do this only on *yasumi* days, but since we had access to only one oil drum for steaming, we were never able to get to everybody on any one day. During the early spring of 1945, a strange biological phenomenon occurred. The crab and body lice disappeared with the coming of the flea hatch in our tatamis. The fleas covered us every night, and they had voracious appetites. We spent most of the nights scratching and cursing. Many of the men hoped that the lice would return and chase away the fleas.

Yasumi day came every two weeks until the Japanese stopped the practice in retribution for the American bombing of Japan. We all looked forward to *yasumi* day for two reasons: rest and a bath. As far as food was concerned, the daily fare prevailed, although occasionally the Japanese threw in an extra issue of pickled daikon or miso, a briny soybean residue that looked like apple butter but tasted like a thick tabasco sauce. For the most part, *yasumi* was just a rest day for us. In our weakened condition we needed all the rest we could get. Many POWs, except for mealtimes, lay as flat as a pancake all day while some of the stronger ones attempted to wash and mend clothing, repair shoes, and do other housekeeping chores.

The highlight of the *yasumi* day was the hot bath in the late afternoon. One large bath facility about twenty by thirty feet in size contained hot water three feet deep. Baths were taken by bay groups (a maximum of fifty people, but gradually less as some of our number died); there were eight British and four American bay groups. For the first group, there was fresh, hot water, but since the water was not changed, each subsequent group added pollution to and took heat from the water. By the time the last group bathed, a heavy film of scum floated on the lukewarm water. Though we were required to take a cold, soapless shower before we got into the hot bath, it did little good. How the order of bathing was determined, I never knew. I always got plenty of scum.

Because the Japanese suspended and finally canceled *yasumi* in the late winter of 1945, from mid-March to V-J Day most of us never had a real bath. Some of our group bathed whenever they could, but others just pursued the wild life. After all, only so much scum and dirt can stick to the body; gravity and friction impose limits.

During the winter of 1944-45, pneumonia was a constant threat to the POWs; most of the sick-call quota were pulmonary cases. The camp clinic was ill-prepared to care for sick people. The U.S. Army doctor and a British Army doctor worked long and hard against great odds to serve their fellow POWs, but few drugs and little medical equipment were available, and the camp Commandant displayed almost no interest in or sympathy for sick prisoners of war. He also insisted that the daily quota on sick call be strictly observed. The clinic had space for only three or four of the most severe cases. The others were retained in the barracks.

About midwinter, I began having fever and chills. I could hardly drag my carcass through the workday. I did not immediately report for sick call because I had heard that the quota was being monopolized by a number of chronic patients. By the third morning of my illness, I felt compelled to go on sick report. After examining me, the American doctor said that I had pneumonia and would be included on the day's sick quota. Before he had completed his conversation with me, however, one of the chronics (a person frequently on sick call) burst into the room, whining that his legs were hurting. After a short discussion with the chronic, the doctor turned to me and, in a profoundly apologetic manner, informed me that he could not keep me on sick call because the quota was full and he was obligated to replace me with the chronic. That was hard to understand since the chronic was one of the more healthy-looking men in the camp. But that was how the cards were dealt. The doctor assured me that I would be placed on the list as soon as there was an opening, probably the next morning. I stumbled to work, but my comrades on the *haikyu* detail helped me a great deal because they knew that I had an officially diagnosed case of pneumonia.

That evening the American doctor came to see me in the barracks. Though he was a dedicated professional whom I respected, he obviously felt some guilt about my case. He again assured me that I would fill the first opening and again predicted there would be room for me the next morning. As he left, he gave me one of his limited number of morphine pills. The morphine soon took effect, and I drifted pleasantly into dreamland. The next morning, just as the doctor had predicted, I was kept in camp among the sick. It was a particularly cold day, and the barracks was without heat because the Japanese were punishing us for the American bombing. The doctor ordered the patients to huddle together as much as possible to keep warm. During the evenings, we returned to our tatami places where we were forced to sleep close together because we had to share a blanket with a bedfellow. After four or five days on the sick list, I returned to work partially recovered but weak. I survived, but even now it seems miraculous.

The greatest general health problem for the POWs in Japan was malnutrition. From our arrival in Japan until the Japanese surrender, we were continuously on a starvation diet. The gnawing hunger indicated that we simply were not getting enough carbohydrates and proteins to sustain life for long. We were all suffering acutely from beriberi, scurvy, and other nutritional diseases. At the Narumi camp we received one small issue of Red Cross goods—some toilet articles, a little food, and some cigarettes. Apparently, the Japanese military confiscated most of the Red Cross supplies. Though our diet was below the subsistence level from the beginning of our stay in Japan, it got even worse after the American bombing began.

By the spring of 1945, practically everyone's health was declining rapidly because of inadequate nourishment. Even the healthiest among us were beginning to stumble. I recall the case of a Navy chief, a rather large fellow, who was barely surviving on our starvation diet. His unrelenting hunger was driving him mad. One day in the early spring his mind collapsed and he attempted to escape, ostensibly to hunt for food. When the guards discovered his absence at the evening *tenko*, they launched a search. They found him nearly dead, hiding in the attic of a storage barracks. The Japanese guards tied chains around his wrists and dragged him around the camp, the chains cutting deeply into his flesh. He was stripped of his clothing and tied to a tree for two or three days in front of the Commandant's office for all POWs to see. During the nights, which were still quite chilly, the guards periodically dashed buckets of cold water on him. Before he died there, the Japanese permitted him a last meal—the scabs from his wrists.

That event was unique during my stay at Narumi. What made it unusual was not the brutality. Japanese brutality remained at a constant level from the beginning. The incident's uniqueness lay in the Navy chief's loss of control. The men who survived as far as Narumi had grown wise in the ways of survival. Only a POW in a state of complete mental derangement, like the chief's, would have knowingly given the Japanese guards the slightest excuse for brutal behavior. Our sense of survival precisely controlled how we behaved around our sadistic masters.

In Japan, opportunities for a POW to stash food away occurred much less frequently than in the Philippines. There was practically no possibility that an American POW could acquire extra food in the Narumi camp because the British controlled the kitchen. Therefore, any additional food had to be found at the factory where the possibilities were less than slim. Nevertheless, a few pickings could be had. American POWs combed the factory grounds for crumbs of food and cigarette butts. Japanese cigarettes had paper filters, thus producing poor butts because most of the tobacco had been consumed. The POWs picked up and carried into camp any kind of food residue that could be found: orange peels and rotten oranges; wild onions and decayed cabbages; the soiled tops of vegetables such as turnips and radishes; an occasional spoiled persimmon or avocado. They even picked up grain that had passed through the horses used at the factory. The recycled grain was available only because there were so few rats and birds. We rarely saw rats at the factory, and birds were almost nonexistent in the Nagoya area. The Japanese were eating both species of wildlife.

Because of the absence of birds, the flea population was out of control. Some small shrubs were literally covered with them like swarms of bees. We did not eat the fleas, but the Japanese did issue some pickled grasshoppers for the soup. We ate them, but I would have preferred grasshoppers dried and crunchy like the dried shrimp we had in the Philippines. Only the final stages of raging hunger could cause anyone to relish soggy grasshoppers floating in his soup.

The great scarcity of food and tobacco in Japan led to a sharp increase in trade in those commodities among the prisoners, an activity rarely seen during my stay in the Philippines. Conversely, trading in items other than food or cigarettes was less intense in Japan than in the Philippines. Though the American POWs were desperately short of wearing apparel, toilet articles, and other personal items lost on board the *Nissyo Maru*, they gave little thought to any of those niceties. In Japan, just staying alive was the name of the game. Since for the majority of men hunger aggravated the addiction to nicotine, only food and tobacco were considered necessary for survival.

In the barracks, trading occurred during the breakfast period and was renewed with our return from work in the late afternoon. Trading in the barracks in the evening did not stop until the Japanese guards conducted the evening *tenko*. Some exchange agreements were made daily on the commuter train going to and from work, but that moving market was hampered by the extremely crowded conditions in the cars.

During working hours at the railway factory, intermittent trading might take place among individuals within a group, but the Japanese normally frowned on communications between different work groups. By far the most important trade center was the *yasumi* shack at the factory during the lunch period. The exchange agreements made there largely determined camp prices and interest rates among the American prisoners for the next twenty-four hours.

Only two food items were normally involved in the trading, steamed grain and small loaves of bread. All other foods were generally unsuitable for trade because of the dreadfully poor quality or the uncertainty of supply. Our steamed grain consisted mostly of a barley-millet mixture we called rice. The rice ration was ideal for trading for two reasons: (1) all prisoners' rice bowls were the same size and thus guaranteed a uniform, easily tradable quantity; and (2) the gummy texture of the cooked grain made it easy to cut into desired fractions without causing the edges to crumble.

The small loaves of bread were issued daily for lunch in the *yasumi* shack at the factory. But the loaves presented some problems in the exchange system. There was the feeling that the bread was overvalued because a loaf seemed to be slightly smaller than a bowl of rice. It was impossible, of course, to compare volume accurately because of the different textures and densities of the two items. Then, too, there was the influence of cultural attitudes. Bread won the allegiance of some simply because of an occidental preference for the loaf as a Western symbol of life. Others felt intuitively that survival lay with the steamed grain. Another problem arose because bread was issued only at noon. Many trading agreements required that the loaves be transported back to camp, an act that was a serious violation of Japanese regulations. I regularly smuggled in half of my loaf and exchanged it for half of Father Reilly's rice. The final solution to the controversy was not an economic one. During the late winter of 1945, B-29s demolished the bakery in Nagoya that supplied the factory, ending the bread issue and thus simplifying the exchange market.

Though most of the traders were hungry people desperately gambling with their lives, a few entrepreneurs were rich enough to participate in the give-and-take of the marketplace in comparative comfort. Some of the affluent prisoners accumulated a considerable supply of food as capital stock that was difficult to maintain because of its perishability. They had to continue lending, to keep juggling the stock to prevent loss of capital by spoilage. To avoid huge debt repayments on a single day, they worked up a complicated schedule of maturity dates. Nevertheless, most of the loans carried interest rates, automatically increasing the amount of capital stock.

Most of those who died failed to consume their daily ration on a regular basis. The POWs who manipulated food rations put themselves at great risk. "Gorgers," who deferred current rations to the future, and "rabbits," who mortgaged future rations to increase current consumption, were flirting with death. At even greater risk were those who gave nicotine a higher priority than food. Most of the men who traded food for cigarettes did not return home.

The gorger loaned part of his daily rations to build up a food supply for a single meal in the future, *Yasumi* Day being the preferred time to receive repayment. The gorger's motive was to enjoy once again the feeling of a full belly. Since the gorger's loans generally earned relatively high interest rates (a half loaf of bread today for a full bowl of rice on *Yasumi* Day), his total consumption of food was greater than that of most POWS. Nevertheless, the gorger's willingness to endure many days of extreme hunger to splurge at one sitting resulted in acute malnutrition.

The prisoners who could not resist the temptation to contract unlimited debt to satisfy their present appetite frequently went bankrupt. They were the rabbits. A rabbit was bankrupt when he would not have enough food to support life if he paid back on schedule all he had borrowed. In short, bankruptcy meant sure and certain death for the rabbit. Though some prisoners favored that type of absolute market discipline, the severity of bankruptcy caused reformers among the POWs to advocate some kind of social welfare for the rabbits. Consequently, an ad hoc group, formed to deal with the bankruptcy problem, established the Rabbit Commission.[9]

The Rabbit Commission acted as receiver of the rabbit's daily rations or other food income and permitted him only that amount the Commission deemed necessary to sustain life. The Commission restructured his debt on a long-term basis, set up a precise schedule of repayment, and saw to it that creditors shared in the debt-discharging process on a prorata basis. Notices of "rabbitcy" were posted, and the Rabbit Commission prohibited everyone from trading with the rabbit under penalty of confiscation of all goods involved in the illegal transaction.

The method of distributing what was called burnt rice afforded the inmates of our camp occasional psychological relief from the torment of existing on the brink of starvation. Burnt rice was the browned, scorched crust that stuck to the metallic interior of the rice cauldrons. Allied prisoners at our camp were divided into twelve sections, four sections per barracks, each section receiving a day's production of burnt rice by turns. Also, there was a distribution to the clinic, and the Japanese took some. Ordinarily the cycle was completed in about two weeks.

In contrast to the desperate condition of the rabbits, those with a helping of burnt rice enjoyed the rare opportunity to feel affluent. The knowledge that his section would eventually receive a ration of burnt rice gave the individual prisoner something to which he could attach his frail hopes and faith. All of us benefitted just knowing that in the near future we could enjoy the notice that came with a bit of luxury.

On any given day, the men in the section scheduled to receive the burnt rice found themselves objects of admiration and envy by their fellow POWs. Though some recipients behaved with pomposity and conceit, most of them responded with a sort of impecunious *noblesse oblige*. After the distribution, the have-nots were prone to engage the fortunate haves in conversation about the burnt rice. As normal young men are "turned on" by discussing sex, so the POWs in our camp were "turned on" by discussing food. The have-nots loved to hear, directly from the lips of the scheduled burnt rice recipient, how he planned to prepare his portion of the scorched crust: he might mix it with tea and allow it to soak overnight to increase the volume; he might blend it into the cardboard (soybean residue) soup until a mushy slurry resulted; or he might convert some of it into sandwiches with soggy-rice fillers to be eaten with a pickled daikon or treated in some other ingenious and delicate manner.

In one respect our health improved with the onset of spring. The coming of warm weather led to gradual recovery from the painful, filthy-looking chilblains most of us suffered during the cold winter of 1944-45. By the early spring my upper front neck and lower chin were almost a solid sore from ear to ear. The chilblains resulted primarily from marching to and standing at the Narumi station on painfully cold mornings. At times, the intense cold caused the greatest suffering during our outside work at the plant; at others, it took its heaviest toll in the heatless barracks.

The shedding of our filthy, nit-ridden winter clothing revealed the frighteningly poor physical condition of the POWs. Except for those swollen with wet beriberi, "skin and bones" was an apt description of almost everyone—exposed rib cages held together by sallow skin that, especially on the back, displayed deadly white splotches, the heralds of starvation. The splotches competed for space with the starlike scars that were remnants of tropical sores incurred in the Philippines. Hollow eyes and distended stomachs hanging to the tops of unsteady, fleshless leg-bones completed the picture of most American POWs in Japan in the spring of 1945. By that time some were losing their eyesight, and a few were nearly blind. The Japanese were reluctant to admit the problem, and in our barracks I recall only one case they accepted. When we were liberated, my malnourished condition was typical of many: I weighed eighty-five pounds.

Given such severe malnutrition, it is not surprising that deviant sexual behavior was not a problem. One of the ex-POWs interviewed by

Donald Knox said that homosexuality was fairly common in his camp in Fukuoka.[10] So far as I know, there was none at Narumi. I believe the POWs in our camp were too starved to be interested in any kind of sex—normal or deviant. Perhaps some sexual activity did occur; if so, I was too distracted trying to survive to recognize it. As a matter of fact, I saw no evidence of homosexuality during my entire imprisonment by the Japanese. Most of the POWs agreed that they had previously overvalued sex, that in reality sex made little sense at best. What was really important was the creative pursuit of *haute cuisine*.

The POWs in our camp devoted much time and energy to the development of recipes and menus. There was keen competition because practically all the prisoners had decided to enter the restaurant business if and when they regained their freedom. Sometimes Japanese guards, during periodic inspections of the barracks, confiscated those records of creative cookery written on scraps of paper, but they were easily reproduced. Some of the exotic recipes suggested the condition of our imaginations, as in the case of the clever Californian who developed an idea he believed would take the States by storm: chocolate-covered hard-boiled eggs.

The year of my life that I left in Japan's industrial heartland was heartbreaking for me. I was surrounded by many things that tantalized the senses and the intellect—the natural beauty of Japan, the power and potential of Japanese industry, the intriguing insights into Japanese culture. But my status as a starving slave laborer made it impossible to enjoy anything about Japan. I could not overcome the craving for food that so utterly defined our existence as POWs. My body, denied essential minerals and nutrients, cried out for physical sustenance so intensely, so single-mindedly, that I could not even think about more subtle, less immediate needs.

12

Fire from the Skies

In Japan in August 1944, the Japanese apparently were serenely confident that the Imperial Wild Eagles (the Japanese Air Force) were invincible. They had completely recovered from General Doolittle's raid of April 1942, of which we knew nothing until after the war. We were not even aware that three of Doolittle's planes had bombed Nagoya. The failure of the United States to bomb Japan in the months and years that followed helped to reestablish Japanese faith in the inviolability of their homeland. In fact, as late as November 1944, the civilian population of Japan was absolutely sure of victory in the war. But in late November and early December our British news source began to pick up hints from newspapers of the American bombing of Tokyo and perhaps adjacent Japanese cities. In mid-December the British obtained from a newspaper a picture and some information about the new American bomber, the B-29. That picture excited us. We reasoned that if Tokyo had been bombed Nagoya would not be far behind, because Nagoya was not only Japan's third largest city (after Tokyo and Osaka) but also one of its most important industrial centers. The Mitsubishi Aircraft Engine Works made Nagoya the center of Japanese aircraft production. During the coming bombing of Japan by the U.S. Army Air Force, Nagoya's industrial sprawl was the number two target, Tokyo, of course, being the first. We did not have long to wait.

From the standpoint of morale, prisoners at the Narumi camp were fortunate to be in such a major target area. The Narumi camp, situated on the southeastern corner of metropolitan Nagoya, was directly in the path of the Air Force's general southeast to northwest approach to the city. All missions over Nagoya were visible from our vantage point, and the sight of those B-29s in the skies probably enabled some POWs to survive the ensuing months of the war.

Some other American and Allied POWs in Japan were not so lucky. For example, Col. E. B. Miller, who was at Zentsuji on the island of Shikoku in the Inland Sea when the bombing of Japan began in the late fall of 1944, did not see a B-29 until March 1945, when a single Super-

196

fortress flew above his camp. Even so, the Colonel's group responded as we did: "It certainly created a great deal of enthusiasm in the camp."[1] Miller and his comrades did not actually see or become aware of the devastation wrought by the huge planes until June, when the group was moved through the Osaka area to a nearby POW camp at Fukui. On their way, the members of Miller's group were so shocked by the destruction in southern Honshu they knew the end of the war was at hand.[2]

Meanwhile, as if preparing Nagoya for the terrible ordeal ahead, nature intervened. In the midafternoon of an early December day, a major earthquake rocked the area. The quake terrified POW workers and Japanese employees alike at the railway factory. We five members of the *haikyu* crew were standing at a doorway to the electric furnaces, having just delivered a carbon stick, when the invisible monster struck. I seemed to be standing on Jell-o, and I was petrified by the unnatural swaying of the great smokestacks (from which the concrete coatings were falling) and by the popping and snapping of broken electric lines. But before I had time to consider any sort of rational response to the situation, a stream of Japanese workers (male and female) poured out of the foundry building, carrying us with them. We were swept into a vacant lot across the street where we all, arms around each other, fell to the ground. On that day nature gave us a taste of the destruction we would soon see in the wake of the bombing runs and also taught us something mysterious about the ties that bind all human beings together, including prisoners and prison keepers.

The earthquake played havoc with the railway factory, flattening a few buildings, throwing assembly lines into disarray, and toppling some smokestacks. The damage would have been much worse, but the Japanese had used rice straw rope as a major structural component in the buildings. The flexibility of the rope no doubt prevented greater losses. John Toland points out that in addition to "crippling a number of munitions plants" and inflicting other industrial damage in the area, the big quake "left a long section of the rail bed in ruin."[3] That meant the train could not run, so we had to walk home, a trek of some ten miles. When we finally got back to the camp after dark, the ill-tempered Commandant, making a bad situation worse, refused to feed us supper because we were late. Our spirits were further depressed by the news that one of our comrades had been killed at the plant in a horrible accident before the quake. A huge power hammer had smashed his head, nearly decapitating him.

By the next day the railroad tracks were repaired, and we returned to work as usual. We could see evidence of the earthquake all along the way to work, and we found extensive damage at the railway factory. Though we had aftershocks from time to time throughout the winter of 1944-45, they did no further harm.

The destruction in Nagoya's future would come from another source. We first saw those beautiful Boeing Superfortresses on a *yasumi* day in mid-December 1944. Flying at about thirty thousand feet, the B-29s looked like toys floating in their vapor trails. We instantly recognized them because we had seen and memorized a newspaper photograph. Their presence high above us sent a thrill through our bodies to our very souls. After all, many of us in the American barracks were members of the U.S. Army Air Corps or service companies attached to the Air Corps. Even though I was not pious, with a little encouragement I could easily have seen the Virgin Mary hovering over the lead plane in that majestic V-formation.[4]

Since most of the air raids on Nagoya in December 1944 and January 1945 were in daylight, we were usually working when the first warnings came. Fearing possible POW escape and sabotage, the Japanese would immediately round us up and hurriedly march us to the train station to be sent back to camp. We were nearly always in camp by the time the huge Air Force birds arrived. A few times, however, the B-29s appeared over the city before we could reach home. That always panicked our Japanese guards, who stopped the train, locked us in the cars, and ran to a nearby air-raid shelter. The train's guard crew was led by a skinny stickman, who wore a black medieval-style suit that made him look like a spider. In fact, we called him "Spider." We would laugh at him when he and his minions returned to the train from the safety of their shelter. The laughter of the lowly POWs always sent him into a rage, causing him to whack the nearest prisoners with his cudgel.

During the early period of the bombing, the Japanese generally punished American POWs after each raid. Two types of punishment were meted out: physical beatings and a lowered living standard. A favorite penalty was to require us to march single file past one of their stronger and more brutish guards, who would slap us or hit us with some object. I shall never forget Joe Louis, one of the meanest guards, hitting us in the face, one after the other, with a shoe. Other punishments included denying us heat in the barracks during cold weather and reducing our food rations. There was no central heating control, but we were not permitted to build fires in the barracks braziers for several days, even though we had a supply of coke we had been permitted to bring from the factory for heating. The reduction in food after the raids threatened us with immediate starvation since our rations could not be noticeably reduced without eliminating our scanty issue completely. As the devastating incendiary raids increased in the late winter and early spring, mass punishment of POWs in our camp declined. Perhaps the Japanese learned that abusing helpless prisoners of war was not going to stop the B-29s.

Throughout the first two months of high-altitude precision bombing, POWs in our camp became disillusioned. As far as we could determine, the big demolition bombs were not hitting the targets. After most raids we could see large holes along the tracks between the camp and the plant where the bombs had obviously missed utility plants, road and railroad junctions, and bridges. The only thing the B-29s hit with any consistency from thirty thousand feet was rice paddies, and we wondered if the Air Force could starve the enemy into submission by blowing up their food source literally at the root.

Once during the period of high-altitude precision bombing (December 1944 to February 1945), the B-29s hit our camp at Narumi, probably accidentally. Our captors had not, of course, marked our POW camp, another instance of their violation of the Geneva Convention. An American bomb landed near our barracks, sending large rocks through the roof and the covered walkway to the latrine. I was just emerging from the latrine when debris from the shattered walkway cover knocked me down, but I was not seriously injured. Fortunately, none of the injuries sustained by the American POWs was severe. The bomb did heavier damage to the British barracks and caused some serious injuries but no deaths. The only deaths were Japanese. A group outside the guards' shack at the front gate watching the bombing was wiped out along with the shack.

Living through the bombing of our camp, I was, oddly enough, absolutely unafraid. In the Philippines I had experienced genuine terror during Japanese bombings. Most of the other American POWs at Narumi had the same curious response; we had no fear of the American bombers. Our hatred of the Japanese, generated by three years of atrocities and indignities, outweighed any anxiety over American bombs. We worshipped the B-29s to the same degree the Japanese feared them. Then, too, we saw in the B-29s our only hope of survival. By the time the bombing began, we were slipping into the last stages of functional starvation. If the B-29s did not bring Japan to her knees, we knew that death would come for us soon. Even though there were periods of low morale, the American bombing of Japan continued to uplift us and encourage our hopes for an end to the war.

The high-altitude precision bombing was probably more effective than we realized. We, of course, were unaware of the damage inflicted on the sprawling Mitsubishi complex, the principal target in Nagoya, or of the problems resulting from attempts to decentralize and relocate units of that massive plant to adjacent areas.[5] We did not know that the first raid on Nagoya (December 13), which seemed rather futile to us, severely impaired some of the Mitsubishi units. Mitsubishi continued to be the major target in the subsequent raids on Nagoya in December. We also knew nothing of the debate within the high command of the U.S. Army Air Force in Washington over bombing policy in Japan—high-level precision bombing or low-level incendiary bombing. The debate revealed much dissatisfaction with the results of precision bombing and a growing sentiment at the White House and among powerful members of the Air Force for a switch to the mass bombing of cities.[6]

Nor did we know that Nagoya had been chosen as the first test target in the proposed experiment with incendiary bombing. On January 3, 1945, ninety-seven B-29 Superfortresses dropped napalm bombs that ignited seventy-five scattered fires. The Air Force viewed the Nagoya test as inconclusive.[7] Having carried out the special directive for the Nagoya incendiary test, Gen. Haywood Hansell, commander of the Air Force bombers over Japan, returned to his top priority—precision bombing. His bombers hit the Mitsubishi plants in Nagoya again on January 14. Though Hansell believed his precision bombing was improving rapidly, his superiors were not impressed. On January 20, 1945, Gen. Curtis LeMay replaced Hansell as head of the B-29 bombing of Japan.[8]

LeMay continued high-altitude precision bombing during the remainder of January, sustaining significant losses over heavily defended Tokyo and Nagoya where Japanese fighters had improved their defensive techniques. The increased aircraft losses led Washington authorities to order another big incendiary test raid on an industrial center. They chose Kobe. The Kobe test raid of February 4 was much more successful than the Nagoya test of January 3. Meanwhile, LeMay returned to precision bombing of Japanese aircraft plants to support indirectly the invasion of Iwo Jima. Some of the most important action of the series was his bombing of the Mitsubishi plants in Nagoya.[9]

On February 19, 1945, Air Force headquarters directed General LeMay to give a higher priority to new test incendiary raids than to precision bombing. On February 25, he carried out the third incendiary test—a raid against Tokyo—with the largest force of B-29s used in a single raid so far. The damage was substantial. But the event that led to the triumph of incendiary bombing came on March 4, when a large flight of bombers utterly failed in a daylight, high-altitude precision attack on an aircraft plant in Tokyo.

As a result of the failed raid, General LeMay "conceived a major and dramatic change in tactics."[10] He decided to remove most of the gunners, guns, and ammunition from a group of B-29s to increase bomb load and to attack in single file at low altitudes (five thousand to eight thousand feet). To implement his newly conceived plan, LeMay carried out five large fire raids, beginning with the first great Tokyo firebombing. On March 10, the Superfortresses burned a big swatch of the city, killing perhaps one hundred thousand people. The third and fourth raids struck Osaka and Kobe on March 14 and 17, respectively. During that series of bombings, the war moved close to home again. Two of the five incendiary raids were on Nagoya. On March 12, 285 B-29s brought devastating fire over Nagoya, dropping seventeen hundred tons of napalm bombs. Then late in March, 290 bombers hit Nagoya with eighteen hundred tons of napalm.[11]

According to Carl Berger, General LeMay was so pleased with the Nagoya raids that following the second one he issued a statement to his bomber crews, praising them highly for their work. Also, immediately following that raid (the fifth of the series), Gen. Lauris Norstad, Chief of Staff, Twentieth Air Force, declared in a Washington press conference that the destruction caused by the five raids was "the greatest ever inflicted upon any people" within such a limited period of time. He praised General LeMay "for solving an acute operational problem by using high altitude Superfortresses at low level to achieve the unloading of a large tonnage of bombs in a short time."[12]

Civilian deaths resulting from the two March fire raids on Nagoya were far fewer than in the March 10 raid on Tokyo because the Nagoya bombing was concentrated on the downtown industrial center where approximately five square miles were destroyed.[13] Nevertheless, the number killed was substantial to the citizens of Nagoya, as rumors circulating at the factory made clear. Some Japanese workers told POWs horror stories about the raids, including accounts of the deaths of family members and friends. At that time we received our first inkling that civilians, including some members of the railway workers' families, were beginning to flee from the city to the countryside. Okadora was the only one of our four Japanese bosses who talked to us about the raids. He described terrible ruin, but he still did not seem bitter toward us.

During the two raids, we were in our barracks, which was not hit. The fires downtown lit up the area like a Christmas tree. The days after each raid were almost dark because of the pall of smoke hanging over the city. As we passed through some of the leveled areas on our way to work on both postraid days, we hoped to find the railway factory in the same condition. No such luck. In spite of heavy damage, there it stood. Located along the edge of the devastated area, it was not yet an important target.

My crew, the *haikyu*, searched the ashes of burned buildings in an attempt to salvage usable materials. I shall never forget the day we were engaged in that salvage work under Sourpuss, our head honcho. He was mean, short-tempered, and vindictive. He worked the hell out of us, but he also worked hard himself. Several times he appeared close to reverting to his old practice of violently kicking us, but he restrained himself. Surprisingly, he did not lay a finger on members of his American *haikyu* crew, for whom he had come to have grudging respect.

The intensity of the all-out fire raids on Japanese cities was reduced during April because the supply of napalm bombs had been depleted and, additionally, the Air Force had to give support to the Okinawa invasion. Nevertheless, the Okinawa diversion did not bring the air attack on Japan to a complete halt. In early April, the Air Force high command in Washington issued a directive for three phases of air raids, each of which included Nagoya. The raids attacked (1) specific aircraft engine plants, including the Mitsubishi plants in Nagoya; (2) designated urban areas in four cities, including Nagoya; and (3) designated targets in seven cities, including Nagoya, to be attacked when targets in (1) and (2) had been destroyed.[14] Consequently, the air attacks on Nagoya (incendiary raids as well as high-level precision bombing) continued hot and heavy through April and early May, during which our plant sustained further damage. For a particularly spectacular high-altitude precision raid on Nagoya on April 7, the Mitsubishi Aircraft Engine Works was the main target.[15] In fact, high-level B-29 traffic—precision bombing, observation planes, and single-plane dump bombing—continued despite the predominance of incendiary mass-bombing after the successful March 10 raid on Tokyo.

During the late winter and early spring of 1945, the single-plane dump bombing over Nagoya became an effective instrument of psychological and physical warfare. On bad-weather nights when the city was closed in by clouds and fog, a lone B-29 would fly over and indiscriminately drop a load of demolition bombs, sometimes wiping out a block or two in a residential district. So frightening was the sound of the "Lone Ranger" to civilians that many Nagoya families spent their evenings in waterlogged and chilly air-raid shelters, thus enduring additional stress imposed by the U.S. Air Force during the first half of 1945. We knew that the Lone Ranger was a specter in civilians' nightmares because of our conversations with Japanese workers at the factory. As for the American POWs, it was hats off to the Lone Ranger.

During the Okinawa-mission period, LeMay was rapidly building up his B-29 forces as new wings arrived. When Admiral Nimitz released LeMay's bombers from the Okinawa mission on May 11, the General was ready to intensify his fiery presence over Japan. He chose Nagoya as the first target of his new series of massive fire attacks. On May 14 and 16, nearly five hundred Superfortresses dropped a total of sixty-one hundred tons of napalm bombs on the city, the primary target being the huge Mitsubishi complex. The two raids destroyed about seven square miles of the city, producing another mass exodus.[16] When LeMay had completed his April-May series, "Japan's six most important industrial cities—Tokyo, Nagoya, Kobe, Osaka, Yokohama and Kawasaki—lay in ruins."[17]

As the incendiary bombing continued through mid-May 1945, when fire rained from the sky over Nagoya, the days were darkened with smoke, but the nighttime skyline was bright with flames raging through newly bombed portions of the city. To us on the outskirts of the city, watching the fires and smelling the acrid smoke, it seemed that nothing could have survived those cataclysmic events. Yet our bomb-scarred factory still functioned. After all, the Superforts were after bigger game, like the Mitsubishi complex. We continued making and repairing steam locomotives and doing some war work, including producing a few *shinyo* (suicide boats).

Morale among the Japanese workers at the factory had plummeted to a new low. Again, they shared with POWs grim tales of the fire raids. Among the stories related to American POWs at the railway plant were heart-breaking tales of families being split up as thousands fled from the city to the countryside or to the far north. I recall an occasion when our *haikyu* crew, soon after the mid-May raids, was sent to help carry the possessions of factory families (mostly women and children) to an adjacent railway station for their exodus from Nagoya. Some of them were going as far away as Hokkaido. Despite my hatred of the Japanese, the pathetic children made me sad. During the bombing of Japan, ten million people from the cities sought safety in the countryside, causing untold problems and hardships for the government and for them.[18] Each encounter with those displaced persons undermined my joy at the performance of the American bombers. Their depression and apprehension forced me to confront the reality that my future was even more insecure than theirs. It seemed that our lot as POWs depended more on the survival of the Japanese than on the success of the bombing raids. If they starved, we starved.

By May, even the iron-hearted stickmen appeared to have lost zest for their jobs. The principal function of the stickmen, some of whom apparently were agents of the Home Ministry's "thought police," was to put down threats to production, including loafing, rowdyism, excessive complaints, and outright sabotage.[19] They now seemed less concerned with keeping lazy Japanese on the job than wreaking vengeance on the American POWs for the air raids. Though punishment for specific air raids had declined in the Narumi camp, at the plant the stickmen and military guards became more cruel after the big incendiary raids. Japanese authorities at the factory were becoming short-tempered because of the declining Japanese fortunes in the war, the American bombing of Japan, and the sagging production as a result of the bombing. It was sometimes obvious that the stickmen, superior in authority to the military guards, instigated attacks on individual POWs and stood by while the brutal peasant soldiers nearly beat Americans to death. Under the goading of the stickmen, the military guards became demons. If an American POW should fall, the guard would stamp his stomach and genitals with his boots. Americans knew that they must stay on their feet or, if knocked down, quickly get up to avoid serious injury or even death. In the attacks on the POWs, the guards seemed to lose control of themselves as they worked their emotions into a frenzy. None of the Narumi camp members was killed in the beatings, but some were severely injured.

Oddly enough, the increasingly vicious attitude of the Japanese stickmen because of the American bombing was not echoed by our fellow Japanese factory workers. From the beginning of our work there, most of the Japanese laborers seemed as intimidated by the stickmen and military guards as we were. Certainly no feeling of solidarity existed between the POWs and the Japanese workers. But as things got worse during the spring and summer of 1945, I sensed that a mutual longing for the war to end was forming a basis of comradeship. Relations between the members of our *haikyu* crew and our honchos remained about the same during those trying times, except for Sourpuss. His attitude toward Americans worsened as Japan's prospects in the war declined. He looked for opportunities to lash out at Americans with his tongue, fists, and feet. Though he did not strike any members of the *haikyu* crew, he used self-control for reasons other than honoring our humanity. Since he came to consider us his valuable personal possessions, he learned to vent his abusive wrath on others. The American bombing merely justified to Sourpuss his original hatred and vindictive treatment of Americans.

There is no doubt in my mind that by the end of the first series of General LeMay's mass incendiary raids in March, most Japanese at the plant wanted the war to cease immediately, even if it meant defeat. Not only were many of them working at jobs they hated; their actual wages were declining because of the dramatic wartime inflation. At the war's close, the factory employees were earning only 40 percent of what they had earned in the mid-1930s. For many, the growing scarcity of food was becoming unbearable. In May 1945, food, clothing, and shelter were barely at subsistence levels. By V-J Day, the American bombers had destroyed almost 24 percent of Japanese dwellings.[20] We could see that the health of the workers was declining. We could imagine the disastrous effects of the bombing on health care services and food supplies. All this brought further apprehension to POWs, many of whom were dying of starvation. We knew that if malnutrition continued to grow among the Japanese, the death rate would accelerate among the POWs. When summer arrived, both POWs and Japanese workers realized that their very lives depended on a quick end to the war. The vast majority of Japanese probably felt relieved by the surrender, which put a stop to the War Ministry's proposal of May 1945 that a major portion of the potato crop be converted into fuel for the Japanese Air Force.[21] For the Japanese, survival was less likely under the policies of their own government than under the bomb bay doors of the American Air Force.

In June and July, the pace of the U.S. Air Force bombing in the Nagoya area slowed down as LeMay turned to incendiary raids on smaller cities. Yet, intermittent attacks, both high-altitude precision and low-level incendiary raids, continued. By now, resistance from Japanese fighters and antiaircraft emplacements had decreased sharply. At the same time, the U.S. Air Force's long-range fighter, the P-51, was establishing a familiar presence in the Nagoya skies, affording superior protection for the B-29s against what resistance was left. In Nagoya in the summer of 1945, the words *B-Ni Ju Ku takusan* (many B-29s) had become the most feared phrase in the Japanese language. When the blue air-warning flag was replaced by the red, terror ran through the civilian population: "By this time, the Japanese people had come to dread the Superfortress more than any other American weapon. . . . It was the major air raids of the B-29 which psychologically affected the opinion among all classes of the population that the war was lost."[22]

I shall never forget an event reflecting both the reversal of Japanese fortunes and the great distance between our two cultures. My *haikyu* crew frequently came into contact with a young Japanese worker whose position and status were unclear. Our four Japanese honchos obviously knew him well and respected him. Perhaps his father or some other relative had political clout at the plant. Even Sourpuss, our bad-tempered senior honcho, was as gentle as a songbird around the young fellow. As time passed, this enigmatic figure seemed to enjoy talking with us Americans. In fact, he and I came as near true friendship as enemies could. He was more gregarious and genial around us than we might have expected a Japanese to be at that time. He and I found that we had a several common interests. He asked many questions about life in America and, in turn, explained various aspects of Japanese life to me. Since he could speak a little English and I a little Japanese, I looked forward to our simple but enjoyable conversations.

After a while my Japanese friend disappeared. I wondered what had happened to him, but the honchos feigned ignorance. Some weeks later a mysterious figure showed up at the plant wearing strange regalia, a black robe to which were attached colorful streamers and a headdress that made him look like a ghost in the Noh theater. As he walked through our part of the factory, everyone—military guards, stickmen, Japanese workers—stood awed as if in the presence of a divinity. When he approached the area where we were standing, I recognized him. It was my missing friend. I did not dare speak to him, and he walked on as if in a trance. Our honchos told us that he had been away training to be a suicide pilot. I never saw him again. I suppose that I am one of few Americans ever to have had as a friend a Japanese kamikaze pilot.

The numerical makeup of the *haikyu* detail—prisoners and honchos —remained constant until late July. By then much of the factory had been destroyed. Eventually, the five POWs on our supply detail were assigned to different projects. I was put to work in the boiler factory with some Koreans who, though they hated the Japanese, apparently despised me. We were using a massive drill, and the Koreans forced me to do most of the heavy work. I was so weak and underweight that I had difficulty lifting the drill; I knew that I would not last long. In desperation, I looked for a new assignment and fortunately landed a job with the crew constructing an air-raid shelter at the camp.

As a result of the stepped-up American bombing of Japan during the winter and early spring of 1944-45, the Japanese decided to construct a system of air-raid shelters connected by a tunnel in the hill under our camp. The Japanese cared nothing about our safety. They wanted to provide shelters for civilians in the neighborhood and Japanese personnel at the camp. Construction of the shelter complex was initiated in late May or early June, using American POWs exclusively. Though only three or four POWs were involved in this project in the beginning, there was a gradual increase until late July when construction was suddenly expanded. I never knew why the Americans were chosen to construct the air-raid shelter rather than the British, who up until then held a monopoly on internal camp jobs. The Japanese may have chosen the Americans because in the beginning they considered the project one of extremely hard labor; assignment to the shelter project was probably considered further punishment for the American bombing of Japan.

For some unknown reason, the Japanese soon lost their enthusiasm for the shelter project, permitting the workers to drift along with construction without interference. They eventually left the supervision of the project entirely to the Americans and assumed a laissez-faire attitude toward the entire undertaking. Because the prisoners were left to work at their own pace, the shelter project provided an opportunity for the weaker workers to recuperate.

For a short time in the summer of 1945, I worked on the camp air-raid detail. One of my duties was to help transport our dead comrades to the crematorium about three miles away. Three of us, supervised by a camp guard, pulled and pushed a rickety two-wheel cart containing the corpses. The wheels, loose on the ungreased axles, wobbled crazily and produced a weird noise. As we three walking skeletons, wearing unsightly rags, dragged our dead comrades across the back country roads in the very shadows of the sky-scraping smokestacks of Nagoya, the Japanese civilians we met paid little attention, apparently regarding the scene as commonplace.

One of the cadavers I helped to haul to the crematorium was a friend of mine, a Navy chief, who literally traded his life for cigarettes. Despite pleas from his friends and his promises to reform, he continued to trade a good part of his food ration for tobacco. In short, he chose starvation for a few more drags of his precious cigarettes.

My new position turned out to be just what I had hoped for—a way to survive awhile longer. The Japanese did not bother us, and we worked just enough to make it appear to be a legitimate job. From all indications, it seemed the situation could continue indefinitely, but we were all aware of the unpredictability of the Japanese. The status quo continued for only two weeks until other events interrupted the work routine of the shelter project.

First, B-29s completely destroyed the railway factory the first week in August. Some of the displaced workers were for a time sent out daily to scattered projects in the Nagoya area. Others were kept in camp and assigned to the air-raid shelter project. With the vastly increased supply of labor, the special advantages and prestige that had been attached to the air-raid shelter jobs disappeared quickly. By that time the Japanese had completely lost interest in the shelter, and it, like the outside jobs, had become a make-work project. Actually, the outside jobs were now attractive because few required much work, and they were located in the suburban areas outside the dirty industrial center of Nagoya.

The Japanese pretended that this particular use of personnel was merely an interlude before making new permanent outside work assignments. Ostensibly, the interim period was to be used to accelerate construction of the air-raid shelter. Yet the failure of the Japanese to show further interest in the project belied the declared goal and purpose. Many of the POWs believed (or at least hoped) that the Japanese were preparing for surrender. All signs indicated that they had no intention of reviving a permanent outside work project. Wild rumors of American landings swept the camp daily, and though we recognized rumors for what they were, we allowed ourselves to believe that the end was near.

Sometime in early August, just two or three days before the final destruction of the railway factory, a memorable event occurred. About midday a lone B-29, producing silver contrails because of its high altitude, flew over Nagoya, passing almost directly above the factory. That was not unusual; the Air Force had been sending single observation planes over Nagoya for a long time, especially after major raids. The number of observation flights had increased from April on, as the magnificent P-51s easily outmaneuvered and downed Japanese fighters and knocked out antiaircraft emplacements.

On that occasion, however, the B-29 dropped leaflets. So far as we POWs knew, leaflets had not been dropped in the Nagoya area before. We did not know that in mid-May, the U.S. Air Force had begun to engage in psychological warfare over Japan with leaflets, carrying some with bomb runs. But in late July, as General LeMay directed the brunt of B-29 bombing to fifty-eight smaller Japanese cities, leaflets containing a list of those to be bombed during a given series were dropped on the cities before the bombings, warning the people to evacuate.[23] The leaflets dropped on Nagoya apparently were different. As the sheets of paper drifted into the plant area, the military guards and stickmen excitedly rushed around gathering them up and ordering Japanese workmen not to touch them. Some of the workers did snatch leaflets, however, and the next day revealed the contents to the American POWs. The leaflets purportedly warned the inhabitants of fourteen major cities, including Nagoya, that the cities on the list were scheduled to be hit with an entirely new kind of bomb, one with unimaginable force. No POW, so far as I could learn, actually read the leaflet. We naturally assumed that the Americans had developed a large new conventional bomb—a "blockbuster." Not until after the end of the war did we attach great importance to that leaflet.

Near mid-August, having spent two weeks on the air-raid shelter project, a second routine-interrupting event occurred. The Japanese discontinued all work details. Everyone remained in camp for two full days as a sense of expectancy grew. We knew that something of tremendous significance must have occurred to disrupt the normal schedule so completely. On the morning of the third day, the camp Commandant announced the surrender of the Japanese. Soon after the surrender, we learned about the destruction of Hiroshima and Nagasaki. Though the leaflet might have been just another of LeMay's warnings of incendiary raids, we assumed, after the fact, that it contained an "atomic bomb" list and that had the war not ended when it did Nagoya might well have been next.

After nearly a year's forced labor under the Japanese, we Americans (along with our British allies) were deprived of our jobs by the American bombing. None of us was sorry. Even under the best conditions, working at the railroad factory was only slightly better than working in Hell. Our pay had been a starvation diet and our retirement plan only a trip to the crematorium. The Japanese policy of slowly but surely starving us to death continued to baffle me to the end. Though food was scarce in Japan during 1944-45, the extra amount required to sustain the strength and health of slave laborers would have been unnoticed among Japan's population of millions. If we had been given an adequate food ration, the Japanese would have profited because of our greater capacity for work. After all, the average American POW was not only larger and stronger than the average Japanese worker, but also superior in mechanical and technical skills.

Yet the Japanese, in both Japan and the Philippines, rarely seemed to value the work or working capabilities of the skilled Americans. When they did, in rare instances, recognize the superior skills of their prisoners, they almost never rewarded them. The only one of our honchos who came to appreciate the skills of the *haikyu* crew was Sourpuss; but as for rewards, that vicious little Japanese tyrant never gave us as much as a kind word. Okadora, of course, esteemed us highly but not because of our labor skills. That gentle soul liked us because we were people.

Any understanding the Japanese might have developed of our actual or potential productivity was outweighed by their need to punish us. On the whole, they seemed to feel that inflicting pain on prisoners of war was necessary to maintain order, discipline, and proper respect. On the rare occasions when the Japanese befriended POWs, it was clear that they viewed themselves as naughty children. They seemed to feel guilty about having permitted compassion for their fellow-man to come before duty to their fatherland. One must remember, however, that it took great courage for a Japanese to extend the smallest humane gesture to the enemy. Apparently, the authorities encouraged the notion among the general population that such action constituted a serious affront to the Emperor's divinity. Also, such a gesture by a Japanese invited severe punishment. Our Blessed Lady of the Executives' Mess was obviously under the pressure of great fear when she courageously extended a helping hand to us. The grand exception to this generalization was Okadora, the *haikyu* crew's beloved number two honcho. He acted without fear or expectation of reward.

By August the prisoners in our camp were drained of energy and near starvation. Those who had survived were clinging to life by their fingernails. Donald Knox's summary description of American POWs in Japan at that time accurately described our predicament in Nagoya:

> More important than their slow physical deterioration, the treatment they received in Japan began to work on the minds and spirits of the prisoners. The threads which precariously laced this captive community together began to unravel. Unable to prevail, the human spirit now endured and hoped only to survive. Under the Japanese, life had always been flint hard. Now, in Japan, it became more and more difficult, and by the summer of 1945 it verged on the impossible.[24]

One survivor interviewed by Knox suggests the extent to which the effort to survive challenged one's humanity: "At the end there was very little decency or human dignity left. Humanity had long since departed from camp. Human worth had disappeared. We were just animals and that's all it amounted to."[25]

The bombing of Japan had the double effect of worsening the lot of POWs and dramatically weakening the enemy. From the beginning of internment in Nagoya until the bombing began in mid-December 1944, all POWs in the Narumi camp were subjected to standard Japanese treatment—hard work, little food, inadequate health care. The bombing of Nagoya, however, increased the pressures on American prisoners of war. Not only did they suffer punishment because of the American raids, but the economic and social disruption produced among the Japanese by the bombing also directly and indirectly made their lives much harder. For example, as supplies grew more and more scarce, the prison administrators found it easier to justify reducing rations. In addition, factory management leaned more and more heavily on slave labor as the paid labor force grew less reliable. Yet the bombing raised POW morale because it was clearly forcing the war to an end.

Because the atomic bombing of Hiroshima and Nagasaki monopolized the press's attention for so long, most Americans lost sight of the crucial importance of the conventional B-29 bombing raids in the defeat of Japan. The attention once focused on the destruction of Japanese cities by massive flights of B-29s was soon refocused on the atomic bombs and the international political questions they raised. And there was the glamour, too. The conventional demolition and incendiary bombs just could not compete with the fascination generated by the mysterious new technology. In the atomic furnace at Hiroshima, Godzilla was born. By the time of the attack on Hiroshima on August 6, the Japanese nation was already on the brink of total collapse, thanks to the *B-Ni Ju Ku*s (B-29s).

Even today, the American public seems to believe that Japan, still strong in the summer of 1945, was abruptly brought to its knees by two atomic bombs. Supposedly a raging war likely to continue for an indefinite time was suddenly stopped by the nuclear explosions at Hiroshima and Nagasaki. The facts are that Japan was in a state of collapse by July and that the vast majority of the Japanese people were psychologically ready for—and actually in favor of—surrender. At the end of the war, the people in Nagoya did not demonstrate any awareness of the fate of Hiroshima. Instead, they thought the surrender was a product of their wrecked city and wrecked lives. Most Americans, familiar with scenes of Hiroshima following the atomic blast, are not aware that by July 1945 the major Japanese cities already resembled postatomic Hiroshima. Americans often quote widely varying figures about the casualties at Hiroshima, but few are aware that larger numbers of Japanese were killed or wounded during the conventional bombing of other Japanese cities.

The major contribution of the atomic explosions of Hiroshima and Nagasaki may have been in providing the most powerful elements of the Japanese military a justification for surrender with minimum loss of face. After all, no one could expect the Bushido spirit to prevail in the face of the new atomic peril. The samurai had been struck down by the divine winds of the nuclear explosions. Had the atomic bombs not been dropped, it is possible that fanatical Japanese military leaders would have been able to prolong the war indefinitely despite the suffering of the people. In that scenario of national hara-kiri, millions of Japanese, hundreds of thousands of American and other Allied servicemen and, most important to me, all of the thirty thousand Allied prisoners of war in Japan would have died.

The bombing of Japan continued for ten months, November to August 1944-45. During that time, the American Air Force dropped thousands of tons of demolition and incendiary bombs on Nagoya. As a resident of one of the most heavily bombed cities in World War II, I had enough fireworks entertainment to last me a lifetime. Today, fireworks of any kind, whether it is the lone kid in the street shooting a firecracker or a giant display on an army base, frighten me. I have a maddening intolerance for this particular American inanity, which always brings back memories of a time long ago in Nagoya, Japan, when the game of fireworks was played for keeps.

13

Liberation

The U.S. Army Air Force's destruction of the Japanese railway system's main factory led to the abandonment of the site and reassignment of all POWs either to the air-raid shelter detail in our camp or to scattered small projects in the Nagoya suburbs. A week later the work assignments, both of which had become merely make-work activities, were canceled, and for two days the POWs remained in camp with nothing to do. We treated them as *yasumi* days, i.e., sleeping, lounging, doing laundry, and scratching flea bites.

At 8:30 on the morning of the third workless day, a guard came up to the American barracks and informed us that all prisoners were to go to their tatami places, there to await an important announcement from the camp Commandant. Quietly but with great excitement, we quickly went to our assigned spaces. It was obvious that everyone was expecting an official statement that the war was over, but no one was saying it out loud as if that would burst the bubble of hope. There were plenty of whispers and knowing glances as we waited and listened.

About 9:00 A.M. we heard from the first British barracks a loud roar that sounded like shouts of joy. In the American barracks, the effect of the noise was a silence so complete that we appeared to be deaf-mutes. With pounding hearts and tense expressions, we waited for a similar roar from the second British barracks, which was next to ours. We did not have long to wait: since they were closer, the second British group's bellow was even louder than the first. Now the tension was greater. My heart beat so hard that it jolted my whole body. It occurred to me that, given our condition, heart attacks might be a real possibility. The tension rose even higher as the Japanese interpreter, accompanied by a guard, entered the American barracks. Breathing seemed to stop as he called out, "The Commandant wishes me to announce that the war is over. You will remain here in this camp until exchanges of prisoners of war can be made."

At that, the pent-up emotions of the American POWs broke loose. It was like Yankee Stadium at World Series time. The interpreter and guard wheeled around and hurriedly left, but not before a chorus of shouts from the Americans bombarded them: "We won the war! We won the war!" Then everyone jumped up from his tatami and began greeting his fellow POWs with shouts of joy, backslapping, and even hugging. The Commandant ordered the American and British officers to report to his office immediately. They told us later that when they arrived, the Commandant, like a reptile shedding its skin, cast off his former hostility and humbly surrendered the prison camp to the four Allied officers (one British and three Americans). As he surrendered, the Japanese officer bowed deeply and tendered his samurai sword to Father Reilly, the American chaplain and highest ranking Allied officer. I do not recall what happened to the sword. I feel certain that Father Reilly did not have it when we left the prison camp. In fact, I do not believe any American POW carried the sword out of camp. At the time we placed little value on things we could not eat or smoke. On the other hand, I am sure that the sword was not returned to the Commandant. The victor returns the sword to the vanquished only when the heroic traits of the latter have earned it, but the Commandant of the Narumi camp had no such qualities. He lacked all nobility.

As part of his act of submission to the Allied officers, the Commandant surrendered the entire camp, including the keys to the food storage house, and gave them control over all Japanese personnel and weapons. He asked for and was granted permission to retain arms for the guards, ostensibly to protect the *ex*-POWs from civilians once the camp was opened. Following the surrender, the Commandant argued that since he and his personnel were now prisoners of war they should be entitled under the Geneva Convention to food and shelter. That, ironically, was the first indication he had given that he knew the terms of the Geneva Convention. Of course his demands were granted; the Commandant continued to occupy his quarters until we left the camp, but the guards no longer hassled the POWs. All of the brutal guards except one had been hurriedly transferred on the eve of the surrender. Old Joe Louis, who used to beat us following American air raids, disappeared as if swept up by the divine winds. Camp commanders had received orders from Tokyo to transfer or otherwise get rid of guards who had abused prisoners of war. Apparently, some camp commanders took the initiative in getting rid of their abusive guards even before the order came from Tokyo. The single brute remaining in our camp was probably left there because of bureaucratic oversight.[1]

At the time of his surrender, the Commandant told the American officers that he had been ordered by Tokyo authorities to inform the Allied POWs that they were to remain in their camps until International

Red Cross representatives came to deliver them to the Allied armed forces. He predicted that it would be several days before the Red Cross arrived.[2]

During the waiting period, an unspoken understanding developed that the Commandant and the guards would no longer have authority over Allied personnel, who would now be under the control of their respective officers. But American officers made little effort to assume control. One lieutenant attempted to exercise authority but failed utterly. For example, he ordered that no one leave camp. In fact, most of us left the camp whenever we wanted to. We spent much of our time roaming the countryside. On the other hand, Father Reilly and the American doctor, both of whom were reluctant to impose military discipline on their fellow POWs, were able to exert considerable influence over the Americans through positive leadership and persuasion but made no attempt to confine them to the camp. Father Reilly did express concern, however, that our running around the countryside might be unsafe. As yet, no one had officially tested the civilians' reaction to the surrender. No Japanese official or guard attempted to prevent us from leaving the compound, although Japanese MPs soon ringed the camp, ostensibly for our protection should the civilians prove hostile. We knew that the MP protection was unnecessary. On our excursions outside the camp, we felt no fear of the local people. It soon became obvious that they were ecstatic that the war was over, acting as if they were as happy as the POWs. They were friendly and hospitable to us as well as humble and contrite. There was absolutely no danger that Japanese civilians would attack the Narumi POW camp.

My contact with the people made it clear that the meekness and kindness displayed toward us were motivated by (1) joy that the war was over, (2) fear of General MacArthur and uncertainty about American policy toward conquered Japan, and (3) the sense that submissiveness disarms the conqueror. Whatever the reason, their pleasant attitude indicated that the Japanese had enormous resilience after adversity.

In the countryside we were looking primarily for food, but the joy of being free again was another motivation for going outside the camp. Most of the farmers in the area still had a few chickens and eggs, which caught our attention. So that we could trade with the farmers, we helped ourselves to the camp food supply: rice, millet, barley, and soybeans. However, trade goods were not really necessary in dealing with the civilians; their fear of us was so great they were ready to give us whatever we wanted without anything in return. Since we had items to trade, our pride would not permit us to accept goods from the Japanese without pay. So far as I know, none of the POWs mistreated civilians in any way;

there was no physical assault against any Japanese person, male or female. Suddenly released ex-POWs, who had been without female companionship for a long time, might have been expected to engage in sexual abuse of the native women. But that did not happen for two reasons: the POWs had not regained the sexual urges lost because of starvation, and those who had survived the terrible ordeal of Japanese imprisonment were too highly self-disciplined to commit sexual or other crimes. Their determination to return home superseded everything else.

As usual, the British were able to establish order much more effectively than the Americans. They did not roam the countryside as much as we did. The British doctor, their only officer, and their army noncoms were aggressive in maintaining discipline.

Soon after the surrender to the Allied officers, the Commandant had red crosses painted on the roofs of all camp buildings, opened the camp store, and paid our officers a lump sum of money declared to be our accumulated wages. We had been paid nothing by the Japanese since our capture on Bataan. All of those things were supposed to have been carried out from the beginning under the requirements of the Geneva Convention. When in January 1945 American bombers hit our camp, it was not marked. It had never been marked, not even during General LeMay's mass bombing. As for the camp store, the Japanese had previously opened it on only one occasion, to mislead the International Red Cross officials in their inspection of our camp. The postsurrender opening of the store was a bitter joke. It contained a pitiful handful of shoddy junk that not even the most poverty-stricken POW would have wanted. It did not even have Japanese cigarettes. So far as I know, no American POW purchased anything.

After the Commandant paid our alleged accumulated wages, American POWs would probably have purchased a few souvenirs at the camp store, but we as individuals did not receive our wages. Before payments could be made, a mass meeting (poorly attended if actually even held) was allegedly convened at which a majority of those present voted to use our lump sum payment to purchase the honey man's bullock. The bundle of yen (as I recall it was nineteen thousand yen) was turned over to certain persons, apparently the self-appointed leaders of that particular cause, to purchase the magnificent bull. The honey man was sent into a state of shock by the proposition. He depended on his bullock for his livelihood. Loss of the great beast of burden would threaten his family's economic security. Besides, paper money in Japan at that juncture was practically worthless. Not only had the yen's value been severely undermined during the previous year because of the general wartime inflation, but the enormous destruction wrought by the American bombing had for all practical purposes placed Japan's economy on the barter system.

For a brief moment the honey man made a feeble attempt to resist, but the transaction was completed and the bag of yen was shoved into his arms while his bullock was being unhitched from the honey cart. Accepting the inevitable, the poor honey man, carrying his bag of unwanted money, walked out of the camp with his head hanging low, obviously defeated in spirit. For a moment, I felt a pang of guilt about the matter. What would he tell his wife and children? But the joyous celebration taking place in the camp soon overrode my compassion.

The honey man had hardly walked through the front gate before the bullock was attacked. Another self-appointed crew of American POWs butchered the sad-faced animal, cutting the tough meat into small, chewable pieces. Soon we all enjoyed the feast despite the difficulty of chewing, which reminded me of eating the tough carabao on Bataan. The feast was supposed to have been in celebration of a sort of revenge-laden victory over the Japanese. Nevertheless, the honey man still occasionally resurfaces in my mind, and I regret having taken his beautiful ox.[3]

Since we had spent our useless yen on the bullock, there was no need for the Japanese to maintain the pretense of a camp store with its few pieces of junk. The Japanese did, however, issue us some new summer clothing, including pants, shirts, underwear, and Japanese tennis shoes. The new clothing raised our already high morale.

One of the first things some of us did as soon as the camp was ours was to seek out and talk to the ten or so Army Air Force personnel shot down during the bombing raids on Nagoya. They had been held incommunicado in cramped quarters behind the Commandant's office, although the British had managed to exchange a message or two with them. We knew they had gone through psychological hell in isolation, and we poured attention on them at their release. Once we saw to their needs, we had a million questions to ask them. Since they were relative newcomers to the camp and had more information about the outside world, the first question was, "Who is now President?" That was when we finally confirmed that Harry Truman had been the Vice-President. We also asked silly questions, some about President Roosevelt's funeral, some about sports—like who had won the World Series for the last four years or what college football teams had done well. And some wanted assurance that the girls were still pretty.

Our chief activities during those first few days were eating, sleeping, walking around the countryside, and just lounging while smoking American cigarettes. In addition to the camp's storerooms being opened to us, the Commandant had quantities of food brought in, especially vegetables. The American and British officers ordered the kitchen to stay open most of the day so that POWs could draw food anyime they desired. Many of us supplemented the regular kitchen issue with chicken and eggs traded for outside the camp. We cooked those groceries in the kitchen or on outside fires, but we did not revert to the quawn system where tolls were paid for cooking. Mostly, we spent the days stuffing ourselves with steamed rice and barley laced with soybeans.

About three days after the war's end, a Navy fighter plane from a nearby carrier found our camp. Within a few hours, the carrier began sending one plane an hour over the camp during the middle of the day for the next two or three days. The Navy planes, using small white nylon parachutes, dropped not only canned goods but luxury items like candy, cigarettes, liquor, and news magazines. At that point, the thing we needed most was medicine. Some American and British POWs in the clinic were close to death, and the doctors wanted a particular medication to try to save their lives. The American doctor directed some of us in making medical symbols out of white papers and rocks on an open place at the highest point in the camp. When the next Navy plane came over, a crowd of us waved our arms and pointed to the symbols. The pilot got the message and returned quickly, dropping the medicine on top of the symbols.

Father Reilly was concerned about the large quantity of liquor being dropped into the camp. He feared the worst. In the name of sobriety, he undertook to gather up all the booze from the skies and place it under his control. The fact that he found it so easy to do should have been a revelation to him. After seizing all of the whisky, he announced the time and place for the first liquor ration, but the event turned out to be a flop. It was like giving a party and having nobody come. The good Father was astounded when only a few people showed up, and even they demonstrated no great desire for the free spirits. The Chaplain came to understand that after three and a half years of slow starvation, even former alcoholics craved food, not booze.

A few days later, the B-29s found our camp, and the skies began to rain all kinds of supplies. The supply drop was something to behold. The goods were placed in containers, each consisting of two 55-gallon oil drums welded end to end. The B-29s carried an unbelievably large number of the 110-gallon drums, each attached to a brightly colored parachute. During the war, the Army Air Force used parachutes of various colors to designate different kinds of materiel, but in dropping our supplies the parachutes were obviously chosen at random. Hundreds of drums packed with food and supplies suspended below red, yellow, white, and blue parachutes were an extraordinary sight. But there were a few problems. The drums descended too rapidly for comfort. Though they were beautiful as they floated down, they hit with force and a pronounced thud. Then, too, some drums came loose from their parachutes and hurtled out of the sky like bombs. The situation became downright dangerous. Fortunately, no one in our camp was hit, but a Japanese residence in Narumi village was struck by a drum full of peaches. According to the report, some or all of the family were killed and the house totally destroyed by the 110 gallons of peaches. We frequently remarked to each other that it would be terrible to have survived three and a half years of agonizing Japanese imprisonment only to be smashed to death by a large can of peaches.

The B-29s flew a number of sorties for two or three days, dropping supplies into the Narumi camp. All told, there were many tons of food in various forms, clothing, toilet articles, medicines, cigarettes, magazines, newspapers, and anything else our liberators could think to drop from the sky. Only a few drums landed directly on the compound; most of them were scattered from Narumi station to the foothills beyond the camp. So many parachutes were hanging from the pine trees in the foothills just beyond the terraces that the area seemed to be a Disney-like forest of Christmas trees. It was obvious that the B-29s were dropping many more supplies in every category than we could possibly consume during the few days remaining for us at Narumi. The word, or rumor, was spread around that supplies for some or all the POW camps in the Nagoya area were being dropped on our location for distribution later.

Even before the B-29s stopped dropping supplies, Japanese MPs had rounded up local people to pick up and bring the drums and parachutes into our camp. The drafted work force consisted of local laborers, farmers, honey men, and village draymen with their bullocks and carts. Some carts came in loaded only with parachutes. The eventual heap amounted to a huge quantity of silk and nylon cloth. Our officers told us that the Commandant had been ordered to save and store the parachutes for return to the U.S. armed forces.

Besides the MPs and the various categories of workers involved in the recovery of supplies, large numbers of civilian spectators lined the roads and paths to watch the process. It appeared that the whole of Narumi village had turned out for the extraordinary affair. The mood of the spectators was almost festive, but their holiday spirit seemed somewhat restrained by what must have been a nagging apprehension and anxiety about the meaning of the event. They also faced the difficult emotional problem of adapting to the new and less ominous overflights of the dreaded B-29 bombers. The local civilians obviously wanted to share in the manna from the heavens. Many of the supply drums and packages had broken open on hitting the ground, spilling items hither and yon. As we POWs moved among the Japanese, we could hear expressions of amazement and surprise about the kinds of goods and their quality and quantity. Despite the desperate needs of the Japanese civilians, I do not believe they stole a single item. American POWs gave many of the goods to the civilians, especially the children. When an American POW challenged Japanese civilians clutching any of the items (I recall one case involving a tiny package of razor blades), they immediately sought out and identified the American who gave them the article.

I do not believe that the Japanese MPs and the conscripted workers stole any of the dropped supplies either. There were too many POWs milling around for them to take goods without being observed. If they had been subjected to close bodily searches such as the Japanese had so frequently used on us, my guess is that the effort would have yielded nothing. Yet the MPs were part of the Japanese military that was guilty not only of committing unspeakable atrocities but also of looting our Red Cross packages.

At the time, we believed that the Japanese refrained from stealing the dropped supplies, even though they were desperately hungry, for fear of General MacArthur. We heard some of the village poor and peasant farmers speak of MacArthur as if he were a god, even superior to Emperor Hirohito. In retrospect, I believe their conduct was a product of cultural and national discipline—the same kind of discipline that during World War II produced probably the best army, man for man, in history and would produce the economic miracle of postwar Japan.

For us POWs, the whole experience was a joy—moving around freely and watching the peasants, herded by the military police, picking up and hauling our supplies into camp and talking with the Japanese civilians, who seemed as delighted as we that the war was over. Part of the joy was seeing them as real, responsive people. During the year I had spent in Japan, the civilians, except for the few workers in the plant whom I knew personally, seemed to be mere automatons. I was aware of them but only as vaguely as they seemed aware of me. For that entire year my only consistent contact had been with Japanese military personnel, civilian stickmen, and factory honchos.

At the time of our liberation, I did not dwell on our relations with the Japanese civilians, but I since have wondered what they must have thought about the American prisoners of war (before whom they were now humble and submissive), who, when the tables were turned, not only did not abuse them but actually shared their newfound wealth with them. I especially have wondered what the Japanese children thought about us. Though they suffered less from malnutrition than we POWs, they were skinny and obviously hungry. The POWs all expressed concern for them and often gave them food. We hated the Japanese military uniform profoundly, but we found it impossible to hate the Japanese civilians. As a result of the events of late summer 1945, I developed a feeling that the plight of the common people in Narumi had been similar to mine: they, too, had been struggling to survive the apocalyptic events unleashed at Pearl Harbor.

In the several days of the supply flights, we were showered with fresh American cigarettes, including all our favorite brands: Camels, Lucky Strikes, Chesterfields, Old Golds, and others. In those days almost everyone was addicted to smoking to some degree. Most of us were delighted to have American cigarettes again; one of the prime joys of being liberated was helping ourselves to the plentiful supply of "coffin nails" dropped from the sky. Unfortunately, our Navy and Air Force benefactors did not drop any matches or cigarette lighters. We had thousands of cigarettes but no "fire." In our barracks, traditional American know-how soon came to the rescue. Some young genius whose name will probably forever be unremembered lit a rope that had been thrown over a rafter in the barracks; it smoldered day and night, providing a light for a cigarette anytime.

During the approximately three-week waiting period in the Narumi camp, some of us eagerly read the American newspapers and magazines. We had been largely cut off from news sources since Pearl Harbor, and almost completely since the fall of Bataan. Articles about the bombing of Hiroshima and Nagasaki caught our eye, but we still thought of the atomic bomb as merely a large blockbuster. None of us, of course, had the scientific knowledge to understand the real significance of nuclear bombs. We certainly did not view them as major factors in ending the war. We assumed that we had beaten Japan through conventional means. The subject lost its interest in the ecstasy of our first days of liberation. Each passing hour brought new ways of enjoying the wonderful pleasures of freedom and food.

Included in the dropped supplies were U.S. Army toilet kits containing scissors, combs, shaving paraphernalia, hair tonic, and soap. After nearly four years of living little better than rats, suddenly we could have our hair cut in World War II styles. For the first time since leaving Manila, we had plenty of soap for bathing, and for the first time since the fall of Bataan, we were rid of prison stench.

The Army toilet kits also contained needles and thread. To kill the time when we were not eating or sleeping, some of us began to compete with each other in making fancy clothing or duffel bags using the silk and nylon of the parachutes. The contest produced many colorful items. An added incentive came from the idea that making those items prepared us for going home.

While waiting in the Narumi camp, I was able once again to enjoy my friendship with Jack Garcia. During those three weeks we frequently talked about our experiences in the Philippines and occasionally discussed vague plans for the future. Being able to talk to Jack again in the absence of terrible hunger and fatigue was a great joy to me.

Three weeks after the Commandant's surrender, word came that the International Red Cross would arrive in our camp the next morning to supervise our return to the U.S. armed forces. Our joy of anticipation peaked at that point. By then our health had improved dramatically; we had been doing little more than eating and sleeping since the war's end. Except for the critically ill, we POWs had rapidly gained weight and looked almost human again. Also, we had regained most of our youthful physical strength, losing that feeling of extreme fatigue. In effect, we had a rebirth of body and spirit.

Our last night in Narumi consisted of joyous but quiet celebrations, mostly by small groups who got together to talk, eat, and smoke those delicious American cigarettes. The mood was relaxed rather than boisterous. Some of the groups broke up after midnight, their members returning to their tatamis for the last time. Others chatted until the wee hours of the morning. Throughout the evening, Americans and British visited each other's barracks. The many sincere good-byes reflected the number of international friendships developed during the year at Narumi, in spite of the periods of tension between the two groups. For most of us there was little sleep.

Though Father Reilly was still in control of the liquor supply, his job remained a pointless one. No serious demand for intoxicants ever developed, not even on that last night. Not only did our appetite for food and cigarettes override our desire for alcohol; just the thought that we were "going home" the next day provided an intoxication greater than that of any alcoholic drink. The most popular beverages our last evening in the Narumi camp were fresh-from-the-sky American coffee and hot Japanese green tea, to which we had become mildly addicted.

The last week in the Narumi camp had been rain-soaked as the tail end of the summer monsoon dragged on in southern Honshu, but the morning of our departure dawned bright and clear. We viewed it as a good omen. We arose from our tatamis still filled with excitement, but since there was no one to push us around anymore, we ate a leisurely breakfast and began to pack our bags for the journey home. Around 8:30 the International Red Cross officials arrived and began consulta-

Plate 8. Father Stanley Reilly (ca. 1965).
*Photo courtesy of the Archdiocese of San
Francisco*

Below:
Plate 9. Jack Garcia with grandchildren,
1973

Plate 10. Preston Hubbard and Jack
Garcia, 1963

tions with the Japanese Commandant and the Allied officers, and within an hour the announcement was made that we were ready to go. With little ceremony or discipline, all of us (POWs, Red Cross officials, and Japanese guards) walked unhurriedly out of the compound and down the hill to Narumi station. On that last journey from the prison camp to the railroad station, none of the POWs looked back nostalgically at the campsite. We were putting a terrible nightmare behind us. The Japanese guards who accompanied us were armed, but they in no way attempted to supervise the ex-POWs. We did not *tenko*, nor did they force us into the usual cattle-herd formation; instead, they walked as a group ahead of us. We were informed as we left camp that the guards were along to protect the liberated POWs from possible assailants.

We left behind large quantities of supplies dropped by the Navy and Army Air Force planes: food of all kinds, American cigarettes, high-grade Army clothing, and many brands of fine whiskies. There was also a small storage house nearly filled with silk and nylon parachutes. Though we had been told that excess supplies had been dropped at our camp to be distributed to other camps, by the time we left not a single item had been sent out from Narumi. We wondered what would happen to that enormous cache of high-quality American goods. Representatives of the International Red Cross informed us that the supplies were now under the control of the IRC and would be used efficiently in the process of liberating Allied prisoners of war. The parachutes, they assured us, would be returned to the U.S. military. Since our experience with the IRC did not encourage us to trust them, we assumed that the Commandant would probably become one of the richest men in postwar Japan.

After a short wait at Narumi station, where during the previous winter we had so often stood at attention while going through *tenko* and freezing in the cold winds and snow, the interurban train, as usual, arrived on time. This time boarding conditions were different. There was no rush to get a seat, and there were no stickmen to pack the last POWs aboard by vigorous use of their cudgels. For our last journey on the train, additional cars were added to provide more than enough seats for everyone. As we headed for the station at Nagoya, the conversations and the general commotion occupied us, leaving no free moment to reflect that we were seeing familiar landmarks for the last time.

We soon arrived at the central railway station near the old factory and walked a short distance to board another train waiting to carry us from the ruin of what once had been a proud industrial center. During that walk we noticed some spectators watching us, and we recognized several of them; they were Japanese personnel (workers, honchos, and stickmen) from the railway factory gathered to bid us farewell. Even Spider, one of the most despicable Japanese stickmen, was there wearing a toothy smile and giving us an emotional send-off as if we were kinfolk. I tried but failed to correlate the two transformations before us: Nagoya's from proud industrial center to smoky ruin, and Spider's from vicious bully to obsequious fan. How or if they related was something I simply could not comprehend.

And then another kind of transformation, secret and internal, took place on the walk across Nagoya station. I saw Father Reilly and a number of other POWs wearing around their necks white silk scarves (no doubt fashioned from parachutes) tied to small wooden boxes containing some of the ashes of our dead comrades, the product of the crematorium. Observing the ritual procession of the ashes led by Father Reilly in a dark priestly robe, I felt for the first time following the Japanese surrender a pang of sadness.

As our train pulled out of the Nagoya station, we slowly moved through a city with the familiar, ghastly appearance of all the Japanese cities, including Hiroshima, devastated by bombs and fire. Soon the train was rolling through the Japanese countryside. We POWs probably could have been recovered right in Nagoya at the city docks, but the Navy apparently did not want to bring large ships into Ise Wan, the almost landlocked shallow bay providing Nagoya access to the sea. Instead, the train carried us about fifty miles to the southeast where we stopped at a fishing village near the mouth of Hamana Ko (bay), a few miles west of the city of Hamamatsu.[4]

When we reached the village, we found the U.S. Marines there. God, it was good to see them! They had just disembarked from several small landing craft that were visble in the background. Since none of the natives spoke English and none of the Marines Japanese, communications were at an impasse. The Marines were nervous, not only because of the difficulty with communications but also, quite naturally, because they were not used to dealing with Japanese civilians. Their previous experience had been with the Japanese military at such places as Guadalcanal, Iwo Jima, and Saipan. The Marines were careful to keep their rear (the area between them and the Navy landing craft) clear of Japanese. We were able to ease the situation by assuring the Marines that they had nothing to worry about. We convinced them that the villagers were harmless civilians who were delighted to have the war over. On the other side, the Japanese guards and Red Cross officials explained to the villagers what was going on. Incredibly, no one had bothered to tell them that their village had been designated a Red Cross station for delivering Allied POWs to the U.S. armed forces.

One of the communications problems developed from the Marines' desire to provide accompanying newsmen electric power to operate newsreel cameras. The villagers were utterly baffled by the Americans' attempt to make this clear. Right after we arrived, a couple of extroverted Italian-Americans, our court jesters during the dark days in the Narumi prison camp, immediately took charge. What those two grandsons of Italy via New Jersey lacked in language skills they made up with their enthusiastic gestures. The electric outlet was promptly set up, and the newsreel cameras rolled.

By popular demand of the American prisoners of war, one of our fellows was persuaded to stand on a platform and have his picture made beside one of the Japanese guards who had accompanied us. The situation was ironic in the extreme. The guard was one of the worst brutes in the Narumi camp. He had severely beaten a number of American POWs, and his last victim was the American standing beside him in the picture, still wearing a head bandage as a result of the beating. Somehow, that Japanese devil had escaped the Commandant's determined effort to get rid of the vicious guards before his surrender to the Allied officers. All of the POWs knew that the rascal had slipped through the Commandant's net, and we kept a wary eye on him. During the waiting period in camp, the brutish guard seemed determined to endear himself to the POWs. He was constantly smiling and doing helpful things for us, and on the train trip to the fishing village, he moved from car to car greeting POWs and generally acting as friendly as a puppy. When he stood on the platform with his last victim, he obviously believed an honor was being bestowed on him. Later, I saw that picture in a national news publication.

We did not tarry long in the fishing village; the Marines seemed to be in a hurry to leave. I would like to be able to recapture the feeling I had as I boarded a small Navy landing craft, a feeling much more positive than three weeks before. My mind no longer lingered on my narrow escape from the jaws of Hell; instead, I felt the beginning of a new life. The Navy craft chugged across the lower part of the bay and through the breakers into the open sea. There, in the distance, we could see ships of the U.S. Navy and other Allied craft. In a short time we were boarding a new Navy hospital ship, the USS *Rescue*. No palace in an Arabian Nights dream could have been more beautiful to me.

As we walked up the gangplank, the newsreel cameras filmed us. I recall that I was proudly carrying all of my possessions in the duffel bag I had made in camp from parachute material. My bag was constructed of white nylon trimmed in blue, and on the side I had sewn letters cut from red silk reading, MACY'S - FIFTH AVENUE. The newsmen thought that was good copy, and their attention helped me regain a little human dignity lost much earlier on the Bataan Death March.

Stepping onto the deck, we were greeted by the ship's captain and other Navy and Marine officers who welcomed us back into the fold of our people and our country. Old Glory flying in the Pacific breeze from the ship's mast had a special meaning for me, for on that day I was officially liberated from the Japanese.

Plate 11. Hospital Ship *Rescue*

14

Homecoming

On the Navy hospital ship USS *Rescue*, the personnel fed us, issued us new fatigues, and gave us physical examinations. Those who seemed to be in reasonably good health were dispatched to other American or Allied ships in the area; those who were obviously ill, together with those who appeared to have some serious health problems, were retained aboard the hospital ship. Since the Navy doctors considered me below the median, they kept me aboard. The examinations were too cursory to detect problems hidden by recent gains in weight. For example, my friend Jack Garcia suffered from health problems that were far more serious than mine. During the summer and fall of 1942, he had lain at death's door for many weeks. But Jack was sent to a British destroyer where, he later complained to me, the cuisine consisted solely of bully beef and hardtack.

The food service on the hospital ship could not have been better; the culinary efforts of those Navy cooks deserved a four-star Michelin rating. Furthermore, the Navy doctors ruled that, except for a few serious cases, the ex-POWs could eat all they wanted. And did we eat! By now most of us had regained near normal weight, and some were overweight. Nevertheless, our bodies were still starved for all the basic nutritional elements—proteins, fats, and carbohydrates. While lounging on deck, I overheard a group of mess attendants expressing amazement at how much food the ex-POWs were eating. One of them said he had seen an ex-POW eat a whole loaf of bread along with an otherwise enormous meal. I can still hear another's reply: "He sho' gonna be constipated!"

Life was luxurious on the *Rescue*, a magnificent craft that had seen its first and only action in the Battle of Okinawa. We, along with a convoy of other naval craft, leisurely steamed a generally eastward course along the southern coast of Honshu, picking up groups of ex-POWs here and there. All of us felt as rich as Croesus: plenty of excellent food, American cigarettes, and new marine fatigues. Yet, some of us felt the Navy personnel were patronizing. They treated us as if we were liberated missionaries or businessmen getting a free ride from the Navy. They seemed totally unaware that we were veterans of Bataan and Corregidor, surviving members of General MacArthur's "Battling Bastards," who, in the First Battle of Bataan, had defeated General Homma's Fourteenth Army, thereby probably saving Australia and providing the first American victory during World War II.

After three days of just poking along the southern Honshu coast, we entered Tokyo Bay and docked at Yokohama harbor, where, apparently, the central processing facilities for ex-POWs were being established.[1] As we sailed into Tokyo Bay, we were privileged to see one of the most awe-inspiring sights of American history: the ships of the U.S. Navy, in all their glory and majesty, riding at anchor almost in the shadow of Emperor Hirohito's palace. Those beautiful ships dominating the horizon across the Bay symbolized for me the American victory over the Japanese.

At Yokohama, our Navy hospital ship eased up to the dock and berthed alongside the harbor wall just behind an ugly, rusty tub, which I unhappily discovered was an Army hospital ship.[2] All of us Army personnel (which included members of the Air Corps) aboard the Navy hospital ship were suddenly dejected at the prospect of being transferred to the filthy-looking Army vessel. Our depression was aggravated by our Navy comrades, sailors and marines, who were to remain aboard the modern, comfortable Navy ship. They sarcastically expressed condolences on our impending decline in life-style. As we marched down the gangplank, a couple of Army MPs were waiting for us. We fell in behind them and, crestfallen, began walking toward the unsightly Army hospital ship. When we came abreast the ship, lo and behold the MPs did not slow their pace. We kept on walking for two or three hundred yards past the old ship to a large pier building where cots were waiting for us. We rested while a sumptuous meal was prepared in our honor.

When we heard what was awaiting us at the pier building, our happiness was only partially restored. We had not yet heard the answer to the big question: Will we be put aboard that rusty old Army hospital ship? We were elated when the MPs informed us that the Army ship had nothing to do with us. They went on to assure us that after we had finished our hot meal we would be trucked out to Atsugi Airfield, where a fleet of C-54s, the Army Air Force's first-class passenger aircraft, was waiting to fly us to Okinawa on the first leg of our journey back to the Philippines. In a spasm of delight, several of us ran back to the Navy hospital ship to tell the sailors and marines about our good fortune. Our revenge was complete when some of our former Navy comrades expressed the desire to go with us and set about getting permission from their Navy superiors.

When we returned to the pier, I stretched out on a cot to wait for chowdown. While I was smoking an American cigarette and contemplating my good fortune in having survived the post-Pearl Harbor apocalypse, an American general accompanied by a couple of Australian officers walked up. I almost fell out of the cot trying to get to attention while getting rid of my cigarette. The American general, a huge man, stuck out his enormous hand and wrapped mine in a warm, effusive greeting. "Son," he said, "my name's Eichelberger." I responded brilliantly: "Glad to meet you, sir! What outfit you in?" "Son," the General answered, "I'm Commander of the Eighth Army, occupying Japan."

After the introduction of the Australian officers, I said, "General, how did you people get back into the Philippines?" Down the General went to his knees, drawing a rough map of the Philippines in the dirt floor of the pier house. "Now, here's Luzon, here's Mindanao, here's Panay, Cebu, Negros, etc." He went on to explain that General Krueger's Sixth Army had fought the bloody Battle of Manila while his Eighth Army had cleaned up the Visayan Islands and Mindanao. General Eichelberger seemed to enjoy his talk with me immensely. I have thought many times since then that he would have been a wonderful teacher.

Following a bountiful Army meal, we boarded trucks for the trip to Atsugi Airfield, about twenty miles from the Yokohama docks. As we passed through Yokohama, the familiar scene of destruction greeted us. Yokohama resembled Nagoya, tangled piles of burned debris and an occasional burned-out building standing forlornly amidst the ruins. It was nearly dusk by the time our C-54 lifted us from the airfield. Thus ended my year's sojourn in Japan. In spite of the warm and, for the most part, respectful care given us by our liberating brothers, as the plane lifted off I could not suppress a feeling of escape and of great good luck in still being alive. We had plenty of room on the C-54 transport. Canvas seats were rigged around the sides of the passenger area, but most of the space was bare deck with some kind of fairly soft covering. Most of us ignored the seats, stretched out on the deck, and went to sleep. I awoke around midnight as the plane landed at Okinawa. After landing, we learned that a decision had been made not to continue the flight to the Philippines because of an approaching typhoon. The ex-POWs were to be farmed out to local Army units until the storm was over. Meanwhile, Red Cross personnel brought us drinks and sandwiches, and like the Navy personnel previously, they were amazed at the amount of food we consumed. On the average, each of us probably disposed of a dozen sandwiches and three or four Cokes.

We stayed three days in Okinawa as the typhoon swept through. The wind was strong but not particularly damaging; the rain came down in torrents. Because of the enormous amount of construction going on (especially roads and airfields), the place was a sea of mud. Barely a month earlier, Okinawa had been preparing to be the center for the coming invasion of Japan.

While in Okinawa, my group was attached to a nearby unit of Army Engineers, who set up some tents for us. The next morning, I, along with about two hundred other ex-POWs, reported to the engineer company's mess building for breakfast. We were lined up outside and given a skimpy breakfast of fried bologna, toast, and coffee. Like locusts, we were perpetually hungry. As soon as we went through the line, we practically inhaled our small portions and immediately lined up again. The mess sergeant gruffly informed us that seconds were not allowed, that the food issued on the first round was all we were going to get, and that we were to clear out immediately. We refused to budge and demanded more food. Meanwhile, the mess sergeant reported our insolence to the mess officer, an arrogant lieutenant who ordered us out. When we refused to go, he declared that we had committed a court-martial offense and were subject to arrest. He said he would give us a second chance to follow his orders or be arrested. We laughed in his face and stood our ground. The mess officer, his face now purple with rage, climbed into a jeep with one of his men and took off hurriedly, presumably to bring back the MPs.

Meanwhile, we waited in line for more food, and none of us feared the consequences. That was one of the few times in my life I felt invulnerable because threatening us with jail was like threatening B'rer Rabbit with the briar patch. In a short time the lieutenant returned; he seemed greatly disturbed but no longer angry. He called the mess sergeant in for a conference, and within two or three minutes the mess sergeant emerged, announcing not only that we could go through the food line again but that we could continue to do so as long as we wished to. In addition, new items were added to the breakfast menu, including fried eggs and ham. Soon we learned that General MacArthur had issued an order throughout his command that the ex-POWs were to be given royal treatment. After all, those men were "MacArthur's Magnificents" of Bataan and Corregidor. For the next three days, Okinawa was ours. The local company messes were open to us at all hours. We could go by the canteens and order anything we wanted at no charge, and when our clothes became soiled, we could just cast them aside and go by the supply tent to choose whatever clothing we wanted. At Okinawa every ex-POW was a king. We knew that the fantasy became a reality because no one dared to risk the wrath of General MacArthur.

Walking through our tent city, I ran into my tatami mate from the Narumi camp. He had been the most successful and affluent trader in the American barracks. Sadly, his whole personality now seemed shaped by the trading instincts so carefully cultivated at Narumi. He was going through the tents buying cigarettes, putting his purchases into a large barracks bag. "What the hell are you doing?" I asked. In a tone chillingly reminiscent of our days at Narumi, he answered that he was accumulating cigarettes for shipment home to Missouri. He said he had been informed that cigarettes were extremely scarce in the States because of the war. He expected to make a killing in the Missouri cigarette market. True to his opinion of me at Narumi as economically inept, he scolded me for not also taking advantage of the market opportunities. I could see at a glance that some of his Lucky Strikes had the green tint of tropical mold. Throwing the bag across his shoulder, my former blanketmate stumbled on through the tent city, muttering to himself.

Soon after the typhoon passed, Army trucks carried us back to the airport. I was in a small group of six or eight Americans assigned to a B-24 Liberator bomber for passage to the Philippines. I remember the face of the pilot as clearly as if it were yesterday. To me that young Irish-American from upstate New York, clean-cut and self-assured, sparkled with heroic confidence. He greeted us Americans with sincere enthusiasm but then grimaced when he discovered that most of his passengers would be foreigners—Indonesians from the Dutch East Indies and English and Indians returning to Singapore. The pilot obviously did not welcome them aboard his ship. Before he was ready to begin boarding passengers, those Dutch and British nationals rushed pell-mell aboard the bomber, rudely occupying the best seats. That made the pilot extremely angry, but he remained calm and did not try to stop them, though he muttered some torrid expletives. We Americans continued our conversation with the pilot, waiting for his signal to board. After a while that green-eyed son of a Celt boarded his ship, ordering us Americans to remain standing where we were. Entering the plane, he sternly ordered all of the foreigners into the bomb bay or into the tail section, areas where they were tightly packed. Initially, they resisted the move, but just one slap of the pilot's hand on his side arm proved persuasive. He then put us in the passenger compartment. We American ex-POWs, of course, nearly worshiped him.

We left Okinawa on a bright and beautiful day, flying over the southern half of the island, which had literally been cut to pieces by the construction of military roads and airfields. From that point the invasion of Japan would have been launched in 1946 had Japan not surrendered. As the B-24 lumbered southward across the China Sea, the powerful harmony of the four big engines was the very sound of confidence and strength. It was a thrill for me when we roared over the green northern coast of Luzon, flying down the east side of Lingayen Gulf and over the northern half of the great central plain of Luzon to Clark Field, where we landed.

At Clark Field we were greeted by a crew of Red Cross ladies with a wagonload of food. Like others before them, they were startled by the incredible appetites of the ex-POWs. Food served in the finest French restaurant could not have been better than those peanut butter and jelly and ham salad sandwiches. We went for the sandwiches like wolves for rabbits.

We had only a short wait before we boarded a smaller plane, a C-47, for the flight to Nichols Field, which was too small for the B-24 to land. Again, the British and Dutch nationals rushed the plane and grabbed the seats. Since I was the last one to board, I found only standing room left. Seeing my predicamant, the pilot solved the problem by inviting me to sit with him and the copilot in the cockpit. That was wonderful. Within a few minutes we were over Manila, and the pilot flew a complete circle just outside the old walled city to show me the destruction done the beautiful "Pearl of the Orient" during the Battle of Manila earlier in the year.

As soon as the C-47 lifted from Clark Field, anticipation began to build. Returning to Nichols Field was special for me—somewhat like returning home after a long absence. Nichols Field had not been the most important base for the U.S. Army Air Corps in the Second World War, but there were those of us who loved it. We had memories of happy times on the base and in nearby Barrio Baclaran.

The C-47 landed on a steel-link runway, commonly used on small bases in the southwest Pacific during World War II. While waiting for transportation to a destination unknown, I noticed a number of Filipino laborers working on a small construction project close by. I sauntered over and began talking to them, but they responded sullenly to my questions. Finally, I asked, "Did any of you serve on Bataan? I'm a Bataan veteran." That did it. Some of them were Bataan veterans, and their attitude changed immediately and completely. They all began to talk excitely and at once. They gave me a hearty welcome back to the Philippines but told me they did not like the American Army that returned with MacArthur. They felt that the newly arrived Americans treated Filipinos with contempt and said that they much preferred the relationship between the Filipinos and the soldiers of the prewar American Army.

A huge Army installation south of Manila where a tent city had been set up was to be our stopping place. The Army unit occupying the area was the Twenty-ninth Replacement Depot, and I was told, or at least got the impression, that all ex-POWs from U.S. Army (including Air Corps) units were to be funneled through that facility, even though we knew that a few had been able to fly back to the States directly from Japan.[3] As we were walking toward our tents about a hundred yards from the parking lot, we passed some Japanese POWs working under the supervision of Army MPs. We seemed to attract their attention, and they made uncomplimentary remarks about us, not realizing that we, unlike the other American GIs they had met, had some understanding of Japanese, especially the kind the prisoners were using. Suddenly one of our group walked over to them and shouted "keyoski," the Anglicized form of *kiwotsuke*, the order to stand at attention. The shocked POWs snapped to and stood as stiff as boards while the American ex-POW cussed them out in their own street language. Everyone except the Japanese thought it was great fun.

As soon as we began settling into our tents (six or eight to a tent), the MPs brought around Japanese POWs to be our servants, allotting one for each tent. That was something we had been looking forward to for a long time—having a Japanese soldier under our control. We waited with eager anticipation for our allotted "Jap," or "coconut head," as we often called Japanese soldiers. While we were waiting, we discussed subtle means of torture and cruel humor to use in tormenting our POW. We thought up ways to subject him to the kinds of deprivation so prized by the Japanese military: denial of water, food, and hygiene. Of course, we would force him to do all of our housekeeping: cleaning the tent, laundry, shoe shining, and the like. We did not have long to wait before the MPs shoved the victim into our tent. Our chance to get even had arrived.

What we saw shocked us. Stumbling into our tent was a Japanese soldier who might have weighed 110 pounds wringing wet. His face, a bloody mess of flesh on one side, was a perfect study in terror. We originally thought the MPs had worked him over, but he explained that he had been beaten by a fellow Japanese POW who had confiscated his American-issue jacket. Rather than put him to work or pull mean tricks on him as planned, we sat him down on a cot, tended to his face, and gave him candy and Cokes. During the short time I was in the camp, we treated him as if he were an important guest, despite the fact that he vainly tried to perform domestic duties for us. It became ludicrous, a bunch of American ex-POWs waiting hand and foot on the only available symbol of the conquered enemy. We proved utter failures at the art of revenge.

The VIP treatment of American ex-POWs continued unabated; we got virtually anything our minds, or appetites, could imagine in the way of material goods or food. We could go into the canteens at any time and get all the candy and Cokes we wanted. More important, we had free access to all the beer we could hold, even though regular Army troops had a limited beer ration. As I recall, they were permitted only three or four cans a week. At any rate, the GIs were desperate for beer, and we became popular with them because we could get the weak Army brew on demand. I remember going to a nearby Army barbershop where the barber, after completing my haircut, refused my money but let me know that if I could get him an extra can of beer he would be grateful. I immediately headed for the local canteen where I picked up a half-dozen cans and carried them back to him. He was ecstatic, and I felt powerful.

At the Twenty-ninth Replacement Depot, the medics looked us over, but only superficially. Although we were required to take off our shirts and submit to perfunctory stethoscopic examinations, the Army doctors were too hurried to uncover internal medical problems. They probably assumed that since most of us were near our normal weight (we had been eating like pigs for nearly a month) we were reasonably fit. I did, however, benefit from a thorough examination and sound treatment by an Army dentist at the Depot.

We were also issued some pay but were not fully compensated until after returning to the States. We had planned to spend some of our money in the Manila area, but we had no need for it in the Army camp. Everything, including movies, was free to us. Here, again, we were issued new clothing. This was to be an officially recorded issue beginning a new clothing record. But when we arrived at Ft. Lewis, Washington, the Army issued us yet another full set of clothes and restarted our record.

Once settled in our canvas accommodations, we were permitted to sign up for one of three choices of transportation to the States: (l) the first aircraft available, (2) the first ship available, or (3) the first transportation available. Though many ex-POWs chose the first aircraft available, Jack Garcia and I, reasoning that the first transportation available could possibly get us home quicker, chose that option. After only a few days in the Philippines military camp, we drew a Liberty Ship (an eleven-thousand-ton supply vessel). We had planned to spend some time in Manila. I had especially wanted to see Bilibid Prison again as well as visit Pasay and Barrio Baclaran. But our call to go home came before we could undertake those expeditions. The thrill of starting home completely outweighed the minor disappointment of having to cancel our planned visits in Manila.

Jack and I boarded the homeward-bound Navy Liberty Ship *Gosper* at Manila Port Area late in the afternoon on September 20. Offshore from the city, Manila Bay was dotted with U.S. naval vessels. When I arrived at

Manila Port Area in August 1941, masts and parts of hulls of Spanish ships sunk by Commodore George Dewey during the Battle of Manila in 1898 rose above the bay's water line in silent testimony to U.S. naval power. During the war, the sunken Spanish ships were salvaged by the Japanese for scrap iron. As we sailed out of the port, I was struck by the irony of it all. The area once occupied by the hulks of the Spanish fleet was now littered with sunken Japanese ships.

As we moved west across Manila Bay, the skies were dark with storm clouds, and a rising wind churned the water. By the time we sailed past Corregidor into the South China Sea, rolling waves were tossing the *Gosper* around like a cork. Standing at the rail, I took one last look across the island of Corregidor toward Bataan, but the poor visibility prevented me from identifying either Mariveles or Cabcaben. Silently, I took the MacArthur oath in reverse: "I shall *not* return!"

During the night, as we rounded the coast of Batangas and worked our way through the passage between Batangas and Mindoro into the Sibuyan Sea, the storm's ferocious winds and flashing sheets of rain dampened our high spirits a little. After a difficult breakfast, some of us stood at the rail trying to enjoy the storm scene, but the first wave that broke across the deck sent us scurrying below. By the time we reached San Bernardino Strait, the storm gave up trying to dash our enthusiasm for the trip. There we rescued a Filipino fisherman from his capsized boat, but the poor fellow had to go with us to Ulithi in the Caroline Islands before he could find passage home. As we sailed into the Philippine Sea, the storm evaporated, and a bottle-glass calm greeted us as we steamed through the Carolines.

We spent a full day at Ulithi, where we saw Navy tankers and other naval craft in the lagoon. The atoll had only recently played a significant role in MacArthur's return to the Philippines, and the large number of huge ships riding at anchor astounded me. While there, we picked up a small group of sailors returning to the States after a few months of duty on Ulithi. After they stored their baggage, some of them began telling members of the ship's crew about the hardships of duty on Ulithi. I just happened to be standing close by and overheard the talk. They told about their traumatic experience some months earlier when Ulithi was bombed by a single Japanese plane from Yap (a Japanese island in the Carolines not invaded by American forces but merely isolated). They complained about the boredom and lack of entertainment. Their food had been barely tolerable, not at all to their liking and well below their expectations. Moreover, one of them lamented that he had gone as long as six weeks without mail. At that point, I rudely interrupted. I expressed sympathy for the poor fellow, saying something like, "Hey, I know what you mean. I've had a similar experience. The last mail I received was during the first week of December 1941." The sailors looked at me as if I had just broken out of a mental institution. Then a crew member explained that most of the passengers were ex-POWs who had been on the Death March. To my knowledge, the Ulithi sailors complained no more.

As we were sailing through the Marshall Islands, a Navy plane from Bikini flew a circle around our ship towing a target for the ship's gunnery. All of the guns opened up, but as I recall, none hit the target. Now that the war was over, the target practice seemed wholly unnecessary. We suspected the crew of doing it just for fun. The weary veterans on those decks had heard all the heavy gunfire and exploding bombs they ever cared to hear. We were less than amused.

Though we were a little crowded and the *Gosper* seemed to be in no hurry to get across the Pacific, we were, nevertheless, a happy bunch of ex-POWs. We had two formal meals a day, breakfast in the midmorning and a midafternoon meal. The food was good, and we could eat all we wanted. In addition, refreshments from the ship's stores were distributed from time to time, and the ship's canteen was open several hours each day. Hunger was certainly not a problem. What problems there were arose from the spartan design of Liberty Ships, which were uncomfortable for troops. Under the tropical sun the ship was hot above deck and below; the canvas bunks had no padding; and once out of the bunk, the passenger had no place to sit, lie, or stretch out except on hard steel. Even so, I did not hear a single ex-POW complain, or anyone else for that matter, because the ship's crew and the picked-up Ulithi sailors felt ashamed to grumble because of the ex-POWs aboard.

We all looked forward to going ashore when we reached Honolulu. But we anchored in Pearl Harbor instead of Honolulu Harbor, and the ship's captain refused permission (with apologies) for us to go ashore on the grounds that he might have a hard time rounding us up before weighing anchor. His statement, given over the ship's intercom system, revealed that he was afraid the ex-POWs would not be able to handle alcoholic drinks. He did not know that we still preferred eating to drinking and that it would be extremely unlikely any POW would miss the ship. Nevertheless, we accepted the captain's decision with little grousing.

In compensation for denying us shore leave, the captain arranged for a USO (United Service Organization) show aboard ship. The show was locally produced and featured primarily Hawaiian residents. Most of the "Hawaiian girls" were Japanese rather than Polynesian-Hawaiian. The USO troupers apparently were surprised that we were able to distinguish

Japanese from Polynesian. They did not know or fully realize that we had been living with the Japanese for three and a half years. We were just beginning to notice women again and found the Japanese girls as attractive as any others.

After staying at Pearl Harbor two or three days, we weighed anchor still assuming that our destination was San Francisco. At Pearl we took aboard some Canadian military personnel we were to transport to Victoria, British Columbia. Not long after rounding Diamond Head, we were informed that our destination had been changed from San Francisco to Seattle, the more logical port just south of Victoria. Having had our hearts set on San Francisco, we were disappointed by that news. But as the days passed and we drew closer to Puget Sound, anticipation began to mount. The long voyage into the north Pacific was uneventful, and we were delighted with the cooler weather in the higher latitudes. Our adrenalin began to rise when the captain announced that we were approaching the Strait of Juan de Fuca, where we ran into heavy fog. We spent a day slowly plowing our way through the soup, finally emerging clear of it just outside Victoria. At nightfall when we dropped anchor in Victoria harbor, I realized that Victoria was the first fully lighted city we had seen since the lights of Manila went out on December 8, 1941. It seemed that all of Canada had come down to the docks to greet us. The Canadians threw apples aboard and carried on whole cases of the beautiful fruit. Bands played and practically all of us had tears in our eyes. The Canadian welcome, which far surpassed the one we would receive in the States, will always have a special place in my heart. That night the *Gosper* made its way south to Seattle, where, on the morning of October 12, 1945, we were greeted with a cold fog and a small Army band. Army trucks carried us to Ft. Lewis in the shadow of Mt. Olympia, traveling in a light rain all the way.

When we arrived at Ft. Lewis, the trucks parked next to a compound containing German POWs. Naturally, we greeted them with "Heil Hitler!" and other derogatory clichés. The Germans, looking fat and lazy, seemed not to mind. After all, they were living like kings compared to what we had undergone as Japanese prisoners of war.

We were, of course, treated royally at Ft. Lewis. Beds had been reserved for us at the Army hospital (Madigan General), and we underwent thorough physical examinations for the first time. The food was everything we had dreamed of for three and a half years. We were given new sets of clothing and were issued medals and ribbons for the first time. The Red Cross ladies helped us fit our new uniforms, sewing on our Hershey bars and other citations.[4] We were especially proud of our

Presidential Unit Citations with two oak-leaf clusters because they provided a nostalgic link with President Roosevelt and our prewar youth.

Soon after our medical examinations at Ft. Lewis, all of the ex-POWs who were physically able to get around were given weekend passes. Everyone with a pass felt like a kid on the last day of school. Jack Garcia and I headed into town together. First we rode an Army bus a few miles to Tacoma. There we wandered up and down the main street and had a beer or two, though neither of us had as yet regained his prewar taste for alcoholic drinks.

As we were walking down a side street, Jack and I noticed a sign advertising the "Bataan Barber Shop." We went in and, sure enough, found the owner, employees, and all patrons to be Filipinos. As we entered, they eyed us suspiciously as if we were intruders. When we explained that we were Bataan veterans, they welcomed us like close relatives, inviting us to join them in the back room for drinks and billiards. The owner insisted that we have dinner with him and some friends that evening at a wonderful Chinese restaurant. I remember that Jack and I insisted on eating with chopsticks. The Chinese cooking staff gathered in the back of the room to watch us. They were amazed that a couple of American GIs could use chopsticks so well. Our thirteen months of intense training impressed even the Chinese. In fact, we could easily retrieve small solid particles of meat, vegetables, or rice from the bottom of a bowl of soup. Alas, after forty years with little practice my fingers have stiffened. Unlike my memories of life under the Japanese, my skill with chopsticks has faded and almost gone.

After dinner, and a few departing toasts to American-Filipino friendship, Jack and I thanked our hosts and walked back to the main street. There we met a couple of ex-POWs who had obviously been drinking too much. They joined us in sauntering down the street, but they were becoming so loud and boisterous I began to feel conspicuous. As we were passing in front of a large hotel, an immaculately dressed woman wearing a fox fur around her shoulders emerged and started walking in the same direction. Suddenly, one of our drunk friends hurriedly walked to her side, took hold of her fox fur, and asked her for a date. I was completely flabbergasted. Jack's face was a mask of helpless frustration. We were both certain that she would call the police, so we got ready to withdraw unobtrusively from the scene. Before we could collect our wits, the handsome woman, without a hint of a smile, said that if we liked she would drive us to a nightclub we might enjoy. We, of course, accepted the invitation; she had her car brought from the hotel garage and off we went down the Olympia road. On the way, she told us that her husband was a high-ranking naval officer still overseas and that she wanted to help lonely GIs find some place to go. Our drunk friends, who had already insulted her, made two or three minor verbal passes as we rolled along, but it was obvious that she could take care of herself. When we came to the nightclub, she let us out and drove off into the night.

At the club, located south of Tacoma on the road to Olympia, everyone wanted to buy drinks for Jack and me, and soon we were drinking too much. By morning, we had been welcomed home by more partying groups than I can remember, all equally eager to toast our health. We wound up in Olympia at a small hotel bar with a group of deer hunters warming up before setting out on their hunt. They, too, insisted on buying us drinks. About that time, a young female American Indian came into the barroom. She was wearing a dirty dress, and her hair was disheveled. The bartender cursed her and ordered her to leave, but she paid him no attention. Instead, she concentrated on soliciting drinks from the deer hunters. They readily bought drinks for her, but they also cursed her and called her names like "dirty bitch," "dirty Indian," and so on.

About eight o'clock, the deer hunters announced that they were going to a restaurant for breakfast, insisting that Jack and I join them. Outside, all of us, including the dirty Indian woman, got into the deer hunters' cars and went down the street a few blocks to a restaurant within sight of the Washington State Capitol Building. The whole group, including the Indian, had coffee laced with whisky while we waited for breakfast to be served. Everyone was as high as a kite. As soon as our hosts had bolted their breakfasts, they set out for the hunt, leaving the drunken, unsightly Indian with Jack and me. The jukebox started playing, and the music prompted the woman to jump on top of a vacated table and begin dancing. As she danced she pulled up her dress, sans underwear. That produced traumatic shock among the restaurant's other patrons, and when the proprietress came out of the kitchen, she was horrified by the exotic activity taking place on the table. She rushed over to Jack and me, shouting, "Get your damn dirty Indian out of here or I will call the police!" Jack and I protested that she was not "our Indian," but to no avail. The owner ran to the phone, screaming that she was going to have us arrested. Since our bill had already been paid by the deer hunters, Jack and I made a quick exit out the back door, leaving the Indian performing her lurid, erotic dance. By this time, we were thoroughly exhausted and headed back to Ft. Lewis.

The large quantities of nutritious food I ate during the weeks following the end of the war finally restored my sexual appetite. It was during my brief stay at Ft. Lewis that I suddenly became aware of delicate and delicious female odors, of the attractiveness of the female form, of the beauty of the female face—all those things that make women physically mysterious and wonderful to men. And all at once I became aware that the state of Washington had an abundance of good-looking women.

One of the ex-POWs I got to know on the Liberty Ship met, romanced, and became engaged to a Tacoma girl during our first weekend pass from Ft. Lewis. I had met him through a friend, a member of the 409th Signal, on the homeward voyage. The week following the announcement, the newly engaged fellow invited me and his 409th friend to accompany him to his fiancee's home in Tacoma to meet her family. I was reluctant to accept, but the two of them practically dragged me to the bus station.

When we arrived, we found the fiancee's home filled with kinfolk— her mother and father, brothers and sisters, grandparents, uncles and aunts, cousins, as well as family friends. When I saw the girl, I was astounded by both her beauty and her bearing. I had assumed that the ex-POW probably had picked up a tramp plying her trade on the streets of downtown Tacoma. Instead, she was a stunning blonde with limpid blue eyes, petite but strikingly built. Her dress and her carriage virtually defined neatness. She was a charming, lovely girl, probably around eighteen years of age. I was also favorably impressed by her family and friends, all of whom seemed to be prosperous, working-class Scandinavian-Americans.

At the rehearsal dinner that night, I had several conversations with various male members of the group, but I had my eyes on the girls, all buzzing around the bride-to-be. Once the rehearsal was over, the party broke up, depriving me of an opportunity to make substantial progress with any of the girls. Though I had planned to attend, for some reason I missed the wedding at which my fellow 409th member was best man.

After the wedding, the Georgian newlywed made reservations for his bride on the same train scheduled to transport us to Atlanta. In fact, all of those whose homes were in the Southeast had received orders to report to Ft. McPherson, where my wartime adventure had begun back on June 13, 1941. We thought we would be on the same train, but a typical Army snafu intervened. When the first orders came listing those to catch the train for Atlanta, the new bridegroom's name was missing. He had been placed on the next train, which would be leaving a couple of days later. As luck would have it, the bride was booked with our group on the first train. At first the poor fellow was frantic; he did not know what to do, because there was no possibility of his changing trains or rearranging passage for his bride. Finally, he asked me in a pleading tone if I would escort his wife on the long train trip to Atlanta. When I said that I would, he relaxed and seemed to be happy about the arrangements.

I was eager to begin the cross-country trip, but in my heart I was not as comfortable in my new role as I pretended to be. In fact, I was torn between excitement and apprehension. I had a feeling that I really could not trust myself, but I certainly had no intention of going back on my word. Anyway, the Georgia-bound bride and I, along with a number of ex-POWs, were soon whisked to Seattle where we boarded a train for Chicago. All of us, including the bride, were assigned places in Pullman cars. One of the most pleasant experiences of my life was lying in a bouncing, swaying Pullman berth being lulled to sleep by the click-clack of steel wheels on steel rails. Throughout the trip, everyone was extremely friendly and courteous to me and the other ex-POWs. I especially enjoyed the attention we received from other military personnel. They were amazed by our Hershey bar patches indicating the maximum of forty-two months overseas. Actually, all of us had been away longer than the Hershey bars indicated. My tour of duty was nearly fifty months.

Across the northern Rockies and Great Plains all the way to Chicago, I was a military model of circumspection in carrying out my duties as guardian and protector of the beautiful young bride. Three times a day I accompanied her to the dining car where I enjoyed being the recipient of envious glances from other GIs as well as civilians. When we arrived in Chicago, I supervised the new wife's transfer across town from one of the great railway stations to another, where we had a multi-hour layover before boarding the Florida train to Atlanta.

In Chicago, that sin-filled Babylon of the prairies, the Devil seized me. Like everyone else, he, too, was on his way to Atlanta. I steered the bride into a cocktail lounge and began to ply her with drinks. As the alcohol loosened my tongue, I falteringly brought up the subject of sex. She looked at me and smiled, apparently thinking that I was trying to be funny. When I looked into those baby blue eyes, which were plainly telling me that she trusted me completely, my devilish intent collapsed and I immediately gave up the quest. Actually, I realized that I did not have any sensual desire for her; making a sexual advance toward her was like making a pass at one's baby sister. So, I disappointed the Devil and delivered my charge to Atlanta safe and unsullied.

When we boarded the train in Chicago, the Pullman beds were already made since it was late evening. I was assigned an upper berth, but I was by no means ready to retire for the night. I decided to go to the club car for a drink, and as I started down the aisle I came to a lower berth where an attractive woman was lounging in her nightgown, her berth curtains fully opened. She greeted me in a friendly manner and after an exchange of pleasantries invited me to sit on the edge of her bed. She appeared to be about thirty years of age, was slightly plump, and exuded a magnetic sex appeal. Her breasts were almost spilling over the top of her nightgown, the smooth, sheer fabric revealing more of her prominent nipples than it concealed. As I desperately tried to remember how to deploy what social charm and wit I once had, I became increasingly distracted by what for me was the essence of her sexuality— her splendid breasts. The longer we talked, the more I became distracted. She was shifting before my eyes into an illusion. She became a pair of extraordinary breasts attached to which, in a vague sort of way, was a nice, talkative woman. As we talked (and I looked), the more I assumed that I would be sleeping with her that night. When I was about to explode, she suddenly shocked me back to reality. She informed me that her husband was on the train in one of the day coaches. They had been able to reserve only one Pullman berth, and her husband had insisted that she have it alone so she could get a good night's sleep. It was about time, she said, for her husband to tuck her in. I bade her goodnight and hurriedly left for the club car. Again, for me it was love's labor lost.

When we arrived at the Atlanta station, where I had begun my westward journey four years and four months before, the bride's new in-laws were there waiting for her. They greeted her with their honey-sweet Georgia drawl, which seemed strange even to me since I had been away from the South for such a long time. The new bride and I exchanged good-byes, and I watched with some sympathy as she disappeared into the bosom of her new family, her new culture.

I arrived at Ft. McPherson with Eugene Coxey of Dayton, Tennessee, also a member of the 409th Signal Company. We were given a royal reception, many people there wanting to talk with us about Japanese imprisonment. That evening Coxey and I went to a small PX beer garden where we compared notes on our POW experiences. We drank too much, and a post taxi driver had to find our assigned lodgings for us. The next morning we went by post headquarters to pick up the orders that gave us a leave until early January, when we were to report to Kelly Field, San Antonio, Texas. Coxey and I then separated, heading for our respective homes.

The excitement of liberation, extended over such a long period, had made me somewhat numb as I began the last leg of the journey to my home in Lawrenceburg, Tennessee. The bus ride from Atlanta gave me time to reflect on the events of the past weeks and to collect my thoughts about the event ahead—my arrival home. Everything about the ride seemed related to homecoming. All along the way from Atlanta to Chattanooga to Nashville to Lawrenceburg, soldiers were going home. Every stop was someone's home, someone's journey ended, someone's reason for having stayed alive. Slowly the numbness began to wear off and be replaced by an eagerness to see old friends and old places, to see and hold my family, to be home.

Late October in the central South is a beautiful time. From the bus window that day, it seemed to me that nature had prepared for a homecoming. The weather was mid-South autumn at its best: a chilly morning followed by Indian-summer warmth at midday. Across the rolling hills and up the long slopes of Monteagle Mountain, the dark green of the cedars competed with the reds, yellows, and mottled browns of the other trees. I particularly remember the cotton fields, much more numerous than now, still deep in drifts of unharvested white. I was surprised at how many other fields, recently planted in pasture or wheat or oats, showed the tracks of new tractors rather than the prints of old mules and horses. Through the open windows of the bus came the smells of the plowed fields, burning leaves, and the season's last-mown grass. Towns and small farms passed by like a great parade of Americana. The towns seemed generally active and the people occupied with work. Everything looked as it should.

As I look back now, I wonder that I never considered it might be otherwise. I never worried that my parents, out of touch with me for over four years, might not be well, that the family might be rent by some calamity, might not be there at all. It never occurred to me to fear that my dream of their continued existence and well-being was illusion. The look of the world from the bus window gave me no reason to doubt the rightness or reality of the dream of homecoming.

Finally, around four o'clock, the bus pulled into Lawrenceburg. It was only a short walk from the station to the feed store, Robert Hayes and Son, where I had worked with Mr. Hayes's son James before enrolling at Austin Peay. He and I were good friends and often double-dated in the old days. I had not had time to alert anyone that I was coming. Few of my acquaintances in Lawrenceburg had telephones in those days; my family did not. In short, I was not expected and had no reason to suppose that James Hayes or anyone else I knew would be in town. But he was. As I walked through the door, he saw me and let out a whoop. It was great to see him. James had served in the Seabees (the Navy's construction battalion) in the Pacific theater and had only just returned home himself. He and the other folks in town had heard that I was a POW and had survived the war, but that was all they knew.

After warm handshakes around the store and a brief account of how I got back to Tennessee, James drove me over to my parents' house. It was not the house where I grew up; my family had moved from the country into Lawrenceburg only the year before the beginning of the war. The emotions I was feeling at that moment had nothing to do with places of residence. When James pulled into the drive, no one was in the yard or around the house. They could not have been expecting me, yet I knew my parents were there. I knew they were well. I knew I was home.

It was late in the afternoon that golden October day when my parents rushed outside to greet me. They had not seen me since Easter Sunday 1941, four and a half years earlier. When my mother saw me, she came running and threw her arms around me, half shouting, half crying, "You did come back! You did come back!" At that moment I understood why I had been so determined to survive, so staunch in my resolution to live. In my mother's embrace I realized why I had fought so hard to undo for myself the apocalypse unleashed at Pearl Harbor.

15

Readjustment to Life,
Dreams of Death

When I arrived home, I found that not until a month after V-J Day did my family know I was still alive. Everyone, especially my mother, was still anxious about me and my welfare. None of them had been able to correspond with me since early December 1941. I had received none of the letters they had written me during the war, and they had not received the one message I had been permitted to send them from Bilibid. I was listed as missing in action until May 1943, when the War Department informed my parents that I was a prisoner of war. They had no further word of me except for some papers of mine retrieved from Bilibid Prison during the liberation of Manila in February 1945.

After I was freed, the Navy Medical Corps assured me that parents of POWs would be notified immediately; the U.S. Army authorities at Yokohama gave the same assurance. By the time I reached the Philippines, I felt confident that my parents knew I had survived. I then had an opportunity to send a Red Cross telegram, never suspecting it would be my parents' first news that I was alive. Members of my family were unable to respond to my telegram until I arrived at Madigan General Hospital, Ft. Lewis, Washington. As far as I could tell, all of my comrades experienced a similar communications problem. At the end of World War II, the military authorities and the civilian officers of the War Department seemed to place a low priority on relieving the emotional stress of the families of prisoners of war.

My leave at home in the fall of 1945 was a memorably happy period in my life; I became reacquainted with my family and friends. My twin baby brother and sister, Kenneth and Kathryn, had grown up during the war. I had missed them more than anyone except my mother. Now they were on the eve of their twelfth birthday, practically teenagers, and I was a stranger to them. The contrast disturbed me; it was difficult to remember that they were the earlier baby twins. Their childlike faces and mannerisms, which were etched in my memory and helped to sustain me during my ordeal overseas, had been replaced by more individual features and more self-conscious behavior that, for a while, seemed strange. The changes in their appearance and demeanor, even more than the deaths of my comrades, reminded me of the mutability and brevity of life.

Though we were not a family whose members ordinarily showed open affection toward one another, it was obvious that my mother, Rachel, was extremely happy about my having survived the war. I could see the delight in her face as she went about her household chores. Her behavior made plain her love for me. Before Pearl Harbor, I had taken my mother for granted: she was always there when I needed her. During the war years, however, I developed a new and profound appreciation of her. For the first time I began to understand that all her effort to keep us fed, clothed, in school, and out of trouble grew out of a deliberate, daily choice and not out of some automatic response mothers are born with. I came to appreciate more fully the true value of the woman who had made so many personal sacrifices for her family during the dark days of the 1930s. I suddenly understood that for three and a half years under the Japanese the things I craved most, what so many of my fellows died longing for, were the very things my mother had chosen to provide me every day: good food, clean clothes, and a clean space in which to live. Her love had so often expressed itself in hard, thankless work. How fortunate I was to have such a mother.

Of course my father, Jim, was also happy about my return, but his masculine code would not permit him to express his emotions, and my family upbringing made it difficult for me to initiate expressions of affection toward him. My father and I did not have close personal relations before the war or after my return. Except for occasional brief discussions of politics or sports, we had no common interests.

Though I had never been particularly close to my three other sisters, they all joyously welcomed me home, two of them coming from distant locations to see me. Next to my mother and the twins, I was most eager to see my oldest sister's daughter, a bright-eyed tyke two years younger than the twins. Her father had deserted her mother, Helen, during her pregnancy. The image of the baby niece had also helped sustain me during the war. Helen and her second husband, a Navy man still on duty in the Pacific, also had a new son, born in December 1944, who soon won my heart as well.

As soon as I became reacquainted with my family, I began to seek out my prewar friends. I was eager to find out which of my classmates had been in the military during the war and to learn their fates. It was not an entirely happy pursuit. Some of my high-school acquaintances had lost their lives on the various battlefields around the world, and I recall that one of them, a former captain of the football team, died at Iwo Jima.

I visited Austin Peay Normal School in Clarksville, where I made the decision to volunteer for military service in 1941, and discovered that a number of my friends and acquaintances had been killed in action. Shortly after the fall of France in 1940, the Civil Aeronautics Administration began enrolling civilian trainees at colleges like Austin Peay that were situated close to an airfield. Roosevelt had become keenly interested in preparing a pool of trained civilian pilots to furnish recruits for the rapidly expanding military air forces. Most of the boys from Austin Peay who died during the war had been enrolled in the Civil Aeronautics training program at Outlaw Field in Clarksville and were military pilots at the time of their deaths.

A pilot I particularly remember was Wiley "Nailhead" Wyatt of Denver, Tennessee. I especially liked Nailhead because we were so much alike. Both of us lacked self-confidence because of our poverty-stricken background and, even more important, because we were physically small and weak in comparison with most males our age. When I grew up during the 1920s and 1930s, large males, brawny as well as obese, were generally viewed as being mentally superior to small, underweight males. There was a strong Darwinian element in that kind of thinking. Large males were apparently the best survivors in an economy of limited resources. It also seemed to Nailhead and me that size often played a rhetorical role as well: somehow big males seemed to be right far more often than small ones. Nailhead wanted to become a pilot to prove to himself and other students that he had "the right stuff." He died flying his B-17 in the European theater.

While I was on my ninety-day leave, I was ecstatically happy but at the same time often emotionally numb. Everything seemed unreal. The haunting melodies of two popular songs at the time, "It Might as Well Be Spring" and "It's Only a Paper Moon," reflected my feelings. My problem of psychological adjustment lay more or less dormant during the period because I felt no real pressure. I ran around with some friends, drinking quite a lot of beer and meeting other old friends I had not seen since before the war.

I spent much of my leave on the prowl for available females. I dated several women but met only one who really attracted me romantically. She soon let me know that she did not reciprocate my feelings toward her. I realized that she had dated me because she was a friend of my family.

My relations with all the other women soon came to naught, leaving me quite frustrated. Most of them wanted to get married right away. I knew I was not ready for marriage and was frightened away. I only wanted to fool around, have fun, make up for lost time. I sensed that the scarcity of eligible men during the war had made women anxious about marriage. By the fall of 1945, most of the GIs had not yet returned home because of the point system, which determined the eligibility for release from the military. During my leave I met a couple of war widows, one of whom had children. They were so desperate they probably would have readily married almost any returning GI, even an irresponsible person like me.

Despite women's employment in the war industries, the feminist revolt had not yet begun. Few of the young women I met during that period had plans for permanent employment. Instead, they wanted a husband and children. They were looking for a man who would provide economic support for a home and family. It was not until the early 1950s, when I was a graduate student at Vanderbilt University, that I became aware of the new feminist.

I had viewed the world so long as a POW that part of my readjustment to civilian life was learning to tolerate the reaction of many people (including members of my family) to the continued rationing of some consumer goods. Despite the fact that controls had been lifted from many items, people complained about scarcities and wallowed in self-pity over their alleged suffering. It was obvious to me that the economic condition of every local family I knew had improved throughout the war years. I considered the shortage of consumer goods barely noticeable. The supply of items in the stores seemed to me a virtual cornucopia. On some occasions when store clerks informed me that the item I had requested was not in stock, they went on to reprimand me with the exclamation, "There's been a war, you know!" I had the feeling that the homefolks were trying to justify their new-found prosperity by exaggerating their inconveniences.

In some cases store owners saved scarce items for their regular customers. When I returned home, white shirts were in short supply; in fact, returning GIs just could not find them. That posed a problem for me because at the time practically all dress shirts were white. I remember going into a shirt shop in Memphis and being informed that no white shirts were available. Somewhat angrily, I lectured the proprietor on the ignobility and low-downness of discrimination against returning veterans. I had intended to follow my reprimand with a sharp about-face and stalk stiffly out of the store, but the proprietor responded, "What size do you wear?" He immediately "found" two white shirts for me.

A more annoying problem was the shortage of beer in my home county, but that had nothing to do with rationing. While a majority of young males were away fighting the fascist dictators, the local politicians, preachers, and bootleggers devoted themselves to the common purpose of eliminating beer sales in the county. As a result, most of the returning GIs were forced to go to neighboring counties for beer.

I was pleased to learn about the educational benefits through the GI Bill of Rights. My extended tour of duty qualified me for the maximum amount of college support allowed. During my leave period, I applied for admission to three great universities: the University of California at Los Angeles, the University of Michigan, and Vanderbilt University in Nashville. I was accepted by all three institutions. At the time of my graduation from high school, a college education seemed a remote, unattainable dream. I did not imagine that I would one day not only have the opportunity to go to college but also be able to choose from a list of the nation's finest institutions. My choice of Vanderbilt was strongly influenced by its proximity. I might have chosen UCLA or Michigan, but the idea of leaving home so soon was something I found emotionally difficult to face.

The fall of 1945 passed so quickly that it was soon time for me to return to the Army for discharge. In early January 1946, I reported to Kelly Field, San Antonio, Texas. There I was hospitalized for six weeks before my final separation from the U.S. Army Air Corps. Though I felt reasonably well, the Air Force physicians realized that I had some residual problems, especially acute anxiety and hidden malnutrition.

While at Kelly Field, I got the feeling that the permanent party there had developed noticeable callousness toward combat veterans. Wounded GIs, who had suffered on battlefields around the world, did not appear to elicit much sympathy from the medical personnel, except for the MDs. The overwhelming numbers of paraplegics and otherwise crippled, disfigured, and deranged GIs (a much higher percentage of the patients there than at Ft. Lewis) produced a regrettable superciliousness among the permanent staff in the enlisted men's wards. I found the attitude at the Kelly Field hospital to be wholly different from that at Madigan General, Ft. Lewis. At the latter institution the word *care* set the dominant theme. The Ft. Lewis hospital had begun my readjustment in the best way possible, but at Kelly Field my morale plummeted.

Even so, at Kelly I gained a better perspective on what had happened during World War II. There I met GIs from all theaters of operation, especially Europe and the Pacific. I was pleasantly surprised to learn that Kelly Field was a home base for important elements of the Twentieth Air Force, which had devastated Japan. I was fortunate to meet and talk with some veterans of that great organization, but for a while I was unable to find anyone who had flown over Nagoya. In my final checkout for discharge, I met a number of pilots and navigators who had traversed the skies of that city. In fact, most of the personnel manning that checkout post were members of an air group whose primary target had been Nagoya. They seemed to be just as enthusiastic about meeting me as I was them. I was the first person they had met who had been on the receiving end of those bombing raids. Most of them had flown many missions over Nagoya. One pilot told me that he knew Nagoya "like a housewife knows her kitchen."

On February 26, 1946, after serving nearly four years and nine months in the U.S. Army Air Corps, I was discharged. I immediately returned home to prepare for enrollment in Vanderbilt University, which I entered a few days later.

During the first year after the war, I frequently had the feeling that I was living on borrowed time. It seemed incredible that I had survived an ordeal in which so many of my comrades had died. The incredulity was increased by the fact that, as compared to the average American soldier in the Philippines, I had not been a good candidate for survival. Physically, I was weaker than the average. I often wondered how I had been able to overcome the odds against me—why I had been able to undo the terrible apocalypse unleashed at Pearl Harbor.

I realized during my months of internment that some of my comrades had died because they could not cope psychologically with the life-strangling conditions of Japanese imprisonment. From time to time, I suspected that many of the survivors had been able to use psychological and emotional aids that enabled them to divert their minds from the stench of life as well as the stench of death. I concluded that a profound religious faith was an important factor in some survivals, though I also saw some evidence to the contrary.

I came to believe that a lack of religious faith was a serious handicap, making my survival more difficult. At times I wished I were a believer in the Christian faith of my family, but I knew it was impossible for me to overcome my religious doubts. My mind had been steeped in agnosticism for too long. As I reflected on the subject after the war, I realized that my ability to survive had probably been enhanced by the religious faith of others. On Bataan, my association with devoutly religious friends improved my morale and gave me a more optimistic outlook. On the other hand, my association with numerous friends who seemed to have a Faustian compact with the Devil also bolstered my morale. I think my believing friends contributed the most in the long run, but everywhere I happened to be as a POW, my friends, the devout as well as the impious, played an essential role in my survival.

Father Reilly, the chaplain so important on the voyage of our Hell

Ship and in our Nagoya camp, had a strong influence on me. I greatly admired him from the days of the *Nissyo Maru*, and I continued to have a deep respect for his integrity and for the care he demonstrated for all members of our Japanese camp without sectarian regard. Everyone felt his cheerful optimism. As much as I admired Father Reilly, however, I had to face one fact: finding comfort in religion was not a matter of choice for me. Though my heart was with Father Reilly, my head could not share his belief.

Lacking a religious faith, I had to find some other way to help divert my mind from the deadly realities of a Japanese prison camp. I developed my capacity to fantasize. At first, I found my imagination weak and ineffectual, but as time went by it grew stronger, more responsive, and eventually adept at transporting me from the real world of the prison camp. I experienced that particular phenomenon without the aid of drugs except for a little tobacco occasionally. Though I was never able to transcend my squalid environment completely, I did achieve a kind of mental escape often enough to provide relief from my fear, pain, and hunger.

Since an active imagination has to be fed, my mind developed an enormous appetite for new ideas. Initially, I attempted to satisfy that appetite by talking with comrades, but generally speaking, conversation proved unsuccessful. In sorrow rather than contempt, I came to view my comrades as either intellectually numb or puerile. Increasingly, I chose silent contemplation as a way to generate new fantasies. Also, I developed a ravenous appetite for reading and devoured everything I could find to read. In Japan, my sole reading matter was a one-volume French encyclopedia someone found in the barracks shortly after our arrival at the Narumi camp. I knew almost no French, but my hunger for reading was almost as acute as my hunger for food. It was slow going, but what I could translate, along with the many pictures, provided dozens of ideas for my active imagination. There in the enemy's industrial center, I frequently fantasized that I was being interned in a large library for the duration of the war.

One of the silliest of my fantasies concerned food. By late 1944 in Japan, I was able to sustain for extended periods the illusion that the slop fed us in prison was high-quality American food. My most elaborate food fantasies occurred during the evening meal. In the afternoon while I was still at work at the railway factory, I often carried on a silent debate with myself, sometimes heated, over the menu for my evening meal. If I were properly stimulated psychologically by mealtime, I seemed to taste the desired item, whether it was fried chicken with my mother's gravy, roast beef with baked sweet potatoes, or whatever. In the late spring of 1945, when I was near starvation, I liked to imagine at mealtime that I was aboard a U.S. government research ship sailing to various ports around the world in search of new foods.

As useful as it was, fantasy was not adequate protection against the deeply scarring traumas suffered in the camps and aboard the *Nissyo Maru*. After I entered Vanderbilt University in the spring of 1946, I buried myself in my schoolwork and was largely free of the symptoms of any psychological problems I might have brought home from the war. By the time I was awarded the B.A. degree in August 1948, I had become quite tired mentally and emotionally depressed. About that time I began to have a problem with dreams. I do not know how long I had been having them, but gradually I realized that I was having a recurring nightmare about Japanese prison camps. For the next twenty years I returned to Japanese camps on the average of three or four nights a week, some weeks every night and other weeks not at all.

On a typical night, my dream would begin as a rather pleasant episode, but after a while the setting and thematic structure would break up, producing strange and often grotesque images. Suddenly, I was again in a Japanese prisoner of war camp. My prison-related dreams were nearly always filled with horrible images: executions, beatings, bloated or emaciated dead bodies, and human feces—always human feces. The feces seemed to take the place of blood.

I also frequently dreamed that members of my family were being held in the prison camp with me. There was an especially harrowing version in which the Japanese were torturing my mother, the baby twins, and the baby niece. The children, of course, always appeared as I last saw them before Pearl Harbor. Some of the dreams, especially those involving my mother and the children, seemed to take place in a Japanese-controlled camp in America.

Through the 50s and 60s the dreams consistently plagued me, but the 1970s brought some relief. In the 1980s, after I assumed additional job responsibilities, the night horrors returned. The dreams have always been enervating, generally leaving me depressed and anxious the next day. To overcome the dreams, I eventually found myself resorting again to fantasy. I crowded my mind with images and events of pure fabrication, a world of surreal escape, if not from the dream at least from its memory. That sort of escape effort sometimes loomed as a greater threat to sanity than the dreams themselves. Whereas my escapism as a POW was the result of a determination to survive, my efforts to escape the pain of dreams became more and more a flight from the real and permanent world. From time to time after 1950, I often overtly struggled to keep a firm grip on reality.

It has now been nearly a half-century since my liberation from Japanese imprisonment and my homecoming. I have had to come to terms with my nightmarish dreams by realizing that I shall probably never be wholly free of them and that I was never fully able to come home. I know now that I shall never be able to escape the frightening images of the Bataan Death March, the living hell of the sealed boxcars of San Fernando, the stench of death at O'Donnell, the green hell of Tayabas, the mental rot of Bilibid, the unspeakable holds of the *Nissyo Maru*, and the starvation of Nagoya. A part of my soul that I visit on many evenings was left in the Philippines and Japan, never to be set free during my lifetime. Perhaps this is as it should be. As long as the bad dreams continue, a part of me will remain close by my many comrades who returned home only in dreams, their bodies left forever in those faraway places of death and despair. Whatever I was before the war, before the dreams, I am not now. I cannot stop the dreams any more than I can change history or who I am. It now seems clear to me that there is no healthy escape. For me, to flee dreams is to flee reality.

I have written this book near the end of my life because of the pressure produced by a great irony. Though throughout my adult life my experiences as a prisoner of war have worked to isolate me and my views from the rest of the civilization I have so painfully served and about which I care so deeply, it is also those wartime experiences that represent my service, formed my views, and are much of the reason for my care. The sense of internal conflict between the horror of war and the love of country is common among soldiers, especially POWs, who have seen and experienced the indescribable agonies that live on in unending nightmares. The most common symptom of that internal conflict is silence. Refusal to speak of experienced atrocities is not simply avoidance of painful memory. It is often the only response to the overwhelming questions I and others like me hear inside our private selves: "How can they hope to know? How can I begin to make them understand?" My need to speak of these matters arises not because I want anyone to see what I have seen, but because the pressure of the conflict between horror and love demands release. Though a gulf has been set between us that I cannot reach across, I want to leave a record for those on whom the future depends. There may be value in their knowing such things can happen, that such things have been survived.

During the first months after I returned home, I felt among the people an optimism about the future that I had not known since before the crash of 1929. Most of my homefolks had a good feeling about World War II, which had produced the highest standard of living they had ever known at a cost of relatively few of their countrymen. Everyone was talking rosily about the future. The unleashing of atomic power during the war presaged an era when an unlimited supply of electrical energy would produce permanent prosperity for the United States as well as the entire world. Our people had great faith that American scientists and engineers, who had performed many miracles during the war, were bringing about a marvelous new age in which American technology could solve any problem. The GI Bill of Rights would tap hitherto neglected scientific and technological talent by providing a college education for poor ex-GIs. Undoubtedly the American cornucopia would always remain full to the brim. There was nothing that Americans could not do—and do in a hurry.

Over the years, I have observed that faith in American stability and invincibility has diminished. Just as my nightly dreams frequently devolve into distorted images, the images of the American postwar dream seem to be devolving more and more into the grotesque. The failure of the promise of atomic fission, not to mention the threat it poses, the squandering of natural and economic resources, the pollution of the environment, and the decline of the American economy have led to new anxieties. I fear that the ultimate consequence of the apocalypse unleashed at Pearl Harbor will be the failure of what we harrowed Hell to preserve—the American dream. The dream of establishing world democracy and world prosperity threatens to degenerate into a nightmare of apocalyptic anarchy.

One of the horrors unleashed by the apocalypse is the new attitude toward war that has formed in the minds of American leaders since 1941. For the first time in American history, war is now a permanently considered alternative of foreign policy. Never before in our history has the possibility of engaging an opponent in battle sat like a member of the cabinet at the President's elbow, by its very presence a vote for armed conflict. The policy of war as a ready response is not the result of a new blood thirst among the people of the United States. The policy is, rather, the natural and necessary component of supporting at huge cost a military establishment that cannot and will not exist without the belief that war is a viable alternative. Every generation since 1941 has discovered the horror anew, has felt the sudden shock of the old apocalypse. But only the relative few who have indelibly experienced the horror of the apocalyptic nightmare of war firsthand can know how utterly damned is the view that war is an easily justified alternative of American foreign policy. Only they can know with perfect certainty that this view clouds and distorts the American dream. The dream of shaping the world in our image is increasingly a nightmare fostered by a belief in the necessity of a huge and complex military establishment. So integrated into our policies of governance is the military alternative that the night-mare is self-sustaining. Our military capacity can, will, and does seek out opportunities for its exercise. It must do so to sustain the position of war as a ready alternative.

Our politicians continue to pretend that the American postwar dream is real. Perhaps we force them to. We do not want to be awakened from the dream-like illusion that we are the leading economic power in the world. It is grating to hear that other nations no longer wish to mold themselves in our image. The idea that resources, room, and answers to severe problems are finite, precious, and expensive beyond imagining does not support the old American dream. The dream is no longer vision; it is fantasy—fantasy that is deluding, escapist, and dangerous. The old dream will never undo the damage of the unleashed apocalypse. Only when our society awakens to a new dream, as unpleasant as some of its realities may be, can dream and vision coincide. Only then can the apocalypse unleashed in 1941 be the apocalypse undone.

Notes

Chapter Three

1. Though the terms *Air Corps* and *Air Force* were used more or less interchangeably, there was a technical distinction. The Air Corps was a branch of the service connected to the Army. An air force was a command structure within the Air Corp, as in *Far East Air Force*.

2. John S. Coleman, Jr., *Bataan and Beyond: Memories of an American POW* (College Station: Texas A&M University Press, 1978), 7.

3. Cal Borden is a fictitious name to avoid possible embarrassment to persons still living.

4. Sidney Fine, *Frank Murphy: The New Deal Years* (Chicago: University of Chicago Press, 1979), 175.

5. Fine, 32.

6. Coleman, 7.

7. Fine, 4.

Chapter Four

1. USAFFE was a new command created for MacArthur on his recall to active duty in July 1941. Louis Morton, *The Fall of the Philippines*, vol. 4 of *The History of the War in the Pacific* (Washington, D.C.: Department of the Army, 1953), 19-30.

2. Morton, 161. For a summary of these developments see Morton, 64-71 and John Jacob Beck, *MacArthur and Wainwright, Sacrifice of the Philippines* (Albuquerque: The University of New Mexico Press, 1974), 5-6.

3. Morton, 71-72.

4. Morton, 72.

5. Ibid.

6. The first news of the Pearl Harbor attack was received in Manila at 2:30 A.M. on December 8. See Charles Bateson, *The War With Japan: A Concise History* (East Lansing: Michigan State University Press, 1968), 50.

7. For a discussion of this theory, see Beck, xi; Gordon W. Prange, *At Dawn We Slept: The Untold Story of Pearl Harbor* (New York: McGraw-Hill, 1981), 553ff.; John Toland, *Infamy: Pearl Harbor and Its Aftermath* (Garden City, N.Y.: Doubleday, 1982), 316ff.

8. Morton, 80.

9. See Bateson, 52.

10. Morton, 80.

11. For a typical description of the bombing of Clark Field, see Ward Rutherford, *Fall of the Philippines* (New York: Ballantine Books, 1971), 43.

12. Bateson, 52-53; Carol Morris Petillo, *Douglas MacArthur: The Philippine Years* (Bloomington: Indiana University Press, 1981), 202; Rutherford, 43.

13. See Morton, 85; Rutherford, 43.

14. See Morton, 84-85.

15. Morton, 77.

16. For a more recent and balanced view of this controversy, see Beck, 15.

17. Col. E. B. Miller, *Bataan Uncensored* (Long Prairie, Minn.: The Hart Publications, 1949), 67. A conversation with Albert Stahl in December 1981 indicated to me that I had failed to sense fully the paranoid response to the possibility of Japanese paratroops.

18. Morton, 105.

19. Morton, 115; Juanita Redmond, *I Served on Bataan* (New York: J. B. Lippincott Co., 1943), 23.

20. Morton, 115-19.

21. Bobette Gugliotta, *Pigboat 39: An American Sub Goes to War* (Lexington: The University Press of Kentucky, 1984), 110-11; Redmond, 20.

22. Morton, 115.

23. Bateson, 62; Morton, 127-38; Beck, 32.

24. Morton, 161-64.

25. Morton, 162-64.

26. Morton, 164; Carlos P. Romulo, *I Saw the Fall of the Philippines* (Garden City, N.Y.: Doubleday, Doran & Co., 1943), 59, 64, 65; Bateson, 62-63.

27. Ostensibly, the reason for General MacArthur's dispatching General Brereton and most of his FEAF staff to Australia was "to organize advanced operating bases" that would protect the sea route from Australia to the Philippines. See Morton, 156.

28. Morton, 96-97, 155-56; Beck, 16-17.

Chapter Five

1. Apparently, troops being evacuated through Manila Port Area on the previous day also believed they were going to Australia. See John S. Coleman, Jr., *Bataan and Beyond: Memories of an American POW* (College Station: Texas A&M University Press, 1978), 15.

2. For an account of the bombing of Mariveles on December 24, 1941, see Coleman, 16.

3. Coleman, 17.

4. Louis Morton, *The Fall of the Philippines*, vol. 4 of *The History of the War in the Pacific* (Washington, D.C.: Department of the Army, 1953), 156, 359.

5. Morton, 156, 488; Col. E. B. Miller, *Bataan Uncensored* (Long Prairie, Minn.: The Hart Publications, 1949), 181ff.

6. Morton, 230, 265; Miller, 38-43.

7. Morton, 265ff.; Miller, 144ff.

8. Morton, 265ff.; Miller, 144-70.

9. Morton, 290-91.

10. Morton, 263-65.

11. Morton, 296-346.

12. Wolfe Boney is a fictitious name to prevent possible embarrassment to persons now living.

13. Morton, 169ff.; 372.

14. Miller, 192. See also Morton, 390-404.

15. Morton, 345-52.

Chapter Six

1. For further information concerning health and food problems on Bataan, see Louis Morton, *The Fall of the Philippines*, vol. 4 of *The History of the War in the Pacific* (Washington, D.C.: Department of the Army, 1953), 258, 380, 381.

2. For information concerning the location of General Hospitals No. 1 and No. 2, see Morton, 258, 380, 381.

3. Juanita Redmond, *I Served on Bataan* (New York: J. B. Lippincott Co., 1943), 121-27, 149-59; Donald Knox, *Death March: The Survivors of Bataan* (New York: Harcourt Brace Jovanovich, 1981), 103-8, 326-27; Ronald H. Bailey, *Prisoners of War* (Alexandria, Va.: World War II, Time-Life Books, 1981), 19.

4. The American soldier's attitude toward the gas mask was similar in other places during World War II. See Eric Morris, *Salerno: A Military Fiasco* (New York: Stein and Day, 1983), 70, 71.

5. Morton, 458.

6. Morton, 353-66, 454-56.

7. Morton, 411-17.

8. Morton, 421-31.

9. Morton, 442.

10. As soon as word was received during the morning of April 9 about General King's surrender of Bataan, some Americans and Filipinos began assembling at Mariveles and other places for the surrender before the Japanese arrived. Stanley L. Falk, *Bataan: The March of Death* (New York: W. W. Norton, 1962), 77.

11. This was the smoldering ship we saw when we disembarked at Mariveles on Christmas Day.

12. Falk, 114, 116.

13. Concerning Japanese looting of American POWs, see Falk, 82-83.

14. Falk, 84, 99, 115-116.

15. Falk, 69ff.

16. Falk, 114.

17. See Falk's chapter "Up From Mariveles," 113-24.

18. Falk, 158-59.

19. Falk, 161.

Chapter Seven

1. Stanley L. Falk, *Bataan: The March of Death* (New York: W. W. Norton, 1962), 190.

2. Falk, 192.

3. Falk, 192-93. Falk's summary of the "welcome speeches," including his description of the circumstances in which they took place, matches my recollection.

4. Donald Knox, *Death March: The Survivors of Bataan* (New York: Harcourt Brace Jovanovich, 1981), 157.

5. Alfred Eckles of Hopkinsville, Kentucky, a member of the 409th Signal Company and a close friend of mine, went along with those officers as an orderly.

6. Knox, 168.

7. Knox, 163, 165, 167-69.

8. Knox, 163.

9. Knox, 164.

10. Ibid.

11. Knox, 161.

12. Knox, 169-70.

13. Knox, 162.

14. Knox, 159, 161-162.

15. Knox, 165.

16. Ibid.

17. Knox, 160.

18. Knox, 169.

19. Knox, 160.

20. Knox, 175-97.

Chapter Eight

1. Donald Knox, *Death March: The Survivors of Bataan* (New York: Harcourt Brace Jovanovich, 1981), 199.

2. Knox, 175-97.

3. Knox, 176.

4. *Tilley* and *Batey* are fictitious names used instead of real names to avoid possible embarrassment.

5. *Quawn* is an Anglicized form of the Tagalog word *quan*. I believe Kerr is wrong in using *quawn* (quan) as a verb form (i.e., quanning). I heard it used only as a noun or an adjective. See E. Bartlett Kerr, *Surrender and Survival: The Experience of American POW's in the Pacific, 1941-1945* (New York: William Morrow, 1985), 99.

6. Frederick L. Wernstedt and J. E. Spencer, *The Philippine Island World: A Physical, Cultural and Regional Geography* (Berkeley: University of California Press, 1967), 420-21.

7. By my recollection, Kerr is incorrect in stating that at Tayabas "a fairly adequate supply of American canned goods was on hand." The few rejects the Japanese gave us were only an infinitesimal portion of our food ration. See Kerr, 86.

8. Knox, 180-85.

9. Near the end of the project, the Japanese provided an old tarpaulin that was thrown across a wooden frame and used for shelter for those who were ill but

still working. Beneath the tarp, the ground was caked with human feces. Up to fifty could crowd under the tarpaulin shelter during a downpour, but it generally accommodated only about thirty, leaving most of us continually exposed.

10. As I recall, no Americans left Tayabas until the project was closed down, at which time all survivors were transported to Bilibid. But Kerr (86-87) states that Dr. Brown, "along with thirty other seriously ill men, left the work camp to return to the prison hospital at Bilibid." Comdr. Thomas Hayes's diary seems to support Kerr. See *Bilibid Diary: The Secret Notebooks of Commander Thomas Hayes, POW, the Philippines, 1942-45*, ed. A. B. Feuer (Hamden, Conn.: Archon Books, 1987), 13, 16-17, 35.

11. Letter, Jack Garcia to Preston Hubbard, December 1, 1984.

12. Captain [Paul] Ashton, *Bataan Diary* (Santa Barbara, Calif.: privately printed by the author, 1984), 219.

13. Kerr's statistics concerning the number of American POWs sent to the Tayabas Project confirm my figures—i.e., approximately three hundred. Kerr, 86.

Chapter Nine

1. Charles Brown, *Bars From Bilibid Prison* (San Antonio, Tex.: Naylor Co., 1947), 6-7.

2. Comdr. Thomas Hayes, *Bilibid Diary: The Secret Notebooks of Commander Thomas Hayes, POW, the Philippines, 1942-45*, ed. A. B. Feuer (Hamden, Conn.: Archon Books, 1987), 35.

3. My change of opinion was largely the result of my having been a student of Professor Norman Parks at Vanderbilt University, who influenced my thinking more than any other person in my life.

4. Brown, 28.

Chapter Ten

1. Donald Knox, *Death March: The Survivors of Bataan* (New York: Harcourt Brace Jovanovich, 1981), 337.

2. John S. Coleman, Jr., *Bataan and Beyond: Memories of an American POW* (College Station: Texas A&M University Press, 1978), 105-9; Col. E. B. Miller, *Bataan Uncensored* (Long Prairie, Minn.: The Hart Publications, 1949), 253ff.

3. See Knox, 349; Coleman, 105; Miller, 259.

4. For example, see Coleman, 105; Miller, 259; Knox, 349.

5. Miller, 260.

6. Coleman, 104.

7. Miller, 259.

8. Miller, 260.

9. Miller, 260-261.

10. As quoted in Knox, 349.

11. Manny (Marion R.) Lawton, *Some Survived* (Chapel Hill, N.C.: Algonquin Books, 1984), 29.

12. Knox, 343.

13. Lawton, 156-57.

14. Knox, 350.

15. Lawton, 160; Knox, 350.
16. Knox, 350.
17. Ibid.
18. Knox, 347.
19. Miller, 261.
20. Ibid.
21. Knox, 355.
22. Coleman, 108.
23. Miller, 264.
24. Lawton, 221.
25. D. Clayton James, ed., *South to Bataan, North to Mukden: The Prison Diary of Brigadier General W. E. Brougher* (Athens: University of Georgia Press, 1971), 46.
26. *New York Times*, September 21, 22, 24, 25, 26, 1945.

Chapter Eleven
1. Thomas R. H. Havens, *Valley of Darkness: The Japanese People and World War II* (New York: W. W. Norton, 1978), 62.
2. Havens, 74.
3. A. J. Barker, *Suicide Weapon* (New York: Ballantine Books, 1971), 144-47.
4. Havens, 92, 96-97, 104.
5. Havens, 92, 96.
6. Ibid.
7. Havens, 92-93, 106-13.
8. Havens, 124-26.
9. Louis Goldstein of Philadelphia and Father Reilly, the Catholic chaplain, took the lead in establishing the Rabbit Commission. Goldstein was a natural leader who did not permit the savage conditions of Japanese internment to destroy his human decency or blunt his sensitivity to the suffering of his comrades.
10. Donald Knox, *Death March: The Survivors of Bataan* (New York: Harcourt Brace Jovanovich, 1981), 419.

Chapter Twelve
1. Col. E. B. Miller, *Bataan Uncensored* (Long Prairie, Minnesota: The Hart Publications, 1949), 338.
2. Miller, 344-45.
3. John Toland, *The Rising Sun: The Decline and Fall of the Japanese Empire, 1936-1945* (New York: Random House, 1970), 305.
4. According to Carl Berger, *B29: The Superfortress, Ballantine's Illustrated History of World War II* (New York: Ballantine Books, 1970), 117-18, the date was December 13 and there were seventy-one B-29s in the flight.
5. Ibid.
6. For the landmark events of the American bombing of Japan during World War II, see Berger, *B29: The Superfortress*; Charles Bateson, *The War With Japan: A Concise History* (East Lansing: Michigan State University Press, 1968); John Costello, *The Pacific War* (New York: Rawson, Wade Publishers, 1981); Edwin P. Hoyt,

Closing the Circle: War in the Pacific, 1945 (New York: Van Nostrand Reinhold, 1982); Gilbert Cant, *The Great Pacific Victory: From the Solomons to Tokyo* (New York: John Day Co., 1946); Toland, *The Rising Sun*; Ronald H. Spector, *Eagle Against the Sun: The American War With Japan* (New York: Free Press, 1985); and Thomas R. H. Havens, *Valley of Darkness: The Japanese People and World War II* (New York: W. W. Norton, 1978).

7. Berger, 120; Bateson, 154.

8. Berger, 120-22.

9. Berger, 122-23.

10. Berger, 128.

11. Berger, 129-35; Toland, *The Rising Sun*, 676; John Costello, 552; Havens, 177-81.

12. Berger, 135.

13. Ibid.

14. Ibid.

15. Berger, 134.

16. Berger, 139.

17. Berger, 141.

18. Havens, 154.

19. Havens, 99.

20. Havens, 114-24.

21. Havens, 129.

22. Berger, 145.

23. Berger, 147.

24. Donald Knox, *Death March: The Survivors of Bataan* (New York: Harcourt Brace Jovanovich, 1981), 362.

25. Knox, 420.

Chapter Thirteen

1. E. Bartlett Kerr, *Surrender and Survival: The Experience of American POW's in the Pacific, 1941-1945* (New York: William Morrow, 1985), 280.

2. For a brief but excellent summary of the post-Japanese surrender period in American POW camps, see Kerr, 274-86. Also see Col. E. B. Miller, *Bataan Uncensored* (Long Prairie, Minn.: The Hart Publications, 1949); John S. Coleman, Jr., *Bataan and Beyond: Memories of an American POW* (College Station: Texas A&M University Press, 1978), 172ff.; Manny (Marion R.) Lawton, *Some Survived* (Chapel Hill, N.C.: Algonquin Books, 1984), 234-38; and Donald Knox, *Death March: The Survivors of Bataan* (New York: Harcourt Brace Jovanovich, 1981), 439-82.

3. There is an account of the bullock incident in Knox, 449.

4. Apparently large numbers of POWs from the greater Nagoya area were brought here for liberation. See Kerr, 287.

Chapter Fourteen

1. E. Bartlett Kerr, *Surrender and Survival: The Experience of American POW's in the Pacific, 1941-1945* (New York: William Morrow, 1985), 287.

2. The Army hospital ship was probably the *Marigold*, which had been anchored there as part of the processing facilities for liberated POWs. See Kerr, 287.

3. That most but not all ex-POWs came through the Twenty-ninth Replacement Depot is confirmed by Kerr, 291.

4. Each of the Hershey bars, named after the head of the Selective Service System, Gen. Lewis B. Hershey, represented six months of wartime service overseas. All survivors of Bataan and Corregidor had served a minimum of forty-six months overseas.